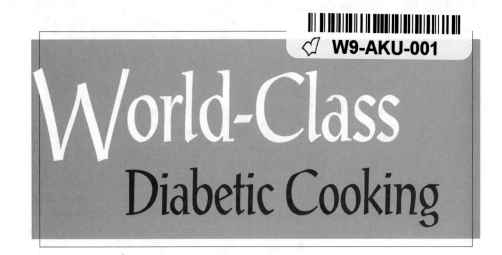

World-Class
Diabetic Cooking

Great-Tasting Recipes
From Around the World

KAY SPICER

American Diabetes Association

Publisher: Susan H. Lau
Editorial Director: Peter Banks
Acquisitions Manager: Susan Reynolds
Book Editor: Karen Lombardi Ingle
Production Director: Carolyn R. Segree

Cover Photography by Aldo Tutino
Cover Design by Wickham & Associates, Inc.
Page Design and Typography by Harlowe Typography, Inc.
Original Page Design by Mary O'Neil
Original Typography by Martin Crawford
Interior Photography by Fred Bird

Spicer, Kay.
    [Multicultural cooking]
    World-class diabetic cooking : great-tasting recipes from around
the world / Kay Spicer.
       p.   cm.
    Originally published: Multicultural cooking. Campbellville, Ont. :
Mighton House, © 1995.
    Includes bibliographical references and index.
    ISBN 0-945448-70-8
    1. Diabetes—Diet therapy—Recipes. 2. Cookery, International.
I. Title.
RC662.S65 1996
641.5'6314—dc20   96-27568
                                                CIP

Published by the American Diabetes Association, Inc.
1660 Duke Street, Alexandria, VA 22314

Printed in the United States of America

CONTENTS

ACKNOWLEDGMENTS

This cookbook is the result of a dream I have had for some time, but had set aside until now. With encouragement from fellow home economist and dietitian Valerie Bell, the idea became an undertaking. And I appreciate her unfailing loyalty and help with this project.

Many coworkers helped make this cookbook possible, and I would like to thank:

- The dietitians at Doctors Hospital, Toronto for contributing some ethnic recipes that were adapted for this collection.

- Bertha Skye for her insight into traditional foods of aboriginal Canadians.

- Cathy Lewis, Patricia Spicer, and Yvonne Tremblay for testing the recipes, tasting the resulting dishes, approving of their inclusion here, and preparing food for photography. And, also, Yvonne Tremblay for proofreading the recipes.

- Kathy Younker, KEYS Nutrition Services, for her expertise in doing all the nutrient analysis of the recipes.

- Mary O'Neil for her creative design.

- Fred Bird for the pleasing photography.

- Debby Boyden for coordinating photographic props.

- Martin Crawford for his expertise in typography.

Many thanks to my husband and my family for their steady support, enthusiasm, patience, and love through all the months, days, and hours of testing, tasting, and typing, plus their honest opinions and great advice.

Dedication

This cookbook is dedicated to my grandchildren and to all children of different cultures. May they enjoy the foods of their heritage and those of other ethnic groups.

Kay Spicer
1996

INTRODUCTION

Cooking is a fascinating subject and enormous in its scope. That became clear to me as I started to gather recipes for this collection. This collection forms what I would like to call a global table. I feel food knows no boundaries. It can be, and is, in my mind, the common denominator among people of many different cultural backgrounds. These ethnic recipes were brought to this country by our immigrants from many different geographical locations.

I have adapted these traditional recipes from all parts of the globe to fit into the food plans of people with diabetes. It has meant addressing the need for dishes that are high in fiber and complex carbohydrates, low in calories, and low in fat and sodium. This has resulted in dishes that are heart-smart and healthy for everyone.

At the same time, I have streamlined their preparation to suit both the equipment and time restraints we have today. As such, they can become a part of our daily lives and can be included in the healthy eating style more and more of us are endorsing as we approach the 21st century.

Printed beside each recipe are the American Diabetes Assocation/The American Dietetic Association Exchanges for Meal Planning for single servings of each specific dish. The energy (caloric value) and nutrient information is also included.

The biggest challenge for me in compiling this collection was not in the gathering but rather in the selecting of the recipes that I could put into a cookbook of this limited size. There were hundreds and hundreds of wonderful recipes—literally a world of choices.

In many cases, there were not only several different names for similar dishes, but also different spellings of the names. I found the Middle Eastern dish tabbouleh spelled tabouli and tabooley. And Middle Eastern pilaf also appeared as pilau and pilaff, depending I think on its regional origin and the interpretation of various writers.

However, after 4 months of researching and developing these recipes, cooking, then testing and retesting, with my assistants, these are the ones that survived the cut.

These recipes are for specialties that are full of the evocative flavors, aromas, colors, and textures from cultures with their roots in far-flung lands in South America, Africa, Europe, and Asia. The cuisine of the people who have emigrated from those lands and become part of our country mirrors their country's character. It's their legacy.

Most people seem to have an enduring sense of pride about the food of their country of origin. Over time, the native language, dress, literature, and music are often set aside as individuals become integrated into their new country. But the traditions pertaining to food for everyday meals and celebrations are passed on from generation to generation and become long lasting.

By cooking and eating the foods of other ethnic groups, we learn about their culture and traditions. That, alone, is bound to develop a better global understanding. Better still, is eating together at the same table. That is an important activity in all cultures, and it provides a medium for sharing our lives and building friendships.

It is no wonder then, that an intense interest has developed in duplicating ethnic dishes. I think it is a delicious trend that is here to stay, and here are some of the reasons:

- Large numbers of immigrants from a multitude of different cultures have settled in Canada and the United States during the 20th century. With them, they have brought their traditional foods and customs.

- To celebrate this influx of immigrants, many cities and towns hold annual multi-cultural festivals. Edmonton's Folklorama and Toronto's Caravan are examples of these festive summer events. Ethnic music, dance, arts, crafts, and food are featured, giving others an opportunity to experience the culture and taste the food. Folk festivals, such as Toronto's Caribana, Dauphin's Ukrainian Festival, and Kitchener's Octoberfest, also offer foods to sample and savor. Once tried, many people yearn for more and want recipes.

- Over the past 20 years, more and more of us have visited foreign countries. And one of the pleasures of travel is enjoying the foods of those far-off lands. Once home,

we have the urge to reproduce some of the specialties in our own kitchens, or at least search for ethnic eateries that serve them.

- International guests to this country, over the years, have introduced us to the tastes of their homeland. Also, many North Americans, after having had the opportunity to live in other countries, have brought back food ideas and recipes to try here at home.

- Because of all of the above, all kinds of ethnic eateries have opened. In any cosmopolitan city or town, look through the restaurant guide. In it, you will find not only pizza parlors but also Middle Eastern falafel counters, Japanese sushi bars, and Jamaican patty houses. One can choose from Spanish, Italian, Thai, or East Indian cuisines, to name a few, on any given day. The tastes, aromas, and textures of the foods of the world are ours for the asking—Chinese hot and sour soup, Greek tzatsiki, German rouladen. And happily, good ethnic restaurants are usually casual, pleasant, and reasonably priced.

- Cookbooks focusing on ethnic cuisines fill bookstore shelves. Their titles alone take us on a trip around the world. My reference page is just a short list of ones that have helped me discover the exotic ingredients and unique tastes popular in other cultures.

- Magazines, many devoted to food alone, and newspaper lifestyle sections continue to bring us food features with titles such as *Portuguese Country Cooking, Ukrainian Christmas,* and *Finnish Festival of Lights.* These whet our appetites for typical ethnic dishes.

- Cooking classes across the country, focusing on Caribbean, Asian, Mediterranean, Italian, and other ethnic foods, become completely booked in no time, confirming the growing interest in ethnic cooking.

- Gourmet clubs for food lovers have sprung up here and there. They function as interest groups within most university women's clubs. In the one that I belong to, some of the meals my friends and I have prepared and shared over the past 25 years include a Strasburg Christmas, Mexican fiesta, Greek Easter, Swedish smorgasbord, and an Arabian picnic. Occasions such as these please the palate and provoke a passion for the foods of other cultures.

■ And last, but not least, some ethnic diets seem to be healthier than ours in the West. Chinese, Japanese, and Mediterranean diets are now considered to be the healthiest. They rely primarily on complex carbohydrates—lots of fresh fruits and vegetables, grains and cereals (rice, pasta, bread, polenta), and legumes—as the mainstay of their daily fare with small amounts of meat, poultry, or fish and dairy products used as an accompaniment or garnish rather than the centerpiece of a meal. That automatically cuts down on saturated fat and increases dietary fiber, which is exactly what the U.S. and Canadian dietary guides are recommending today.

What has been extremely fascinating to me as I have searched through cookbooks and magazines, chatted with individuals of different races, and tasted ethnic dishes has been the discovery of the number of similarities in cooking. The differences come from the variety of agricultural products and the nuances of aroma and flavor from the herbs, spices, and seasonings indigenous to different regions.

For a moment, just think of the foods that are put together in little bundles. Every culture, it seems, has morsels and mixtures wrapped with dough or pastry. These packages are boiled, steamed, baked, or deep-fried (but none of the latter in my kitchen). The Chinese wonton, Italian ravioli, Ukrainian perogie, and South American empanaditas are just a few examples.

Starters or appetizers are a part of most national cuisines. For Italians, antipasti are the hot and cold little things served before the pasta. The meze table of tasty morsels is set out by Greeks and Middle Easterners before their souvlaki or shish kebobs. For the Spanish, tapas is the small meal before the main one, and for Russians it is zakouski.

Every nationality seems to have its own great tossed green salad. The French call theirs salade verte and dress it with a vinaigrette. The Portuguese green salad is salada verde with cilantro as one of the prominent greens. In Italian homes, it's insalata mista, usually made with olives. For Greek diners, the operative name is salata meze made with traditional Greek vegetables—tomatoes, cucumbers, spinach, artichokes, onions.

Legumes, grains, and pasta with plenty of vegetables play a significant role in many ethnic cuisines. And, fortunately, all these foods have moved up on the social ladder in the West. Dishes such as East Indian dal, Portuguese feifoes assados (baked beans), Italian polenta, and Middle Eastern couscous are winning places at our tables.

Soups and stews originated in most lands as basic country or peasant cooking. Simmering vegetables, meats, and seasonings indigenous to a region resulted in satisfying repasts that could feed a few or many. One example is the three sisters soup from Canadian aboriginals with an Iroquois background. Squash, corn, and green beans (the three sisters) were planted together, grown together, and cooked together with wild game from the hunt and water from the stream.

Barbecuing meat probably comes from the days when Turkish hordes roamed and conquered large areas of Asia and Europe and roasted whole sheep and goats over their campfires. Today, chefs all over the world grill all sorts of items, and barbecuing is a universal cooking style practiced by most nationalities.

Chicken finds itself on the table of nearly every ethnic group. For Jamaicans, it will likely be jerk chicken. For the East Indian, it will likely be tandoori. Greek cooks roast it with lemon, and Russians grind it to make cotletki.

When the entrée is meat, British cooks are likely to roast beef. In Greek kitchens, lamb roasting with rosemary is common. In German homes, thin slices of breaded veal or pork turn into schnitzel. In Italian kitchens, the thin slices of breaded veal are called scallopine and are flavored with lemon juice to make piccata al limone. Meatballs made by Scandinavian cooks are dill-scented frikadeller, while those made by Latin Americans are spicy albodigintos.

Fish dishes range from grilled, steamed, and baked steaks and fillets to fish pies and patties. Of course, they are most popular among people from islands in the Caribbean or Pacific or from countries with large sea coasts, like the ones bordering the Mediterranean, the North Sea, and the China Sea.

Every nationality has its own bread. Basic recipes are similar. It is the type of flour used, the treatment of the ingredients, and the way in which the bread is baked that make one different from the other. Portuguese broa is made with corn flour, and Irish soda bread is made with oatmeal. Italian pizza and foccacia are baked as flat breads (so is the East Indian naan). Cakes range from the rich milk cake of the Portuguese to the light chocolate chiffon cake of North America, used for making the German Black Forest cake.

In all cultures, fruits native to the geographic area make perfect low-calorie, luscious desserts. For the Chinese, it is usually orange slices and lychees, sometimes accented with a touch of fresh or candied ginger. Cooks from the northern hemisphere make wonderful puddings and whips from berries that grow in those regions. Russian kissel, Scandinavian rodgrod, and British berry fool are a few of them.

Then, there are the desserts of celebrations. Believe it or not, rice pudding is one of them. For Scandinavians, it is ris a l'amande, and for the Chinese it is eight treasures pudding, studded with candied fruit. In French haute cuisine you find riz a l'imperatrice, and in Middle Eastern cookery it is shiri berenj. Light meringue also makes its presence in many different desserts, such as Italian biscuit tortoni, French meringue torte, and French Canadian floating islands.

Fortunately, since it is natural to share food with others, many of the world's best dishes now have a place in our lives. We can make East Indian tandoori and pilaf, Mexican mole and salsa, Chinese wontons and egg foo yung, Italian risotto and polenta, Portuguese bacalhoa and broa, and much more, all in our own kitchens.

Some ethnic recipes call for exotic and unfamiliar ingredients, but as much as possible I tried to make these with readily available ingredients. In doing so, a degree of authenticity has been sacrificed. Even though our supermarkets have shelves lined with various ethnic products and a wider selection of herbs and spices than ever before, the best selection and price for these are in ethnic and foreign food stores, such as the Greek, Oriental, and Caribbean ones that I visit regularly for my supplies. I also go for the joy of seeing, smelling, and sampling the food and meeting the people.

From out of this incredible array of influences, cross-cultural cooking is emerging. Food writers, chefs, and creative cooks are mixing ethnic cuisines on the contemporary food beat. And now we see fusion cooking, which is sort of a marriage between East and West, on magazine pages and in cookbooks—pita pizzas, beef tortilla pizzas, and Asian risotto.

These recipes will add great variety and flexibility to what you cook. In preparing these world-class dishes, your kitchen will take on fascinating, multicultural characteristics. And above all, there will certainly be good healthy eating at your global table, a precious gift to be enjoyed by your family and friends of all nationalities.

Kali orexi! Itadakimasu! Buon Appetito! Guten Appetit! Enjoy!

Kay Spicer, 1996

NUTRIENT ANALYSIS OF RECIPES

Nutrient analysis of recipes was performed by KEYS Nutrition Services, using the 1991 Canadian Nutrient File Nutrient Analysis Program, copyright Elizabeth Warwick, BHSc, PDt. Analysis was based on imperial measures. The analysis accounted for cooking methods, yields, and resultant changes in nutrient profile. Carbohydrate values are calculated as total carbohydrate minus dietary fiber.

Fiber Values in Individual Servings

Moderate Fiber	2.0–4.0 grams/serving
High Fiber	4.1–6.0 grams/serving
Very High Fiber	greater than 6.1 grams/serving

Recipe variations were averaged when the energy difference was minimal (less than 10 calories). When the recipe stated "salt to taste" and/or "salt and pepper to taste," these were not added to the recipe.

Recipes that are high in sodium, that is, 400 mg or more of sodium per serving, are marked with a ❀ symbol.

Canadian Diabetes Association Food Choice Values from the *Good Health Eating Guide System*, 1994, have been converted to the American Diabetes Association/The American Dietetic Association Exchanges from *Exchange Lists for Meal Planning*, 1995, by Madelyn L. Wheeler, MS, RD, CDE.

These recipes have not been tested or analyzed by the American Diabetes Association. Therefore, we cannot guarantee their accuracy.

Appetizers & Snacks

Hummus - *Middle Eastern*

Skordalia - *Greek*

Baba Ghannooj - *Middle Eastern*

Guacamole - *Mexican*

Chili con Queso - *Mexican*

Antipasto di Funghi Crudi - *Italian*

Brandade de Saumon Fumée - *French*

Brandade de Truite Fumée - *French*

Brandade de Huitres Fumée - *French*

Saté Ajam - *Indonesian*

Sushi - *Japanese*

Empanaditas - *South American*

Pirozhki - *Russian*

Pyrohy - *Eastern European*

Boureka - *Middle Eastern*

Dolmates - *Greek*

Fruit & Nut Dolmates - *Greek*

Quesadillas - *Mexican*

Huanese Dipping Sauce - *Chinese*

Chun Juan - *Chinese*

Mushroom Phyllo Nests - *Canadian*

Phyllo Nests or Shells - *Canadian*

Jia Chang Pai Gu - *Chinese*

Hsia Ch'iu - *Chinese*

Lemon Cilantro Dipping Sauce - *Chinese*

Cha Yun T'uns - *Chinese*

Hummus (Middle Eastern)
Light Hummus

Hummus is a staple for the Mediterranean or Middle Eastern meze (appetizer table). Torn pieces of pita bread and/or vegetable sticks and slices for dipping are served alongside the hummus.

1½ cups	cooked chickpeas	375 mL
	(19 oz/540 mL can, drained)	
2	cloves garlic	2
¼ cup	tahini*	50 mL
2 Tbsp	lemon juice	25 mL
½ tsp	salt	2 mL
6	drops hot pepper sauce	6
	Hot water	
	Chopped fresh chives or parsley	
	Paprika	

▪ Set aside 7 whole chickpeas for garnish.

▪ In food processor or blender, combine remaining chickpeas, garlic, tahini, lemon juice, salt, and hot pepper sauce. Puree, adding hot water to thin to consistency of thick paste.

▪ Transfer to serving plate or shallow bowl. Spread in circle, creating raised edge and indentation in center. Garnish with chives, paprika, and reserved chickpeas.

Makes about 1¾ cups (425 mL), 16 servings.

*TIMELY TIP
Tahini is sesame seed paste, available in specialty food stores that carry ingredients for Mediterranean and Israeli-style cooking. If tahini is unavailable, substitute 2 Tbsp (25 mL) peanut butter plus 2 Tbsp (25 mL) sesame oil.

Skordalia (Greek)

Country Bean Spread

In this variation of traditional skordalia, white beans are used in place of the potatoes. The resulting smooth, garlicky sauce makes a superb dip. It is also great as a sauce for steamed vegetables or fish.

1½ cups	cooked white kidney beans	375 mL
½ cup	fresh breadcrumbs	125 mL
2	cloves garlic, chopped	2
½ cup	low-fat yogurt	125 mL
1 Tbsp	lemon juice	15 mL
2 tsp	extra virgin olive oil	10 mL
	Chopped fresh mint or dill	

∎ In food processor, combine beans, breadcrumbs, garlic, yogurt, lemon juice, and olive oil. Puree until smooth. Transfer to serving bowl. Swirl top. Garnish with mint.

Makes about 2 cups (500 mL), 15 servings.

EACH SERVING
1/15 of recipe

½   Starch

46 calories
1 g total fat
0 g saturated fat
0 mg cholesterol
3 g protein
8 g carbohydrate
75 mg sodium
108 mg potassium

Baba Ghannooj (Middle Eastern)

Eggplant Dip

Mashed baked eggplant is the base for this dip or salad. Folklore indicates baba ghannooj was first made for an older, toothless Lebanese man, and the name means "spoiled old daddy."

1	medium eggplant (about 1 lb/500g)	1
1	onion, quartered	1
1	clove garlic, halved	1
	Juice of 1/2 lemon	
1 Tbsp	olive oil	15 mL
	Salt and freshly ground black pepper	

∎ Prick eggplant 4 or 5 times. Place on rack in small pan. Bake in 400°F (200°C) oven for about 40 minutes or until tender. Set aside to cool to room temperature. Peel and cube.

∎ In food processor or blender, combine eggplant, onion, garlic, lemon juice, and olive oil. Process until smooth. Season to taste with salt and pepper.

Makes about 1¾ cups (425 mL), 16 servings.

EACH SERVING
1/16 of recipe

1   Free

17 calories
1 g total fat
0 g saturated fat
0 mg cholesterol
0 g protein
2 g carbohydrate
1 mg sodium
66 mg potassium

Guacamole (Mexican)

Low-Fat Guacamole

True Mexican guacamole calls for avocados only. In this variation—half avocado, half zucchini—the fat content is substantially lower and so is the calorie count, but the flavor and texture are like the real thing.

2	small zucchini, shredded	2
1	green onion, finely chopped	1
1	small clove garlic, minced	1
1	jalapeno pepper, minced or 1 Tbsp (15 mL) chopped pickled jalapeno peppers	1
1 Tbsp	lime juice	15 mL
1/2 tsp	salt	2 mL
1	ripe avocado	1

■ In steamer or boiling water, steam or cook zucchini for 5 minutes or until tender. Drain well and mash. Cool.

■ In bowl, combine green onion, garlic, jalapeno pepper, lime juice, and salt.

■ Peel, seed, and mash avocado. Add to green onion mixture along with zucchini. Mash and stir until mixture is smooth with some small chunks.

■ To help prevent browning, squeeze a little lime juice over top. Cover with plastic wrap snug against top of dip. Refrigerate for up to 2 days. Stir before serving.

Makes 1½ cups (375 mL), 15 servings.

Chile con Queso (Mexican)

Hot Cheese Dip

Here is a warm cheesy dip accentuated with the heat of chili peppers. It is kind of a Mexican fondue, perfect as a dip for crisp vegetables or snappy tortilla chips.

2 tsp	canola oil	10 mL
1	onion, finely chopped	1
1	clove garlic, minced	1
2 tsp	all-purpose flour	10 mL
2 tsp	chili powder	10 mL
1 cup	drained canned tomatoes	250 mL
½ lb	shredded cheddar or Monterey Jack cheese	250 g
1	jalapeno pepper, seeded and finely chopped or 1 Tbsp (15 mL) finely chopped pickled jalapeno peppers Salt and freshly ground black pepper	1

▪ In saucepan, heat oil over medium heat. Cook onion and garlic for 5 minutes or until onion is translucent. Stir in flour and chili powder; cook, stirring constantly, for 1 minute.

▪ Stir in tomatoes; cook, stirring, for 4 minutes or until thickened. Reduce heat. Gradually add cheese, stirring constantly until cheese melts. Remove from heat. Stir in peppers and season to taste with salt and pepper.

▪ Serve hot in fondue pot or small chafing dish.

Makes 2 cups (500 mL), 20 servings.

EACH SERVING
1/20 of recipe

½ Meat, lean
½ Fat

55 calories
4 g total fat
2 g saturated fat
11 mg cholesterol
3 g protein
1 g carbohydrate
98 mg sodium
44 mg potassium

Antipasto di Funghi Crudi (Italian)

Marinated Mushrooms

For Italian cooks, these little mushroom "pickles" are ideal for the antipasto tray. They are just as great with a sandwich platter. Each one delivers a mouthful of flavor with almost no calories.

EACH SERVING
1/12 **of recipe**

1   Free

   12 calories
   0 g total fat
   0 g saturated fat
 0 mg cholesterol
   0 g protein
   2 g carbohydrate
67 mg sodium
158 mg potassium

1 lb	button mushrooms	500 g
½ cup	water	125 mL
¼ cup	white wine vinegar	50 mL
2 Tbsp	lemon juice	25 mL
8	black peppercorns	8
2	green onions (with tops), thinly sliced	2
2	cloves garlic, minced	2
½ tsp	salt	2 mL
¼ cup	chopped fresh parsley	50 mL

▪ Rinse mushrooms, set aside.

▪ In large saucepan, combine water, vinegar, lemon juice, peppercorns, green onions, garlic, and salt. Bring to boil. Add mushrooms, and boil for 1 minute. Stir well. Stir in parsley.

▪ Transfer to screw-top jars.

▪ Refrigerate for 6 hours or overnight for flavors to blend. (Keeps, refrigerated, for 3 weeks.)

Makes about 4 cups (1L), 12 appetizer servings.

Brandade de Saumon Fumée (French)

Smoked Salmon Spread

This light spread seems to stretch the delightfully smoky taste of the fish. Spread it on melba toast or zucchini slices, and pipe it into little cherry tomato cups.*

¼ lb	smoked salmon	125 g
½ cup	light cream cheese (125 g)	125 mL
½ cup	1% cottage cheese	125 mL
1	small clove garlic, minced	1
2 tsp	lemon juice	10 mL
2 tsp	horseradish	10 mL
1 tsp	tomato paste	5 mL
1½ tsp	chopped fresh dill	7 mL
	or ½ tsp (2 mL) dried	
¼ tsp	freshly ground black pepper	1 mL

▪ In container of food processor, combine smoked salmon, cream cheese, cottage cheese, garlic, lemon juice, horseradish, tomato paste, dill, and pepper. Process for about 2 minutes, scraping down processor bowl frequently, until pureed and smooth. Spoon into serving crock or dish.

▪ Cover and refrigerate overnight for flavors to blend, or keep refrigerated for up to 3 days.

Makes 1¼ cups (300 mL), 15 servings.

VARIATIONS

Brandade de Truite Fumée (French)
Smoked Trout Spread

• In place of smoked salmon, use smoked trout; in place of tomato paste, use Dijon-style mustard.

Brandade de Huitres Fumée (French)
Smoked Oyster Spread

• In place of smoked salmon, use 1 can (3½ oz/92 g) smoked oysters, well drained. In place of dill, use 1 Tbsp (15 mL) chopped fresh parsley.

For Dips: Blend ¼ cup (50 mL) skim milk into spreads.

EACH SERVING
¹⁄₁₅ of recipe

½ Meat, lean

33 calories
1 g total fat
0 g saturated fat
6 mg cholesterol
3 g protein
1 g carbohydrate
144 mg sodium
40 mg potassium

*TIMELY TIP
To make cherry tomato cups: Slice stem end from cherry tomato. With small spoon, scoop out seedy interior. Place cut side down on paper towels to drain. Just before serving, pipe or spoon filling into cavity. Garnish with chopped parsley or chives.

Calculations approximately the same as above.

Saté Ajam (Indonesian)

Chicken Satay

Satés or satays are the Indonesian version of kebabs. Small pieces of marinated meats or poultry are skewered, grilled, or broiled and served with a hot, spicy, nut-based sauce. They make great appetizers for a crowd or tasty light fare with rice and a salad.

2 lbs	boneless chicken breasts	1 kg
3/4 cup	boiling water	175 mL
1/2 cup	unsweetened desiccated coconut	125 mL
1/3 cup	smooth peanut butter	75 mL
2 Tbsp	sesame oil	25 mL
2 Tbsp	lite soy sauce	25 mL
2 Tbsp	lemon juice	25 mL
1 Tbsp	shredded fresh ginger root	15 mL
1	clove garlic, minced	1
6	drops hot pepper sauce	6
24	wooden or bamboo skewers*	24
	Sugar substitute equivalent to 1/2 tsp (2 mL) sugar	

▪ Cut chicken into strips about 1/4 inch (5 mm) thick, 3/4 inch (2 cm) wide, and 3 to 4 inches (8 to 10 cm) long.

▪ In small bowl, pour boiling water over coconut. Let stand for 20 minutes. Strain liquid into another bowl. Discard coconut.

▪ To coconut liquid, add peanut butter, sesame oil, soy sauce, lemon juice, ginger root, garlic, and hot pepper sauce; mix thoroughly.

▪ Add chicken, coating pieces with peanut butter mixture. Cover and refrigerate for about 30 minutes to marinate.

▪ Remove chicken strips from marinade. Thread accordion-style on skewers. Pour marinade into saucepan.

▪ Place skewers on a rack in shallow baking or roasting pan.

▪ Bake in 350°F (180°C) oven for about 10 minutes or until meat is no longer pink. Alternatively, place on grill and barbecue over hot coals, turning once, for 10 minutes.

▪ Bring marinade to boil; cook for 1 1/2 minutes. Cool. Sweeten to taste with sugar substitute. Transfer to flat dish for dipping satés.

Makes 24 satés, 12 servings.

*TIMELY TIP
Soak wooden or bamboo skewers in water for about an hour before using to help prevent scorching of the ends as the satay cooks.

Sushi (Japanese)

Sushi

Takeout from sushi bars became popular in the early '90s. Even though it may seem daring, it is easy to make sushi, or "vinegared rice," at home.

2 cups	short-grained rice	500 mL
2 ¼ cups	water	550 mL
¼ cup	rice vinegar	50 mL
	Sugar substitute equivalent to 2 tsp (10 mL) sugar	
¼ tsp	salt	1 mL
4	sheets nori* (toasted seaweed)	4

FILLINGS
(each combination will fill 2 sheets of nori)
1) 8 imitation crabmeat legs, 4 slices avocado, 4 green onions
2) 4 large steamed spinach leaves, 4 long thin slices of seedless cucumber, 8 cooked shrimp cut in half lengthwise

GARNISHES
pickled ginger, Japanese soy sauce, wasabi, mixed with enough water to form a paste

▪ Rinse rice; drain well. In saucepan, combine rice with water; let it stand for 30 minutes. Bring to boil. Reduce heat, cover and simmer for 12 minutes or until water is absorbed. Remove from heat, uncover, and drape a clean tea towel over the saucepan. Replace cover and let stand for 15 minutes to steam.

▪ Combine rice vinegar, sugar substitute, and salt.

▪ Place cooked rice on shallow platter and run wooden spoon through it to separate grains. Gradually fold in vinegar mixture as rice cools.

▪ To make sushi, lay sheet of nori, crosswise, on bamboo mat or heavy cloth mat. Spread 1 cup (250 mL) sushi rice evenly on the nori, leaving 1-inch (2.5-cm) strip uncovered at the upper edge.

▪ Make an indentation across rice about ⅓ of the way from the bottom. Lay fillings in rows across indentation.

▪ Starting with closest edge, and using mat to help, begin rolling nori tightly. Moisten uncovered edge and seal.

▪ Wrap the mat around the rolled nori and shape it into a smooth cylinder. Remove mat and with sharp knife slice each cylinder into 8 equal portions. Arrange slices, cut side down, on serving plate.

▪ Serve with separate tiny dishes of pickled ginger, soy sauce, and wasabi for dipping.

Makes 32 sushi, 16 servings.

EACH SERVING
¹⁄₁₆ of recipe

1½ Starch

99	calories
0 g	total fat
0 g	saturated fat
0 mg	cholesterol
3 g	protein
20 g	carbohydrate
81 mg	sodium
55 mg	potassium

*TIMELY TIP
Nori, shitake mushrooms, pickled ginger, and wasabi (Japanese powdered green horseradish) are available at Japanese and Oriental markets.

Empanaditas (South American)

Little Meat Pies

These little pastry turnovers with a spicy, sweet meat filling are mini versions of the Spanish empanadas. The little pies take the place of sandwiches and are popular with Latin American families.

Light Sour Cream Pastry (recipe p. 162)

2 tsp	butter	10 mL
1	onion, finely chopped	1
1	clove garlic, minced	1
½ lb	ground beef	250 g
1	tomato, seeded and finely chopped	1
4	pimento-stuffed olives, finely chopped	4
2 Tbsp	raisins, finely chopped	25 mL
1 tsp	chili powder	5 mL
	Salt and freshly ground black pepper	
2 tsp	dry breadcrumbs	10 mL
1	egg white beaten with 2 tsp (10 mL) water and pinch salt	1

▪ Prepare pastry; wrap it and chill in refrigerator.

▪ In nonstick skillet, heat butter over medium heat. Cook onion and garlic for 3 minutes. Stir in ground beef; cook, stirring to break up meat, for 5 minutes or until browned and crumbly.

▪ Stir in tomato, olives, raisins, chili powder, salt, and pepper. Bring to boil. Reduce heat and simmer, uncovered, for 5 minutes or until thickened. Stir in breadcrumbs.

▪ Divide pastry evenly into 24 balls. Roll or pat out into 4-inch (10-cm) circles.

▪ Place heaping teaspoonful (5 mL) meat mixture in center of each circle. Lightly brush edge with egg white wash, and fold dough over filling to form half circle. Pinch edges together. With fork, prick each one 3 times.

▪ Arrange on nonstick baking sheets. Brush top with egg white wash.

▪ Bake in 375°F (190°C) oven for 20 minutes or until golden brown.

Makes 24.

EACH SERVING
¹⁄₂₄ of recipe

½ Starch
½ Meat, lean
1 Fat

113 calories
7 g total fat
2 g saturated fat
8 mg cholesterol
3 g protein
10 g carbohydrate
120 mg sodium
64 mg potassium

Pirozhki (Russian)

Savory Pastries

This is a baked version of pyrohy, popular with Russians and Eastern Europeans for both celebrations and everyday fare. Pirozhki appear on the zakouski table and make great accompaniments to salads and soups, especially borscht.

Light Sour Cream Pastry (recipe p. 162)

½ lb	lean ground beef	250 g
1	small onion, finely chopped	1
2 Tbsp	chopped fresh dill or 2 tsp (10 mL) dried	25 mL
2 Tbsp	1% sour cream	25 mL
	Salt and freshly ground black pepper	
1	egg white, beaten	1
1 tsp	all-purpose flour	5 mL
1	egg white beaten with 2 tsp (10 mL) water and pinch salt	1

- Prepare pastry; wrap it and chill in refrigerator.
- In nonstick skillet, over medium heat, cook ground beef and onion, stirring occasionally for 5 minutes or until meat is no longer pink. Remove from heat. Stir in dill and sour cream. Season to taste with salt and pepper. Cool to room temperatrure.
- On lightly floured surface, roll out pastry to ⅜-inch (4-mm) thickness. With 3-inch (7.5-cm) cookie cutter, cut into circles.
- Stir egg white into meat mixture.
- Place rounded teaspoonful (5 mL) on center of each circle. Dab outside edge with a little water. Pinch edges of each circle together in thirds to form tricornered patty. Place on nonstick baking sheet. Lightly brush tops with egg white wash.
- Bake in 375°F (190°C) oven for 15 minutes or until golden brown.

Makes 24 pastries.

EACH SERVING
1 pastry

½   Starch
½   Meat, lean
1   Fat

107   calories
6 g   total fat
1 g   saturated fat
8 mg   cholesterol
3 g   protein
9 g   carbohydrate
108 mg   sodium
50 mg   potassium

Pyrohy (Ukrainian, Eastern European)

Pyrohy

To some cooks, these "packages" may seem like large ravioli. The concept is similar. Assorted fillings, such as chopped cabbage, cheese mixtures, chopped meats, fish, mushrooms, and even fruit, are wrapped with pasta-like dough and then cooked. They are also called perogies. They have had the reputation of being fattening, but this slimmed-down version is low in fat.

EACH SERVING
1/12 of recipe

2   Starch
1   Fat

218   calories
6 g   total fat
1 g   saturated fat
10 mg   cholesterol
6 g   protein
33 g   carbohydrate
398 mg   sodium
185 mg   potassium

3 cups	all-purpose flour	750 mL
1 tsp	salt	5 mL
1/4 tsp	cream of tartar	1 mL
2 Tbsp	canola oil	25 mL
1 1/4 cups	lukewarm water	300 mL

FILLING

1 tsp	butter or oil	5 mL
1/2 cup	finely chopped onion	125 mL
2 cups	mashed potatoes	500 mL
1 cup	low-fat cottage cheese, drained	250 mL
	Salt and freshly ground black pepper	

TOPPING

2 tsp	butter	10 mL
1 cup	chopped onions	250 mL
1 cup	low-fat sour cream	250 mL

■ In mixing bowl, combine flour, salt, and cream of tartar. Add oil to water and stir into flour mixture until soft dough is formed: knead well. Cover dough and let stand for 30 minutes.

■ Filling: In nonstick skillet, melt butter; add onion and saute for 3 minutes. Stir in mashed potatoes, cottage cheese, salt and pepper to taste. Set aside to cool.

■ On lightly floured surface, roll out dough to 1/8-inch (3-mm) thickness. Cut into 3-inch (8-cm) squares. Place a generous teaspoonful of filling in center of each square. Fold corner to corner to form a triangle. Pinch edges together until well sealed. Place pyrohy on plate lightly dusted with cornstarch. Cover with tea towel to keep from drying out.

■ Drop 8 pyrohy at a time into pot of lightly salted boiling water. Boil for 10 minutes or until pyrohy rise to surface and dough is cooked. Remove with slotted spoon and drain in colander.

■ Topping: In nonstick skillet, melt butter over medium heat. Cook onions for 5 minutes or until tender. Place in bowl; add pyrohy. Toss to coat. Top each serving with low-fat sour cream.

Makes 24, 12 servings.

Boureka (Middle Eastern)

Meaty Phyllo Squares

Here is a crispy, light finger food using phyllo pastry in a low-fat way. It is similar to the German bierocks and the Greek spinach and cheese bourrek.

2 tsp	olive oil	10 mL
1	onion, finely chopped	1
½ lb	lean ground beef	250 g
1 tsp	ground allspice	5 mL
½ tsp	salt	2 mL
¼ tsp	freshly ground black pepper	1 mL
1	tomato, peeled, seeded, and diced	1
¼ cup	finely chopped walnuts or almonds	50 mL
2 Tbsp	chopped fresh parsley	25 mL
8	sheets phyllo pastry	8
1 Tbsp	butter, melted	15 mL

- In nonstick skillet, heat oil over medium-high heat. Cook onion for 3 minutes. Add ground beef, allspice, salt, and pepper. Cook, stirring to break up meat, until it is crumbly and no longer pink.
- Stir in tomato, nuts, and parsley. Set aside to cool.
- Line 11 x 15 inch (28 x 38 cm) jelly roll pan with 1 sheet phyllo pastry. Lightly dab here and there with melted butter. Repeat with 4 additional sheets of phyllo.
- Spread meat mixture evenly over top. Place 1 sheet of phyllo over filling, lightly dab with butter. Repeat with 2 remaining sheets of phyllo. With scissors, cut off any pastry hanging over edges of pan.
- With serrated knife, cut through top crust layers into 24 squares.
- Bake in 350°F (180°C) oven for 20 minutes or until golden brown.
- Let stand for 10 minutes. Cut completely through top crust and bottom crust to serve.

Makes 24 squares, 12 servings.

EACH SERVING
1/12 of recipe

½ Starch
½ Meat, lean
1 Fat

114 calories
6 g total fat
2 g saturated fat
12 mg cholesterol
5 g protein
9 g carbohydrate
184 mg sodium
108 mg potassium

Stuffed Grape Leaves

In some cookbooks, stuffed grape leaves are listed as dolmathes or dolmas. Turkish cooks call them dolmades. The names come from the Arabic word for "something stuffed." In this case, it is grape leaves. They make a terrific appetizer.

½ cup	long-grain rice	125 mL
36	small grape leaves*	36
½ lb	ground lamb or beef	250 g
1	onion, finely chopped	1
¼ cup	chopped fresh parsley	50 mL
½ tsp	anise seed, crushed	2 mL
½ tsp	chopped fresh mint	2 mL
	Salt and freshly ground black pepper	
2 Tbsp	lemon juice	25 mL
	Grated lemon rind	

- Pour boiling water over rice; let it stand for 10 minutes.
- In steamer or saucepan of lightly salted boiling water, steam or blanch grape leaves for 2 minutes or until limp. Drain and rinse under cold running water.
- Drain rice. In bowl, combine ground lamb, onion, parsley, anise seed, and mint until well blended. Season to taste with salt and pepper.
- Arrange grape leaves, dull side up, on working surface. Place 2 Tbsp (25 mL) lamb mixture on each leaf. Fold lower edge over filling, turn sides in, and loosely roll up.
- Arrange in single layer, in batches, on steamer basket. Cover and steam over boiling water for 20 minutes or until rice is tender and meat is no longer pink. Repeat with next batch.
- Transfer dolmates to serving plate.
- Sprinkle with lemon juice and grated rind.
- Serve hot, at room temperature, or cold.

Makes 36 rolls, 6 servings.

*TIMELY TIP
When fresh grape leaves are not available, use pickled ones. They are found in specialty shops or gourmet shops dealing with Mediterranean foods. Always rinse well to remove the brine.

VARIATION
Fruit and Nut Dolmates
- Delete ground meat.
- Add ¼ cup (50 mL) each currants and chopped almonds or pine nuts. Add a pinch each of ground allspice and cinnamon to the rice mixture.

Quesadillas (Mexican)

Quesadillas

Queso is the Spanish word for cheese, and quesadillas can be called the Mexican version of the grilled cheese sandwich.

4	7-inch (18-cm) flour tortillas	4
½ cup	shredded light mozzarella cheese	125 mL
¼ cup	shredded old cheddar cheese	50 mL
2	slices smoked chicken or turkey, slivered	2
2	green onions, thinly sliced	2
½ cup	finely chopped fresh cilantro	125 mL
1	tomato, finely chopped and drained	1
2 tsp	finely chopped pickled jalapeno peppers	10 mL

▪ Place tortillas, one at a time, on preheated nonstick skillet. Evenly distribute ¼ of mozzarella, cheddar, chicken, onions, cilantro, tomato, and peppers over top.

▪ Cook over medium heat until cheese melts (tortilla shouldn't brown). Fold to make half moon; press firmly in place. Transfer to baking sheet or platter in warm oven.

▪ Repeat with remaining tortillas and remaining ingredients.

▪ Cut each into 2 or 3 wedges. Serve immediately.

Makes 4 servings.

EACH SERVING
¼ of recipe

1   Starch
1   Meat, medium-fat

153 calories
6 g total fat
3 g saturated fat
19 mg cholesterol
10 g protein
15 g carbohydrate
291 mg sodium
171 mg potassium

GOOD
Calcium, Vitamin B$_{12}$

Huanese Dipping Sauce (Chinese)

Hot Sauce

Huanese dipping sauce is hot. Vary the heat by decreasing or increasing the hot Oriental chili paste.

2 Tbsp	each lite soy sauce, lemon juice, and water	25 mL
1 Tbsp	hoisin sauce	15 mL
2 tsp	sesame oil	10 mL
2 tsp	grated fresh ginger root	10 mL
½ tsp	hot Oriental chili paste	2 mL
2 Tbsp	each finely chopped green onions and fresh cilantro	25 mL

▪ In bowl, whisk together soy sauce, lemon juice, water, hoisin sauce, sesame oil, ginger root, and chili paste. Stir in green onions and cilantro.

Makes ½ cup (125 mL), 8 servings.

EACH SERVING
⅛ of recipe

1   Free

14 calories
1 g total fat
0 g saturated fat
0 mg cholesterol
0 g protein
1 g carbohydrate
215 mg sodium
24 mg potassium

Chun Juan (Chinese)

Spring Rolls

Smaller, more delicate egg rolls are called spring rolls. In Chinese culture, the name comes from the custom of greeting friends and relatives on the first day of the Chinese New Year, which occurs in early spring, with tea and these crispy rolls. Filipinos call these lumpia. The Vietnamese wrap the filling in moistened rice paper wrappers and call them cha gio.

2 Tbsp	dried Oriental mushrooms	25 mL
½ lb	cooked lean pork or beef	250 g
6	cooked medium shrimp, peeled, deveined	6
4 tsp	canola oil	20 mL
1	onion, finely chopped	1
2 tsp	grated fresh ginger root	10 mL
1 Tbsp	lite soy sauce	15 mL
3	green onions, finely chopped	3
1 cup	shredded Chinese cabbage	250 mL
1 cup	bean sprouts, chopped	250 mL
1 cup	grated carrot	250 mL
	Salt and freshly ground black pepper	
12	spring or egg roll wrappers*	12
1 Tbsp	canola oil	15 mL
	Huanese Dipping Sauce (recipe p. 15)	

▪ In small bowl, cover mushrooms with hot water and let stand for 20 minutes or until softened. Drain well. Discard stems. Finely chop caps. Set aside.

▪ Cut pork and shrimp into thin strips lengthwise. Set aside.

▪ In nonstick skillet, heat oil over medium heat. Cook onion, ginger root, and soy sauce for 5 minutes or until onion is translucent. Stir in green onions, cabbage, bean sprouts, and carrots. Stir-cook for 2 minutes. Stir in mushrooms, pork, and shrimp. Heat through. Season to taste with salt and pepper.

▪ Lay spring roll wrappers out on clean surface, with one point of each wrapper facing you. Divide filling into 12 equal portions. Place one portion just above the bottom point on each wrapper. Fold side points in, overlapping slightly. Brush top point of each wrapper with water. Starting at the point facing you, roll up, pressing to seal. Place on lightly oiled plate. Cover and chill for 1 hour.

▪ In nonstick skillet, heat oil over medium heat. Cook rolls, turning often, for 3 to 4 minutes or until golden.

▪ Serve with Huanese Dipping Sauce (recipe p. 15).

Makes 12 spring rolls, 12 servings.

Mushroom Phyllo Nests

These filled pastries look much richer than they are.

30	Phyllo Nests (recipe below)	30
1 lb	mushrooms, wiped and stemmed	500 g
1 Tbsp	butter or canola oil	15 mL
½ tsp	minced garlic	2 mL
Pinch	ground nutmeg	Pinch
1 Tbsp	lite soy sauce	15 mL
3	green onions, minced	3
2 Tbsp	finely chopped toasted pecans or walnuts	25 mL
2 Tbsp	light mayonnaise	25 mL
	Salt and freshly ground black pepper	
	Parsley sprigs	
	Red sweet pepper slivers	

▪ Prepare and bake Phyllo Nests.

▪ Finely chop mushrooms.

▪ In nonstick skillet, melt butter over medium heat. Cook mushrooms, garlic, and nutmeg, stirring occasionally, for 7 minutes or until pieces begin to dry and separate. Stir in soy sauce, green onions, and pecans until well mixed. Blend in mayonnaise. Season to taste with salt and pepper. Spoon into phyllo nests.

▪ Garnish each nest with parsley and red pepper.

Makes 30 nests.

EACH SERVING
5 nests

1	Starch
1½	Fat

135	calories
8 g	total fat
3 g	saturated fat
13 mg	cholesterol
4 g	protein
13 g	carbohydrate
262 mg	sodium
369 mg	potassium

TIMELY TIP
The shells or nests can be made ahead and kept in a covered container in a cool dry place for 6 weeks. If baking in batches, keep buttered phyllo squares covered with waxed paper and damp cloth while first batch bakes.

Phyllo Nests or Shells

These buttery tasting, crisp containers for savory or sweet fillings take only minutes to assemble.

4	sheets phyllo pastry	4
1–2 Tbsp	melted butter	15–25 mL

▪ Place one sheet of phyllo pastry on working surface. Using pastry brush, dab here and there with butter; cover with second sheet of phyllo and dab sparingly with butter. Repeat with remaining sheets of phyllo.

▪ Cut in half crosswise. Cut each half crosswise in fifths and lengthwise in thirds to make 15 squares. With fingers, gently press each square (it will be 4 layers) into nonstick 2-inch (5-cm) muffin cups or tart pans.

▪ Bake in 350°F (180°C) oven for 10 minutes or until golden brown.

Makes 30.

EACH SERVING
5 nests

½	Starch
½	Fat

50	calories
2 g	total fat
1 g	saturated fat
5 mg	cholesterol
2 g	protein
8 g	carbohydrate
115 mg	sodium
15 mg	potassium

Shanghai Ribs

These glazed ribs are as close as I could come to the mouth-watering ones that I tasted in Shanghai.

2 lb	pork back ribs	1 kg
8	whole black peppercorns	8
3	cloves garlic, cut in half	3
1	onion stuck with 4 whole cloves	1
1	bay leaf	1

MARINADE

1	can (10 oz/284 mL) beef consommé	1
2 Tbsp	hoisin sauce	25 mL
1 Tbsp	cooking sherry	15 mL
2	cloves garlic, minced	2
1 Tbsp	grated fresh ginger root	15 mL
1 tsp	Chinese five spice	5 mL
1 tsp	toasted sesame seeds	5 mL

▪ Ask butcher to cut strips of ribs in half crosswise, then cut strips into single rib portions.

▪ In medium saucepan, combine ribs, peppercorns, garlic, studded onion, and bay leaf. Bring to boil. Reduce heat, cover and simmer for 40 minutes or until nearly tender. Drain well, rinse under running water, and pat dry.

▪ Place precooked ribs in large shallow baking dish or roasting pan in as close to a single layer as possible.

▪ Marinade: In bowl, mix together consommé, hoisin sauce, sherry, garlic, ginger root, and Chinese five spice. Pour over ribs; cover and marinate, turning several times, in refrigerator for 4 to 6 hours.

▪ Drain marinade into saucepan. Bring to boil; cook for 5 minutes or until slightly reduced. Pour back over ribs.

▪ Bake in 350°F (180°C) oven, turning occasionally, for 35 minutes or until ribs are browned and glazed.

▪ Arrange on serving platter. Sprinkle lightly with sesame seeds.

Makes 30 pieces, 10 servings.

EACH SERVING
1/10 of recipe

3   Meat, lean

166 calories
7 g total fat
2 g saturated fat
43 mg cholesterol
22 g protein
3 g carbohydrate
310 mg sodium
410 mg potassium

GOOD
Phosphorus, Zinc, Riboflavin, Vitamin B$_6$, Vitamin B$_{12}$

EXCELLENT
Thiamin, Niacin

TIMELY TIP
Precooking tenderizes the ribs and helps to eliminate excess fat.

Hsia Ch'iu (Chinese)

Cantonese Shrimp Balls

Chinese cooks from Canton, known as the culinary center of China, cook with a light touch, often steaming their dishes, like these shrimp balls.

1 lb	raw shrimp, shelled and deveined	500 g
6	water chestnuts, finely chopped	6
2	green onions, finely chopped	2
2 tsp	cornstarch	10 mL
1 tsp	finely chopped fresh ginger root	5 mL
1 tsp	sesame oil	5 mL
¼ tsp	salt	1 mL
Pinch	white pepper	Pinch
1	egg white	1
	Lemon Cilantro Dipping Sauce (recipe below)	

▪ Finely chop shrimp. Place in bowl. Add water chestnuts, green onions, cornstarch, ginger root, sesame oil, salt, and pepper. Stir in egg white until well blended. Form into 24 small balls.

▪ Place on cheesecloth-lined steamer basket. Cover and place over boiling water. Steam for 5 to 7 minutes or until firm.

▪ Serve on toothpicks, with Lemon Cilantro Dipping Sauce.

Makes 24, 12 servings.

EACH SERVING
1/12 of recipe

1   Meat, lean

      51 calories
       1 g total fat
       0 g saturated fat
     58 mg cholesterol
       8 g protein
       2 g carbohydrate
    132 mg sodium
     89 mg potassium

Lemon Cilantro Dipping Sauce (Chinese)

Lemon Cilantro Dipping Sauce

This exquisite sauce complements the shrimp balls and will also bring compliments to the cook.

	Juice of half lemon	
1 Tbsp	lite soy sauce	15 mL
2 tsp	rice vinegar	10 mL
1 tsp	sesame oil	5 mL
½ tsp	minced garlic	2 mL
¼ tsp	Oriental chili paste	1 mL
1 cup	packed cilantro or watercress leaves	250 mL
	Salt and freshly ground black pepper	

▪ In small food processor, combine lemon juice, soy sauce, rice vinegar, sesame oil, garlic, chili sauce, and cilantro. Process until pureed.

▪ Season to taste with salt and pepper.

Makes ¾ cup (175 mL), 12 servings.

EACH SERVING
1/12 of recipe

1   Free

       6 calories
       0 g total fat
       0 g saturated fat
       0 mg cholesterol
       0 g protein
       0 g carbohydrate
      87 mg sodium
      17 mg potassium

Cha Yun T'uns (Chinese)

Wontons

All sorts of dumplings or little packages similar to these turn up in Chinese cooking and are an integral part of dim sum. Like pyrohys, they are also similar to Italian ravioli. To turn them into pot stickers, brown the bottoms in a nonstick skillet before steaming.

½ lb	ground chicken or pork	250 g
¼ lb	raw shrimp, peeled and deveined, and finely chopped	125 g
½ cup	finely shredded and chopped cabbage	125 mL
8	water chestnuts, finely chopped	8
2	green onions, finely chopped	2
1 Tbsp	lite soy sauce	15 mL
2 tsp	cornstarch	10 mL
1 tsp	each sesame oil and rice vinegar	5 mL
¼ tsp	hot Oriental chili paste	1 mL
Pinch	each salt and white pepper	Pinch
1	egg white	1
24	wonton wrappers*	24
	Huanese Dipping Sauce (recipe p. 15)	

▪ In bowl, combine chicken, shrimp, cabbage, water chestnuts, green onions, soy sauce, cornstarch, sesame oil, vinegar, chili paste, salt, and pepper until well mixed. Stir in egg white until well blended. Chill for 10 minutes.

▪ Arrange wonton wrappers on work surface. Place spoonful of filling on each. Brush edges with bit of water. Fold dough over into triangle; pinch edges to seal. Press little pleats into the sealed edge for decoration. Place on nonstick baking sheet lightly dusted with cornstarch. Cover with dry kitchen towel.

▪ Lightly oil bottom of steamer basket with sesame oil. Arrange dumplings in basket, about 12 at a time. Place over boiling water. Steam for 4 minutes or until shiny and filling is no longer pink.

▪ Serve with Huanese Dipping Sauce (recipe p. 15)

Makes 24, 8 servings.

*TIMELY TIP
Wonton wrappers or skins are paper-thin squares of uncooked dough and can be purchased in some super-markets or in Oriental specialty stores.

*Chinese Dim Sum,
Cha Yun T'uns (Wontons),
Hsia Ch'iu (Cantonese Shrimp Balls),
Jia Chang Pai Gu (Shanghai Ribs).*

Soups

Sopa Azteca - *Mexican*

Minestrone - *Italian*

Sopa de Feijao - *South American/Portuguese*

Soupe aux Pois - *French Canadian*

Three Sisters Soup - *Canadian Aboriginal*

Soupe aux Tomates et au Lait - *French Canadian*

Vichyssoise - *French*

Bloomkallsuppe - *Scandinavian*

Potage Crème de Champignons - *French*

Potage Crème de Laitue - *French*

Caldo Verde - *Portuguese*

Borscht - *Russian, Ukrainian*

Scotch Broth - *British*

Cock-a-Leekie - *British*

Sopa de Agriao - *Portuguese*

Bouillabaisse - *French*

Soupe a l'Oignon Gratinée - *French*

Tom Yam Kung - *Thai*

Hun T'un T'ang - *Chinese*

Gazpacho - *Spanish*

Jajik - *Middle Eastern*

Sopa Azteca
(Chicken Tortilla Soup),
Guacamole, Tortilla
Chips

Sopa Azteca (Mexican)

Chicken Tortilla Soup

When I make this soup, I'm filled with memories of my early '80s trip to San Miguel Allende in Central Mexico. It was at a cooking school there where I made this and learned about the nuances of aroma, flavor, color, and texture that one finds in Mexican food.

3	6-inch (15-cm) corn or flour tortillas	3
2 tsp	canola oil	10 mL
1	onion, finely chopped	1
1	clove garlic, minced	1
1	jalapeno pepper, minced	1
¼ tsp	ground coriander	1 mL
1	can (19 oz/540 mL) tomatoes	1
3 cups	chicken broth	750 mL
1 cup	shredded cooked chicken	250 mL
1 Tbsp	lime juice	15 mL
	Salt and freshly ground pepper	
	Thin lime slices	

▪ Tear or cut tortillas into 2 x ½ inch (5 x 1 cm) strips. Place in single layer on baking sheet. Bake in 350°F (180°C) oven for about 10 minutes or until crisp and golden.

▪ In large saucepan or soup kettle, heat oil over medium heat. Cook onion and garlic for 4 minutes or until translucent. Stir in jalapeno and coriander. Cook for 1 minute.

▪ Stir in tomatoes, breaking up with fork, and broth. Bring to boil. Reduce heat, cover and simmer for 10 minutes. Add chicken; simmer for 10 minutes or until flavors are well blended. Stir in lime juice. Season to taste with salt and pepper.

▪ Ladle into soup bowls; add tortilla strips. Float lime slice in center of each bowl.

Makes 6 cups (1.5 L), 6 servings.

Minestrone (Italian)

Minestrone

The word minestrone means a "big soup." That's exactly what this one is. Adapted from the Italian classic, it is filled with pasta, beans, and peas. Although meatless and low in fat, it is still hearty enough to be a meal in a bowl.

2 tsp	olive or canola oil	10 mL
1	onion, chopped	1
2	cloves garlic, minced	2
2	carrots, diced	2
2	stalks celery, sliced	2
1	potato, peeled and diced	1
2 cups	shredded and chopped cabbage	500 mL
3 cups	beef broth	750 mL
1	can (19 oz/540 mL) tomatoes	1
2 cups	water	500 mL
1 Tbsp	chopped fresh oregano or 1 tsp (5 mL) dried	25 mL
1	bay leaf	1
1	can (19 oz/540 mL) white or red kidney or Romano beans	1
2 oz	spaghetti, broken	60 g
1 cup	fresh or frozen peas	250 mL
2 Tbsp	chopped fresh Italian parsley	25 mL
	Salt and freshly ground pepper	
¼ cup	freshly grated Parmesan cheese	50 mL

- In large saucepan or soup kettle, heat oil over medium heat. Cook onion and garlic for 5 minutes or until translucent. Stir in carrots, celery, potato, cabbage, broth, tomatoes, water, oregano, and bay leaf. Bring to boil.
- Reduce heat, cover and simmer for about 15 minutes or until vegetables are just tender.
- Add beans, spaghetti, and peas. Cook, stirring occasionally, for 12 minutes or until spaghetti is tender. Discard bay leaf. Stir in parsley. Season to taste with salt and pepper.
- Sprinkle each serving with Parmesan cheese.

Makes 8 cups (2 L), 8 servings.

EACH SERVING
⅛ of recipe

2 Starch
½ Fat

181 calories
3 g total fat
1 g saturated fat
2 mg cholesterol
10 g protein
30 g carbohydrate
602 mg sodium ❆
623 mg potassium

GOOD
Phosphorus, Iron, Magnesium, Vitamin C, Niacin

EXCELLENT
Vitamin A, Folate

VERY HIGH
Fiber

Sopa de Feijao (South American/Portuguese)
Bean Soup

This hearty soup can be served as a meal, on its own. It's wonderful with crusty Portuguese corn bread, called Broa (recipe p. 167).

(recipe p. 167).

1	onion, finely chopped	1
2 tsp	hot chili paste	10 mL
⅓ lb	chourico (Portuguese sausage)	150 g
	or chorizo (Spanish sausage)	
	or ham, pork, beef, or chicken	
½ lb	pork or beef bones	250 g
8 cups	water	2 L
2	potatoes, diced	2
2	carrots, diced	2
1	turnip, diced	1
2 cups	shredded kale or collard greens	500 mL
¼	head cabbage, shredded	¼
2 cups	cooked white fava or kidney beans	500 mL
	Salt and freshly ground pepper	

▪ In large pot, combine onion, chili paste, sausage, bones, and water; mix well. Bring to boil for 2 minutes, skimming foam from top. Reduce heat, cover, and simmer for 10 minutes or until meat is almost cooked.

▪ Add potatoes, carrots, and turnip. Cook for 10 minutes.

▪ Stir in kale, cabbage, and beans. Simmer for 15 minutes or until vegetables are tender.

▪ Discard bones. Dice sausage. Return to soup.

▪ Season to taste with salt and pepper.

Makes 10 cups (2.5 L), 10 servings.

EACH SERVING
¹⁄₁₀ of recipe

1 Starch
2 Meat, lean
½ Fat

220 calories
9 g total fat
3 g saturated fat
32 mg cholesterol
16 g protein
18 g carbohydrate
228 mg sodium
605 mg potassium

GOOD
Iron, Magnesium, Vitamin C, Niacin, Folate, Vitamin B_6, Vitamin B_{12}

EXCELLENT
Zinc, Vitamin A

MODERATE
Fiber

Soupe aux Pois (French Canadian)

Split Pea Soup

Many cookbooks refer to French Canadian pea soup as habitant soup. Dried yellow peas are used in it, just as they are in the Swedish version of this thick and hearty, gold-colored soup. Dutch cooks prefer using dried green peas for their pea soup, which is called erwtensoep.

1 lb	dried yellow split peas	500 g
	Water	
¼ lb	chunk salt pork	125 g
2	onions, chopped	2
1	carrot, chopped	1
1	stalks celery, chopped	1
1	clove garlic, minced	1
1	bay leaf	1
1 tsp	dried summer savory	5 mL
¼ cup	chopped fresh parsley	50 mL
	Salt and freshly ground black pepper	

▪ Rinse peas well. In large soup kettle, cover peas with 4 cups (1 L) water. Bring to a rapid boil for 2 minutes, turn off heat and let stand for 1 hour. Rinse and drain.

▪ Add salt pork, onions, carrots, celery, garlic, bay leaf, and savory to peas in soup kettle. Pour on 8 cups (2 L) water. Bring to boil. Reduce heat and simmer, uncovered, for about 1½ hours or until peas are tender.

▪ Remove salt pork and bay leaf. Stir in parsley and season to taste with salt and pepper. (For a smooth soup, puree in blender or food processor or pass through a sieve or food mill.)

Makes 10 cups (2.5 L), 10 servings.

EACH SERVING
¹⁄₁₀ of recipe

2   Starch
1   Meat, very lean

183 calories
2 g total fat
0 g saturated fat
2 mg cholesterol
11 g protein
29 g carbohydrate
48 mg sodium
458 mg potassium

GOOD
Phosphorus, Iron, Zinc, Magnesium, Vitamin A, Thiamin

EXCELLENT
Folate

MODERATE
Fiber

Three Sisters Soup (Canadian Aboriginal)
Squash, Bean, & Corn Soup

The name comes from the three vegetables—green beans, squash, and corn—that are planted and grown together in Iroquois villages.

1 lb	boneless lean pork	500 g
1	potato, peeled and diced	1
1 cup	diced butternut squash	250 mL
1 cup	sliced green beans	250 mL
1 cup	frozen kernel corn	250 mL
8 cups	water	2 L
	Salt and freshly ground black pepper	
¼ cup	all-purpose flour	50 mL

▪ Cut pork into ½-inch (1-cm) cubes, trim and discard fat.

▪ In soup pot, combine pork, potato, squash, green beans, and corn; stir well. Pour in water. Bring to boil for 3 minutes; skim off foam. Reduce heat, cover and simmer for 40 minutes or until tender. Season to taste with salt and pepper.

▪ In small bowl, whisk flour into ½ cup (125 mL) cold water until smooth. Gradually stir into simmering soup. Cook, stirring, for about 2 minutes or until thickened.

Makes 6 cups (1.5 L), 6 servings.

Soupe aux Tomates et au Lait (French Canadian)
Cream of Tomato Soup

Tomatoes are used in dozens of different ethnic dishes.

2 Tbsp	butter	25 mL
2 Tbsp	finely chopped onion	25 mL
2 Tbsp	all-purpose flour	25 mL
2 cups	1% milk	500 mL
1	can (19 oz/540 mL) tomatoes	1
1 Tbsp	chopped fresh basil or	15 mL
	1 tsp (5 mL) dried	
	Salt and freshly ground black pepper	

▪ In saucepan, heat butter over medium-high heat. Cook onion for 2 minutes. Stir in flour until smooth. Gradually stir in milk. Bring to boil, stirring constantly, for 2 minutes or until thickened. Stir in tomatoes, breaking up with fork, and basil. Heat to simmering. Season to taste with salt and pepper.

Makes 4½ cups (1.12 L), 6 servings.

Vichyssoise (French)

Light Vichyssoise

The classic, creamy, rich potato and leek soup is usually served cold. In my family, we love this light rendition hot, at room temperature, or well chilled.

4	leeks, white part only, sliced	4
2	potatoes, peeled and cubed	2
1	small onion, chopped	1
4 cups	chicken broth	1 L
1	bay leaf	1
½ tsp	salt	2 mL
⅛ tsp	white pepper	0.5 mL
Pinch	nutmeg	Pinch
2 Tbsp	light cream cheese	25 mL
½ cup	1% milk	125 mL

- In large saucepan, combine leeks, potatoes, onion, broth, bay leaf, salt, pepper, and nutmeg. Bring to a boil. Reduce heat and simmer, covered, for 20 minutes or until potatoes are tender. Discard bay leaf.
- Transfer mixture in batches to blender or food processor. Process for 1 to 2 minutes or until pureed and smooth. Return to clean saucepan or refrigerator container. Add cream cheese to last batch.
- For chilled soup, refrigerate for at least 4 hours or overnight. Just before serving, stir in milk until well blended.
- For hot soup, stir milk into pureed mixture in saucepan. Heat to simmering. Ladle into soup bowls.

Makes 6 cups (1.5 L), 6 servings.

EACH SERVING
⅙ of recipe

1 Starch

100 calories
1 g total fat
1 g saturated fat
4 mg cholesterol
5 g protein
14 g carbohydrate
697 mg sodium ❆
413 mg potassium

GOOD
Niacin

VARIATIONS

Bloomkallsuppe (Scandinavian)

Cream of Cauliflower Soup

Here is a lighter version of a popular Scandinavian soup.

- Substitute 1 medium head cauliflower, chopped (4 cups/1 L), for the leeks.

Calculations approximately the same as above.

Potage Crème de Champignons (French)

Cream of Mushroom Soup

- Substitute 1 lb (500 g) mushrooms, sliced, for the leeks.

Potage Crème de Laitue (French)

Cream of Lettuce Soup

When I first made this soup, I used regular iceberg lettuce. Big mistake; it was too delicate.

1 tsp	butter	5 mL
1	small onion, finely chopped	1
2	small bunches romaine, finely shredded (6 cups/1.5 L)	2
1	potato, peeled and shredded	1
3 cups	chicken broth	750 mL
2 Tbsp	light cream cheese	25 mL
½ cup	1% milk	125 mL
	Salt, white pepper, and ground nutmeg	

▪ In large saucepan, melt butter over medium heat. Cook onion for 3 minutes or until limp.

▪ Reserve 1 cup (250 mL) romaine. Stir remaining romaine, potatoes, and broth into onion. Bring to boil. Reduce heat, cover, and simmer for 15 minutes or until tender. Transfer to food processor. Add cream cheese. Puree until smooth. Pour back into clean saucepan. Stir in reserved romaine and milk. Heat to simmering. Season to taste with salt, pepper, and nutmeg.

Makes 4½ cups (1.12 L), 6 servings.

Caldo Verde (Portuguese)

Potato Soup with Greens

This soup is favored by the Portuguese as one way of using potatoes.

¼ lb	cooked smoked garlic sausage	125 g
8 cups	chicken or beef broth	2 L
4	potatoes, peeled and sliced	4
2 lbs	kale, collard greens, or watercress, stems removed and shredded	1 kg

▪ In large saucepan, combine sausage and 4 cups (1 L) broth. Bring to boil. Poach for 10 minutes. Remove sausage, reserving broth. Dice sausage and set aside. Add potatoes and remaining broth to saucepan. Bring to boil. Cook for 20 minutes or until potatoes are tender.

▪ Puree half of potatoes and return to saucepan. Add kale. Cook for 7 minutes or until tender. Stir in reserved sausage. Heat through, season with salt and pepper.

Makes 8 cups (2 L), 8 servings.

Borscht (Russian, Ukrainian)

Country Beet Soup

There are many, many versions of this country-style soup—
Russian, Polish, German. There are almost as many as there
are cooks. One thing is certain: beets are always in the soup,
and it has a vibrant ruby red color. Serve it hot or chilled,
chunky or pureed.

8 cups	beef broth	2 L
2	onions, finely chopped	2
2	beets, peeled and diced	2
2	stalks celery, thinly sliced	2
1	carrot, diced	1
1	potato, peeled and cubed	1
3 cups	shredded cabbage	750 mL
1 tsp	caraway seeds	5 mL
1	clove garlic, minced	1
1	bay leaf	1
1 cup	tomato juice	250 mL
1 Tbsp	lemon juice or cider vinegar	15 mL
	Salt and freshly ground black pepper	
½ cup	sour cream	125 mL
1 Tbsp	chopped fresh dill or parsley	15 mL

▪ In large saucepan or soup kettle, combine broth, onions, beets, celery, carrot, potato, cabbage, caraway seeds, garlic, and bay leaf. Bring to boil. Reduce heat and simmer, skimming foam occasionally, for about 35 minutes or until vegetables are tender. Discard bay leaf. Stir in tomato and lemon juices. Season to taste with salt and pepper.

▪ Let stand for 2 to 3 hours. (Borscht develops a richer flavor after standing for a few hours.) To reheat, bring to boil.

▪ Just before serving, remove from heat and stir in sour cream.

▪ Garnish with dill.

Makes 10 cups (2.5 L), 8 servings.

EACH SERVING
⅛ of recipe

1   Vegetable
½   Fat

    79 calories
     3 g total fat
     2 g saturated fat
     5 mg cholesterol
     5 g protein
    10 g carbohydrate
919 mg sodium ✿
422 mg potassium

GOOD
Folate

EXCELLENT
Vitamin A

Beef & Barley Soup

Some cookbooks may refer to this as barley broth. It is a full-bodied, economical medley of vegetables, bits of meat, and barley that makes a great, satisfying meal on its own.

½ lb	stewing lamb or beef	250 g
6 cups	water	1.5 L
1	bay leaf	1
¼ tsp	whole black peppercorns	1 mL
½ cup	pot or pearl barley	125 mL
2	stalks celery, diced	2
2	large carrots, diced	2
2	leeks, sliced, white part only	2
1	onion, finely chopped	1
1 cup	diced rutabaga or turnip	250 mL
	Chopped parsley	

- Cut meat into ¾-inch (2-cm) cubes; trim and discard fat.
- In large saucepan or soup kettle, combine meat, water, bay leaf, and peppercorns; bring to boil. Reduce heat, cover and simmer for 1 hour, skimming off foam occasionally.
- Meanwhile, in small saucepan, cover barley with water. Bring to boil. Rinse and strain. Add to soup pot with celery, carrots, leeks, onion, and rutabaga; bring to boil. Reduce heat and simmer for about 30 minutes or until barley is tender.
- Ladle into soup bowls or tureen. Garnish with parsley.

Makes 8 cups (2 L), 8 servings.

EACH SERVING
⅛ of recipe

1   Starch
1   Meat, very lean

106 calories
2 g total fat
1 g saturated fat
18 mg cholesterol
8 g protein
15 g carbohydrate
35 mg sodium
257 mg potassium

GOOD
Zinc, Niacin

EXCELLENT
Vitamin A, Vitamin B$_{12}$

MODERATE
Fiber

Cock-a-Leekie (British)

Chicken Leek Soup

Of all the chicken soups in global cuisines, I picked this one because it is similar to the soupe aux poireaux of Belgium. For many of you, it's probably just like Mom's chicken soup.

1 lb	chicken legs and thighs	500 g
4 cups	water	1 L
2 cups	chicken broth	500 mL
6	sprigs parsley	6
2 tsp	butter	10 mL
3	leeks, trimmed to light green part and thinly sliced	3
¼ cup	long-grain rice	50 mL
	Salt and freshly ground black pepper	
	Chopped fresh parsley	

- Rinse chicken; remove and discard fat and skin.
- In large saucepan or soup pot, cover chicken pieces with water, chicken broth, and parsley sprigs; bring to boil. Reduce heat and simmer for 50 minutes or until chicken is tender. Cool slightly.
- Strain broth into glass measure or bowl. Rinse saucepan. Remove chicken from bones. Discard bones and parsley. Return broth and chicken to saucepan.
- In nonstick skillet, heat butter over medium heat. Cook leeks for 10 minutes or until soft.
- Add to chicken mixture. Stir in rice. Bring to boil. Reduce heat, cover and simmer for 15 minutes or until rice is tender. Season to taste with salt and pepper.
- Garnish with parsley.

Makes 6 cups (1.5 L), 6 servings.

VARIATION

Sopa de Agriao (Portuguese)

Watercress Soup

It is the watercress in this chicken soup that gives it both a unique flavor and color.

- Substitute 2 cloves garlic, minced, and 1 onion, finely chopped, for leeks and 1 potato, cubed, for rice. Just before serving, add 2 cups (500 mL) chopped watercress and simmer for 5 minutes or until wilted.

Makes 6 cups (1.5 L), 6 servings.

EACH SERVING
⅙ of recipe

½ Starch
3 Meat, very lean
½ Fat

170 calories
5 g total fat
2 g saturated fat
72 mg cholesterol
20 g protein
10 g carbohydrate
352 mg sodium
307 mg potassium

GOOD
Phosphorus, Zinc,
Vitamin B$_6$,
Vitamin B$_{12}$,
Pantothenic Acid

EXCELLENT
Niacin

EACH SERVING
⅙ of recipe

½ Starch
1 Meat, lean

99 calories
2 g total fat
0 g saturated fat
34 mg cholesterol
11 g protein
8 g carbohydrate
689 mg sodium ✹
385 mg potassium

EXCELLENT
Niacin

Marseilles Fish Soup

Real Marseilles bouillabaisse is made with only Mediterranean fish, particularly the poissons de roc, or fish that live among the rocks. Bouillabaisse, meaning a boiling of fish, is old and probably originates back to the trading days of the Phoenicians.

2 lb	mixed saltwater fish steaks or pieces (bass, snapper, haddock, perch, cod)	1 kg
1 Tbsp	olive oil	15 mL
2	onions, sliced	2
2	cloves garlic, minced	2
1 tsp	fennel seed, crushed	5 mL
1	bay leaf	1
1	strip orange peel	1
¼ tsp	saffron	1 mL
1	can (19 oz/540 mL) tomatoes	1
6 cups	hot fish broth	1.5 L
ROUILLE		
1	clove garlic, minced	1
1 Tbsp	fresh white breadcrumbs	15 mL
1 Tbsp	olive oil	15 mL
1 tsp	paprika	5 mL
2 Tbsp	hot fish broth (from soup pot)	25 mL

- Rinse and cut fish into small pieces; remove any bones and discard.
- In nonstick saucepan, heat olive oil over medium heat. Cook onions and garlic until translucent. Add fennel, bay leaf, orange peel, and saffron.
- Stir in tomatoes. Bring to boil; cook for 4 minutes. Add fish.
- Pour in hot broth; bring to boil. Reduce heat and simmer for 10 minutes.
- Rouille: In small food processor, combine garlic, breadcrumbs, oil, and paprika. Thin by adding hot fish broth.
- Ladle soup into bowls. Top each serving with about 1 tsp (5 mL) rouille.

Makes 8 cups (2 L), 8 servings.

EACH SERVING
⅛ of recipe

½ Starch
3 Meat, very lean
1 Fat

195 calories
7 g total fat
1 g saturated fat
77 mg cholesterol
26 g protein
6 g carbohydrate
774 mg sodium ✿
670 mg potassium

GOOD
Iron, Magnesium

EXCELLENT
Phosphorus, Niacin, Vitamin B$_{12}$

Soupe a l'Oignon Gratinée (French)

French Onion Soup

If I were to list the great soups from ethnic kitchens, dark savory French onion would certainly be in the top ten.

2 Tbsp	butter	25 mL
5	yellow onions, halved and sliced	5
2	slices French bread	2
2 Tbsp	all-purpose flour	25 mL
4 cups	strong beef broth	1 L
1 Tbsp	red wine vinegar	15 mL
1 tsp	Worcestershire sauce	5 mL
2	drops hot pepper sauce	2
	Salt and freshly ground black pepper	
¼ cup	grated Parmesan cheese	50 mL
1 cup	shredded low-fat Gruyere cheese	250 mL

▪ In large saucepan over medium heat, melt butter. Cook onions, stirring occasionally, for 30 minutes or until golden brown and soft.

▪ Meanwhile, cut bread into small cubes. Place on baking sheet. Dry in 350°F (180°C) oven for 10 minutes or until crisp. Set aside.

▪ In small nonstick skillet over medium heat, brown flour, stirring frequently for about 4 minutes. Stir into onions; cook for 1 minute.

▪ Stir in broth, vinegar, Worcestershire, and hot pepper sauces. Season to taste with salt and pepper. Bring to a boil, reduce heat, cover and simmer for 5 minutes.

▪ Spoon hot soup into ovenproof bowls. Float croutons on top; sprinkle with Parmesan cheese, then Gruyere cheese.

▪ Place under preheated broiler. Broil for about 1 minute or until cheese is bubbly and golden.

Makes 6 cups (1.5 L), 6 servings.

EACH SERVING
⅙ of recipe

1	Starch
1	Meat, lean
1	Fat

185	calories
10 g	total fat
6 g	saturated fat
31 mg	cholesterol
10 g	protein
11 g	carbohydrate
742 mg	sodium ✹
190 mg	potassium

GOOD
Calcium, Phosphorus, Niacin, Vitamin B$_{12}$

Tom Yam Kung (Thai)
Hot and Sour Soup

Notes of sour, sweet, salty, and spicy flavors—the essence of Thai cooking—ring through every mouthful of this soup.

12	fresh or frozen raw shrimp	12
3 cups	chicken broth	750 mL
¼ cup	dry lemon grass in cheesecloth bag	50 mL
2 Tbsp	lite soy sauce or fish sauce (nam pla)	25 mL
2	shallots or 1 small onion, thinly sliced	2
1 Tbsp	grated fresh ginger root	15 mL
20	small mushrooms, halved	20
4	thin strips of zest from 1 lime	4
2 Tbsp	lime juice	25 mL
1	jalapeno pepper, seeded and thinly sliced or 2 Tbsp (25 mL) pickled jalapeno peppers	1
2	green onions, thinly sliced	2
	Fresh cilantro leaves	

▪ Shell and devein shrimp. Cut in half lengthwise. Set aside.

▪ In large saucepan, combine chicken broth, lemon grass bag, soy sauce, shallots, and ginger root. Bring to boil for 2 minutes. Add shrimp and mushrooms. Cook for 3 minutes or until shrimp turn pink.

▪ Add lime strips, lime juice, and jalapeno pepper. Cook for 1 minute. Remove lemon grass bag and discard.

▪ Serve hot, sprinkled with green onion rings and cilantro.

Makes 4 cups (1 L), 4 servings.

Hun T'un T'ang (Chinese)

Wonton Soup

Since wonton wrappers are so readily available, making this soup at home is relatively easy, and it duplicates what you find in Chinese restaurants.

WONTONS

½ lb	ground chicken, veal, or lean pork	250 g
2	green onions, finely chopped	2
2 tsp	grated fresh ginger root	10 mL
1 tsp	cornstarch	5 mL
1 tsp	lite soy sauce	5 mL
6	drops hot pepper sauce	6
18	wonton wrappers	18

SOUP

4 cups	chicken broth	1 L
2 tsp	lite soy sauce	10 mL
1 tsp	sesame oil	5 mL
¼ tsp	hot chili paste	1 mL
	Salt and freshly ground black pepper	
1 cup	shredded fresh spinach or watercress	250 mL
1	green onion, thinly sliced	1

■ Wontons: In bowl, combine ground chicken, green onions, ginger root, cornstarch, soy sauce, and hot pepper sauce; mix until well blended.

■ Lay wonton wrappers on work surface. Place spoonful of ground chicken mixture in center of each one. Moisten edges with water. Fold each wrapper in half to form triangle; press edges to seal. Arrange in steamer basket. Cover and steam over boiling water for 3 minutes.

■ Meanwhile, in large saucepan, combine broth, soy sauce, sesame oil, and hot chili paste. Bring to boil. Season to taste with salt and pepper.

■ Just before serving, stir in spinach until wilted.

■ Place 3 wontons in each bowl. Ladle soup over top.

■ Garnish with green onion rings.

Makes 6 cups (1.5 L), 6 servings.

EACH SERVING
⅙ of recipe

1½ Starch
2 Meat, very lean

183 calories
3 g total fat
1 g saturated fat
47 mg cholesterol
16 g protein
21 g carbohydrate
642 mg sodium ✿
340 mg potassium

GOOD
Phosphorus, Iron, Riboflavin, Folate, Vitamin B$_{12}$

EXCELLENT
Niacin

Gazpacho (Spanish)

Cold Tomato Cucumber Soup

When speed is important, all the ingredients in this classic uncooked soup can be chopped in the food processor.

12	plum tomatoes, peeled and chopped, or 6 regular	12
1	slice white bread	1
1	green onion, chopped	1
1	clove garlic	1
1 Tbsp	chopped fresh basil or parsley	15 mL
1 Tbsp	olive oil	15 mL
2 tsp	cider vinegar	10 mL
Dash	hot pepper sauce	Dash
1 cup	tomato juice	250 mL
1	red or green sweet pepper, diced	1
1 cup	finely chopped cucumber	250 mL
½ cup	finely chopped celery	125 mL
	Salt and freshly ground black pepper	

- In food processor or blender, puree tomatoes, bread, onion, garlic, basil, olive oil, vinegar, and hot pepper sauce.
- Stir in tomato juice, red pepper, cucumber, and celery. Season to taste with salt and pepper. Chill for at least 1 hour before serving.

Makes 6 cups (1.5 L), 6 servings.

Jajik (Middle Eastern)

Cold Yogurt Cucumber Soup

- Turn Tzatziki (recipe p. 46) into a chilled soup, similar to jajik and Bulgarian tarator.
- Reserve 12 to 18 of the halved cucumber slices for garnish.
- In food processor or blender, process the remaining ingredients, 1 cup (250 mL) ice water, and 1 Tbsp (15 mL) chopped fresh dill or 1 tsp (5 mL) dried, until pureed.
- Cover and refrigerate for at least 1 hour. Stir well.
- Garnish each serving with reserved cucumber slices and chopped fresh mint.

Makes 6 servings.

Salads

Salada Verde com Coentro - *Portuguese*

Salade Verte - *French*

Insalata Mista - *Italian*

Sienisalaatti - *Scandinavian*

Caesar Salad - *American*

Kal-och Appelsalad - *Scandinavian*

Rotkohlsalat - *German*

Murgha Kari Chat - *East Indian*

Yaam Gai Yai - *Thai*

Kartoffelsalat - *German*

Bean & Bulgur Salad - *North American*

Tzatziki - *Greek*

Agurkesalat - *Scandinavian*

Giardinera - *Italian*

Inkokta Rodbetor - *Scandinavian*

Yasai no Sokuseki-suke - *Japanese*

Caponata - *Italian*

Tabbouleh - *Middle Eastern*

Fatoosh - *Middle Eastern*

Horiatiki Salata - *Greek*

Salada Verde com Coentro (Portuguese)

Mixed Greens with Cilantro

Mixing salad greens makes salad making and eating fun and never boring. Cilantro (fresh coriander) is a green leafy herb that Portuguese cooks rely on for distinct flavor in their salads.

GARLIC LEMON DRESSING

1	clove garlic, minced	1
1 Tbsp	olive oil	15 mL
1 Tbsp	lemon or lime juice	15 mL
1 tsp	salt	5 mL

SALAD

6 cups	mixed salad greens (iceberg, romaine, spinach, curly endive)	1.5 L
¼ cup	chopped fresh cilantro	50 mL
	Freshly ground black pepper	

▪ Dressing: In small jar with tight-fitting lid, shake together garlic, oil, lemon juice, and salt.

▪ In salad bowl, toss together salad greens and cilantro. Shake dressing; pour over greens. Sprinkle to taste with pepper. Toss well.

Makes 6 servings.

Salade Verte (French)

Lettuce with Vinaigrette

When the oil is reduced in a vinaigrette, as it is here, so is the calorie count. It's that simple.

VINAIGRETTE

2 Tbsp	red wine vinegar	25 mL
1 Tbsp	canola oil	15 mL
1 Tbsp	water	15 mL
1 tsp	Dijon mustard	5 mL
½	clove garlic, minced	½
1½ tsp	chopped fresh tarragon or ½ tsp (2 mL) dried	7 mL
	Salt and freshly ground black pepper	

SALAD

2	heads bibb lettuce	2

▪ Vinaigrette: In jar with tight-fitting lid, shake together vinegar, oil, water, mustard, garlic, tarragon, and salt and pepper to taste. Chill.

▪ Rinse, dry, and chill lettuce. Tear into bite-size pieces into salad bowl. Chill.

▪ Just before serving, pour on dressing. Toss well.

Makes 6 servings.

Insalata Mista (Italian)

Greens with Black Olives

Garlic, oregano, and thyme are essential to an Italian-style dressing.

ITALIAN DRESSING

¼ cup	balsamic vinegar	50 mL
1 Tbsp	water	15 mL
2 Tbsp	extra virgin olive oil	25 mL
1 tsp	anchovy paste	5 mL
1	clove garlic, minced	1
1½ tsp	each chopped fresh thyme, oregano, and basil or ½ tsp (2 mL) dried	7 mL

SALAD

1	small head romaine lettuce	1
1	head curly endive	1
½	head iceberg lettuce	½
6	pitted black olives, sliced	6

▪ Dressing: In jar with tight-fitting lid, shake together vinegar, water, olive oil, anchovy paste, garlic, thyme, oregano, and basil. Chill. (Always shake before using.)

▪ Rinse, dry, and chill greens. Tear into bite-size pieces into salad bowl. Add olive slices. Pour on dressing. Toss well.

Makes 6 servings.

EACH SERVING
⅙ of recipe

1   Vegetable
1   Fat

  61 calories
  4 g total fat
  0 g saturated fat
  0 mg cholesterol
  2 g protein
  4 g carbohydrate
  61 mg sodium
348 mg potassium

EXCELLENT
Folate

Sienisalaatti (Scandinavian)

Mushroom Salad

In Finland in the mid-'80s, I tasted this wonderfully different salad. Now, I make it with low-fat sour cream rather than the full cream called for in traditional recipes.

1 lb	mushrooms, coarsely chopped	500 g
¼ cup	finely chopped onion	50 mL
2 Tbsp	lemon juice	25 mL
¼ tsp	salt	1 mL
¼ tsp	freshly ground black pepper	1 mL
½ cup	low-fat sour cream	125 mL
½ tsp	Dijon mustard	2 mL
6	small romaine leaves	6
6	cherry tomatoes, halved	6
	Parsley sprigs	

▪ In bowl, toss mushrooms, onion, lemon juice, salt, and pepper. Cover and refrigerate for 1 hour.

▪ Whisk together sour cream and mustard; stir into mushroom mixture. Cover and refrigerate for 2 to 6 hours.

▪ Line serving plates with romaine; spoon salad over top. Garnish with cherry tomatoes and parsley.

Makes 8 servings.

EACH SERVING
⅛ of recipe

1   Vegetable

  36 calories
  1 g total fat
  0 g saturated fat
  4 mg cholesterol
  2 g protein
  5 g carbohydrate
109 mg sodium
284 mg potassium

GOOD
Vitamin D, Riboflavin

Caesar Salad (American)

Light Caesar Salad

The combination of garlic and other flavorings of this perennial favorite in Canadian and American circles is here. One ingredient found in the original Caesar is missing—the raw egg. Because of all our '90s health concerns, I prefer to leave it out.

CROUTONS

2	slices French-style bread, cubed	2
1 tsp	olive oil	5 mL
½	clove garlic, minced	½

DRESSING

¼ cup	light mayonnaise	50 mL
2 Tbsp	lemon juice	25 mL
1 tsp	Worcestershire sauce	5 mL
1 tsp	anchovy paste or 1 anchovy fillet, mashed	5 mL
½ tsp	Dijon mustard	2 mL
2 Tbsp	freshly grated Parmesan cheese Freshly ground black pepper	25 mL

SALAD

1	head romaine lettuce	1

▪ Croutons: Spread bread cubes on nonstick baking sheet. In small dish, combine oil and garlic. With brush, dab oil and garlic on bread cubes. Bake in 350°F (180°C) oven, turning once, for 5 minutes or until toasted. Remove and set aside.

▪ Dressing: In bowl, whisk together mayonnaise, lemon juice, Worcestershire sauce, anchovy paste, mustard, and Parmesan cheese. Season to taste with pepper. Set aside.

▪ Rinse, dry, and chill romaine. Tear into bite-size pieces into salad bowl. Pour dressing over top; toss well. Add croutons. Toss again.

Makes 6 servings.

Kal-och Appelsalad (Scandinavian)

Apple & Grape Coleslaw

There are as many versions of ever-faithful coleslaw as there are cooks, ethnic backgrounds, and varieties of cabbage—the one common ingredient.

2 cups	shredded regular or Savoy cabbage	500 mL
1	red apple, chopped	1
1 cup	green seedless grapes, halved	250 mL
1	green onion, thinly sliced	1
¼ cup	low-fat sour cream	50 mL
¼ cup	light mayonnaise	50 mL
1 Tbsp	lemon juice	15 mL
	Salt and freshly ground black pepper	
	Sugar substitute equivalent	
	to 1 tsp (5 mL) sugar	

▪ In salad bowl, combine cabbage, apple, grapes, and green onion.

▪ Whisk together sour cream, mayonnaise, and lemon juice. Season to taste with salt, pepper, and sugar substitute. Pour over cabbage mixture. Toss to coat with dressing. Chill.

Makes 6 servings.

EACH SERVING
⅙ of recipe

1 Fruit
½ Fat

  78 calories
  3 g total fat
  0 g saturated fat
  3 mg cholesterol
  0 g protein
  12 g carbohydrate
  82 mg sodium
150 mg potassium

Rotkohlsalat (German)

Red Cabbage Salad

It is the marinating that brings out the full flavor of the caraway, an herb often used in German cooking.

3 cups	shredded red cabbage	750 mL
1	carrot, shredded	1
2 Tbsp	vinegar	25 mL
2 Tbsp	water	25 mL
2 tsp	canola oil	10 mL
1 tsp	caraway seeds, crushed	5 mL
	Sugar substitute equivalent	
	to 1 tsp (5 mL) sugar	
	Salt and freshly ground black pepper	

▪ In glass bowl, combine cabbage and carrot.

▪ In small bowl, whisk together vinegar, water, oil, caraway seeds, and sugar substitute. Season to taste with salt and pepper. Pour over cabbage. Cover and refrigerate, stirring occasionally, for 4 hours or overnight for flavors to blend. Drain before serving.

Makes 6 servings.

EACH SERVING
⅙ of recipe

½ Fat

  30 calories
  2 g total fat
  0 g saturated fat
  0 mg cholesterol
  0 g protein
  4 g carbohydrate
  8 mg sodium
120 mg potassium

GOOD
Vitamin C

Murgha Kari Chat (East Indian)
Curried Chicken Rice Salad

The raisins and the peanuts are counterpoints to the heat of the curry and red pepper flakes in this chilled East-Indian style combination topped with grilled chicken.

¾ cup	low-fat yogurt	175 mL
3 Tbsp	curry powder	45 mL
1	clove garlic, minced	1
½ tsp	salt	2 mL
¼ tsp	red pepper flakes	1 mL
4	boneless, skinless, single chicken breasts (1 lb/500g total)	4
1 cup	basmati rice	250 mL
2 cups	chicken broth	500 mL
1	red sweet pepper, julienned	1
1	stalk celery, cut in 2-inch (5-cm) pieces and julienned	1
1	small red onion, thinly sliced	1
2	green onions, thinly sliced	2
2 Tbsp	chopped raisins	25 mL
1 Tbsp	finely chopped peanuts	15 mL
2 Tbsp	light mayonnaise	25 mL
2 Tbsp	orange juice	25 mL
	Fresh parsley sprigs	

- In bowl, combine ½ cup (125 mL) yogurt, 2 Tbsp (25 mL) curry powder, garlic, salt, and red pepper flakes; mix well. Place chicken in mixture, turning to coat well. Cover, refrigerate, and allow to marinate for 4 hours.
- In saucepan, combine rice and chicken broth; bring to boil. Reduce heat, cover and simmer for 20 minutes or until tender. Cool.
- In bowl, combine cooked rice, remaining curry powder, red pepper, celery, red onion, green onions, raisins, and peanuts; mix well.
- Whisk together remaining ¼ cup (50 mL) yogurt, mayonnaise, and orange juice until smooth. Pour over rice mixture. Toss. Cover and refrigerate for 1 hour or until well chilled.
- Barbecue or broil chicken on grill or broiler pan on medium-high heat for about 5 minutes on each side or until juices run clear when chicken is pierced. Cut into strips.
- Arrange chicken strips over salad. Garnish with parsley.

Makes 6 servings.

Yaam Gai Yai (Thai)

Thai Salad

One of the keys to the unique flavor of Thai dishes is the use of nam pla, which is a pungent, malodorous fish sauce. Even though it is a taste foreign to Western palates, a fondness for Thai food is certainly growing in North America.

DRESSING

¼ cup	strong tea	50 mL
2 Tbsp	lemon juice	25 mL
2 Tbsp	rice vinegar	25 mL
1 Tbsp	sesame oil	15 mL
2 tsp	peanut butter	10 mL
2 tsp	shrimp or fish sauce (nam pla*)	10 mL
1 tsp	chopped pickled jalapeno pepper	5 mL

SALAD

4	dried Chinese mushrooms	4
4 oz	rice vermicelli or cellophane noodles	125 g
2 cups	packed shredded fresh spinach	500 mL
1 cup	bean sprouts, trimmed	250 mL
1	medium red sweet pepper, slivered	1
2 Tbsp	coarsely chopped peanuts	25 mL
2	green onions, thinly sliced	2
2 Tbsp	chopped fresh mint	25 mL
2 Tbsp	chopped fresh cilantro	25 mL
1	cooked, single skinless chicken breast	1
12	cooked shrimp, peeled and deveined	12
8	romaine lettuce leaves	8
	Fresh cilantro or parsley sprigs	

▪ Dressing: In small bowl or jar with tight-fitting lid, whisk or shake together tea, lemon juice, vinegar, sesame oil, peanut butter, shrimp sauce, and jalapeno pepper until well blended. Chill for 30 minutes or up to 2 hours.

▪ In bowl, soak mushrooms in boiling water for 20 minutes. Drain, discard stems. Cut caps into thin slivers. Set aside.

▪ In saucepan of lightly salted boiling water, cook vermicelli for 3 minutes; drain and cut into shorter strands. Set aside to cool.

▪ In salad bowl, combine spinach, bean sprouts, red pepper, peanuts, green onions, mint, and cilantro. Add vermicelli and mushrooms.

▪ Shred chicken and shrimp. Add to salad.

▪ Whisk or shake dressing. Pour over salad; toss well.

▪ Line serving plates with romaine leaves. Mound salad on top. Top with cilantro sprig.

Makes 6 servings.

EACH SERVING
⅙ of recipe

1   Starch
1   Vegetable
2   Meat, lean

220 calories
6 g total fat
1 g saturated fat
44 mg cholesterol
16 g protein
23 g carbohydrate
79 mg sodium
414 mg potassium

GOOD
Phosphorus, Iron, Zinc, Magnesium, Vitamin A, Vitamin B$_6$, Vitamin B$_{12}$

EXCELLENT
Vitamin D, Vitamin C, Niacin, Folate

MODERATE
Fiber

*TIMELY TIP
Nam pla (fish sauce) is available in Asian specialty shops.

Kartoffelsalat (German)

Hot Bavarian Potato Salad

Unpeeled red potatoes are the potatoes of choice when I make this variation of the traditional German salad. Their color adds eye appeal to this fragrant combination.

SALAD

4	potatoes, scrubbed	4
1	bay leaf	1
4	peppercorns	4
1	red onion, chopped	1

DRESSING

¼ cup	finely chopped onion	50 mL
2	slices back bacon, chopped	2
1 tsp	celery seeds	5 mL
2 Tbsp	vinegar	25 mL
2 Tbsp	water	25 mL
2 Tbsp	oil	25 mL
¼ cup	chopped radish	50 mL
2 Tbsp	chopped parsley	25 mL
	Freshly ground black pepper	

■ In saucepan of lightly salted boiling water, cook potatoes with bay leaf and peppercorns for 25 minutes or until tender. (Or prick potatoes and alternatively microwave them on high for 12 to 15 minutes until tender.)

■ While still hot, peel and slice potatoes into salad bowl. Discard bay leaf and peppercorns. Add onion.

■ Dressing: In nonstick skillet, cook bacon, onion, and celery seeds over medium heat for 2 minutes or until bacon is nearly crisp. Stir in vinegar, water, and oil; bring to boil for 30 seconds. Pour over potatoes. Sprinkle with radish, parsley, and pepper to taste. Lightly toss.

■ Serve while still warm.

Makes 6 servings.

Bean & Bulgur Salad

The food guides in Canada and the U.S. recommend eating more grains and legumes and reducing the amount of fat consumed. A salad like this fits that criteria. The calorie count of a serving is low, with a high proportion of the calories coming from complex carbohydrates. Its fiber content rating is tops.

½ cup	uncooked bulgur	125 mL
1 cup	boiling water	250 mL
2 cups	cooked red kidney or black beans, well drained	500 mL
4	green onions, thinly sliced	4
1	medium carrot, coarsely grated	1
1	stalk celery, thinly sliced	1
1	small red pepper, diced	1
1	tomato, diced	1
2 Tbsp	each chopped fresh mint and parsley	25 mL
2 Tbsp	sunflower seeds	25 mL
2 Tbsp	lemon juice	25 mL
1 Tbsp	olive oil	15 mL
1	clove garlic, minced	1
1 tsp	Dijon mustard	5 mL
	Salt and freshly ground black pepper	

▪ In heat-proof salad bowl, combine bulgur and boiling water. Cover and let stand for 20 minutes. Uncover and fluff with fork. Let cool until just warm.

▪ Mix in beans, green onions, carrot, celery, red pepper, tomato, mint, parsley, and sunflower seeds.

▪ In small bowl, whisk together lemon juice, oil, mustard, and garlic. Pour over bean mixture. Season to taste with salt and pepper.

▪ Cover and refrigerate for 1 hour before serving.

Makes 6 servings.

EACH SERVING
⅙ of recipe

2   Starch

159 calories
3 g total fat
0 g saturated fat
0 mg cholesterol
7 g protein
26 g carbohydrate
26 mg sodium
461 mg potassium

GOOD
Iron, Magnesium

EXCELLENT
Vitamin A, Vitamin C, Folate

VERY HIGH
Fiber

Tzatziki (Greek)

Cucumber & Yogurt Salad

Cooks from the Middle East make a salad similar to this, dressing their cucumbers with yogurt and calling it borani.

1	English cucumber, unpeeled	1
	Salt	
1	clove garlic, sliced	1
Pinch	white pepper	Pinch
2 tsp	each lemon juice and olive oil	10 mL
1½	cups low-fat yogurt	375 mL
¼ cup	chopped fresh mint	50 mL
	or 1 Tbsp (15 mL) dried	
	Fresh mint leaves	

▪ Cut cucumber in half lengthwise, scoop out seeds and discard. Cut halves into slices. Place in bowl and toss with ¼ tsp (1 mL) salt. Set aside for about 20 minutes.

▪ In serving bowl, crush garlic with back of spoon and add ¼ tsp (1 mL) salt. Stir in pepper, lemon juice, and olive oil. Add yogurt and mint; mix well.

▪ Drain and rinse cucumbers and pat dry with paper towels. Stir into yogurt mixture. Cover and refrigerate.

▪ Stir just before serving. Garnish with mint leaves.

Makes 3 cups (750 mL), 6 servings.

Agurkesalat (Scandinavian)

Cucumbers & Onions

These cucumbers seem slightly pickled after they marinate in the delicately sweetened vinegar solution.

2	medium cucumbers, thinly sliced	2
2	onions, thinly sliced	2
1 tsp	salt	5 mL
½ cup	white vinegar	125 mL
½ cup	water	125 mL
2 tsp	granulated sugar	10 mL
¼ tsp	white pepper	1 mL
2 Tbsp	chopped fresh dill or parsley	25 mL

▪ Place cucumber and onion slices in glass bowl. Sprinkle with salt, cover with plate, weight down, and let stand for 3 hours. Drain well.

▪ Stir together vinegar, water, sugar, and pepper until sugar dissolves. Pour over cucumbers and onions. Cover and refrigerate, stirring occasionally, for 2 to 6 hours.

▪ At serving time, drain and sprinkle with dill.

Makes 6 servings.

Giardinera (Italian)
Marinated Garden Vegetables

Most Italian cooks always have a medley of pickled garden vegetables on hand, especially for antipasto.

6	thin carrots, thickly sliced	6
2	pickling cucumbers, sliced	2
2	stalks celery, diagonally sliced	2
1	each red and yellow sweet pepper, seeded and cut into strips	1
1	small head cauliflower, cut into florets	1
8	sprigs fresh dill	8
1½ cups	rice or white wine vinegar	375 mL
4 tsp	pickling salt	20 mL
12	black peppercorns	12
3	cloves garlic, sliced	3
1 tsp	crushed hot red pepper	5 mL

■ In glass or plastic container, combine carrots, cucumbers, celery, peppers, cauliflower, and dill.

■ In saucepan, combine 2 cups (500 mL) water, vinegar, salt, peppercorns, garlic, and red pepper. Bring to boil for 2 minutes. Pour over vegetables. Cover and refrigerate, stirring occasionally, for 2 to 6 days until marinated.

Makes 12 servings.

EACH SERVING
1/12 of recipe

1   Vegetable

   32 calories
   0 g total fat
   0 g saturated fat
   0 mg cholesterol
   1 g protein
   8 g carbohydrate
795 mg sodium ✺
258 mg potassium

EXCELLENT
Vitamin A, Vitamin C

Inkokta Rodbetor (Scandinavian)
Pickled Beets

For the Middle Eastern version of this pickle, replace half of the beets with cooked turnips, which turn pink as they marinate.

4	medium beets, scrubbed	4
⅔ cup	vinegar	150 mL
2 tsp	salt	10 mL
1	onion, thinly sliced	1
¼ cup	granulated sugar	50 mL
2 tsp	whole cloves	10 mL
12	whole black peppercorns	12

■ In large saucepan, combine beets, 2 Tbsp (25 mL) vinegar, 1 tsp (5 mL) salt. Cover with water. Bring to boil. Reduce heat, cover and cook for 40 minutes or until tender. Drain and run cold water over beets. Slip off skins. Slice beets into glass bowl or jar. Add onion slices.

■ In saucepan, heat remaining vinegar and salt, ½ cup (125 mL) water, sugar, cloves, and peppercorns. Bring to boil. Pour over beets and onion. Cover and refrigerate for 12 hours or up to 4 weeks.

Makes 3 cups (750 mL), 12 servings.

EACH SERVING
1/12 of recipe

1   Vegetable

   24 calories
   0 g total fat
   0 g saturated fat
   0 mg cholesterol
   0 g protein
   6 g carbohydrate
394 mg sodium
 38 mg potassium

Japanese Pickled Vegetables

The typically Japanese flavorings in this salad—mustard's pungency, rice vinegar's mild acidity, soy sauce's saltiness, and sesame seeds' toastiness—enhance the taste of the vegetables.

EACH SERVING
⅙ of recipe

1   Vegetable
½   Fat

   53 calories
   2 g total fat
   0 g saturated fat
   0 mg cholesterol
   1 g protein
   5 g carbohydrate
192 mg sodium
194 mg potassium

EXCELLENT
Vitamin C

4 cups	assorted vegetables: cucumber sticks, celery sticks, shredded (not grated) cabbage, green and red sweet pepper strips, and bean sprouts	1 L
¼ cup	rice vinegar or diluted cider vinegar	50 mL
2 Tbsp	cooking sherry	25 mL
2 Tbsp	lite soy sauce	25 mL
2 Tbsp	water	25 mL
2 tsp	sesame oil	10 mL
1	1½-inch (3.5-cm) strip lemon rind	1
	Sugar substitute equivalent to 2 tsp (10 mL) sugar	
2 Tbsp	toasted sesame seeds	25 mL

▪ Place prepared vegetables in flat-bottomed dish.

▪ In small bowl, whisk together vinegar, sherry, soy sauce, water, sesame oil, lemon rind, and sugar substitute. Pour over vegetables; toss to coat. Cover and refrigerate, stirring occasionally, for 2 to 4 hours or until marinated.

▪ Serve sprinkled with sesame seeds.

Makes 6 servings.

Caponata (Italian)

Caponata

Eggplant turns up in all sorts of combinations in both Middle Eastern and Mediterranean cooking. Here, it teams up with tomatoes and herbs, plus extra virgin olive oil, for a rich-tasting, low-calorie salad that is popular on its own and as part of an antipasto with Italian families.

1	medium eggplant	1
	Salt	
2 Tbsp	olive oil	25 mL
2	stalks celery, finely chopped	2
2	cloves garlic, minced	2
1	onion, finely chopped	1
1	carrot, finely chopped	1
1	can (19 oz/540 mL) plum tomatoes, drained and chopped	1
4	large green olives, pitted and chopped	4
¼ cup	red wine vinegar	50 mL
2 Tbsp	capers	25 mL
2 tsp	anchovy paste or 2 anchovy fillets, minced	10 mL
	Salt and freshly ground pepper	
¼ cup	chopped fresh parsley	50 mL

▪ Cut eggplant into ½-inch (1-cm) cubes. Sprinkle with salt and spread on paper towels. Cover with more paper towels. Place weighted tray or baking sheet over top for 15 minutes.

▪ In nonstick skillet, heat olive oil over medium heat. Cook celery, garlic, onion, and carrot for 7 minutes or until soft but not brown. Remove from skillet to plate. Set aside.

▪ In same skillet, cook eggplant, stirring constantly, until lightly browned.

▪ Return cooked vegetables to skillet. Stir in tomatoes, olives, vinegar, capers, and anchovy paste. Bring to boil. Reduce heat and simmer, uncovered, for 15 minutes or until eggplant is tender but holds its shape. Season to taste with salt and pepper.

▪ Transfer to serving dish. Cover and refrigerate for 20 minutes.

▪ Stir in parsley just before serving.

Makes 8 antipasto servings.

EACH SERVING
⅛ of recipe

2   Vegetable
½   Fat

61 calories
3 g total fat
0 g saturated fat
4 mg cholesterol
1 g protein
8 g carbohydrate
139 mg sodium
289 mg potassium

EXCELLENT
Vitamin A

MODERATE
Fiber

Bulgur Parsley Salad

Whatever the spelling for this salad—tabooley, tabuleh, tabbouli—it is the classic bulgur, parsley, and mint combination dressed with lemon juice and a little olive oil. This one, adapted from a Lebanese version, is my favorite.

½ cup	bulgur	125 mL
1 cup	boiling water	250 mL
2 cups	finely chopped fresh parsley (1 bunch)	500 mL
1	carrot, coarsely grated	1
⅓ cup	lemon juice	75 mL
⅓ cup	finely chopped fresh mint or 2 Tbsp (25 mL) dried	75 mL
2 Tbsp	olive or canola oil	25 mL
5	drops hot pepper sauce	5
½ tsp	salt	2 mL
¼ tsp	freshly ground pepper	1 mL
2	green onions, with green tops, thinly sliced	2
1	tomato, seeded and diced Romaine lettuce leaves	1

▪ In salad bowl, combine bulgur and water; let stand for 10 minutes or until water is absorbed. Cool for 10 minutes.

▪ Stir in parsley and carrot.

▪ In small dish, combine lemon juice, mint, oil, hot pepper sauce, salt, and pepper; mix well. Pour over bulgur mixture. Toss well.

▪ If not serving immediately, cover and refrigerate.

▪ Just before serving, stir in green onions and tomato.

▪ Arrange Romaine lettuce leaves on platter. Mound salad in center of platter and serve.

▪ If you wish, for eating, tear romaine into pieces and scoop up tabbouleh with each piece.

Makes 4 servings.

EACH SERVING
¼ of recipe

1½ Starch
½ Fat

142 calories
5 g total fat
0 g saturated fat
0 mg cholesterol
3 g protein
21 g carbohydrate
220 mg sodium
434 mg potassium

GOOD
Iron, Magnesium

EXCELLENT
Vitamin A, Vitamin C, Folate

HIGH
Fiber

Fatoosh (Middle Eastern)

Bread Salad

In addition to being popular in the Middle East, bread salads are also specialties of Italian and Greek kitchens. They include panzanella, the famous bread salad of Tuscany, and Crete bread salad, the one known to individuals with a Greek background.

2	whole-wheat pita bread (6-inch/15-cm)	2
¼ cup	lemon juice	50 mL
2 Tbsp	olive oil	25 mL
1	clove garlic, minced	1
1 tsp	salt	5 mL
¼ tsp	freshly ground black pepper	1 mL
8	romaine lettuce leaves	8
8	red radishes, sliced	8
2	tomatoes, cut into wedges	2
2	green onions, sliced	2
½	English cucumber, cubed	½
½ cup	chopped fresh parsley	125 mL
¼ cup	chopped fresh mint or 1 Tbsp (15 mL) dried	50 mL

▪ Cut pitas in half, pull halves apart. Place pieces on nonstick baking sheet. Toast in 350°F (180°C) oven for 5 minutes or until crisp.

▪ Break into bite-size pieces; place in salad bowl.

▪ In small dish or screw-top jar, whisk or shake together lemon juice, oil, garlic, salt, and pepper. Set aside.

▪ Tear romaine into bite-size pieces; sprinkle over bread. Add radishes, tomatoes, green onions, cucumber, parsley, and mint. Gently toss to combine.

▪ Pour dressing over bread and greens; toss well.

Makes 4 servings.

EACH SERVING
¼ of recipe

1   Starch
1   Vegetable
1   Fat

161 calories
6 g total fat
0 g saturated fat
0 mg cholesterol
4 g protein
23 g carbohydrate
699 mg sodium ✿
327 mg potassium

GOOD
Vitamin C

EXCELLENT
Folate

MODERATE
Fiber

Horiatiki Salata (Greek)

Hellenic Country Salad

To many, this is known as kalokerini salata, a Greek summer salad. For others, it is a colorful salad that may have first been tasted in a local Greek restaurant. It is wonderful and easy to make, especially when garden vegetables are at their prime. For best results, always use feta cheese and Kalamata olives.

3	firm, ripe tomatoes	3
1	English cucumber	1
1	green sweet pepper, seeded	1
1	white onion	1
	or 3 green onions	
1 Tbsp	each olive oil, white wine vinegar, and lemon juice	15 mL
	Salt and freshly ground black pepper	
3 oz	feta cheese, broken into small pieces	100 g
12	black Kalamata olives	12
2 Tbsp	chopped fresh oregano or parsley or 2 tsp (10 mL) dried	25 mL
	Romaine lettuce leaves	

▪ Cut tomatoes into wedges and then in half. Place in salad bowl. Coarsely chop cucumber, green pepper, and onion. Add to tomatoes.

▪ Combine olive oil, vinegar, and lemon juice. Season to taste with salt and pepper. Pour over vegetables.

▪ Sprinkle feta cheese, olives, and oregano over top. (If using dried oregano, rub between palms as you sprinkle on salad.) Toss well.

▪ To serve, spoon into romaine lettuce leaf–lined bowl or toss with torn romaine leaves.

Makes 6 servings.

EACH SERVING
⅙ of recipe

1   Vegetable
1½ Fat

105 calories
7 g total fat
3 g saturated fat
15 mg cholesterol
3 g protein
7 g carbohydrate
509 mg sodium ✷
243 mg potassium

GOOD
Vitamin B$_{12}$

EXCELLENT
Vitamin C

MODERATE
Fiber

*Horiatiki Salata
(Hellenic Country Salad),
Shashlik*

Small Meals

Tourtière - *French Canadian*

Pizza Primavera C.P. - *Italian/North American*

Latkes - *Jewish*

Falafel- *Middle Eastern*

Burritos - *Mexican*

Tortillas - *Mexican*

Pomodori Ripieni - *Italian*

Toltott Paprika - *Hungarian*

Courgettes à la Niçoise - *French*

Hoisin Chicken in Crystal Fold -
Chinese, Vietnamese

Five Spice Tomato Sauce - *American/Chinese*

Fu Yong Hai - *Chinese*

Eggah - *Middle Eastern*

Spanakopita - *Greek*

Tortilla de Patatas - *Spanish*

Tortilla Espanola - *Spanish*

Frittata di Spinaci e Capellini - *Italian*

Blintzes - *Jewish, Russian*

*Tourtière, Fèves au Lard,
(Baked Beans), Inkokta
Rodbetor (Pickled Beets)*

Meat Pie

Traditionally, some variation of this meat pie is served by French Canadian families after mass on Christmas Eve. As with many ethnic dishes prepared for special celebrations, recipes for this one have been passed on from generation to generation.

EACH SERVING
⅛ of recipe

2	Starch
4	Meat, very lean
1	Fat

350 calories
11 g total fat
2 g saturated fat
65 mg cholesterol
30 g protein
28 g carbohydrate
855 mg sodium ✛
424 mg potassium

GOOD
Iron, Zinc, Magnesium, Riboflavin

EXCELLENT
Phosphorus, Thiamin, Niacin, Vitamin B$_6$, Vitamin B$_{12}$

1 lb	lean ground pork	500 g
1 lb	ground chicken	500 g
2	cloves garlic, minced	2
1	onion, minced	1
1½ tsp	salt	7 mL
1 tsp	crumbled sage	5 mL
¼ tsp	nutmeg	1 mL
¼ tsp	black pepper	1 mL
Pinch	each ground cloves and allspice	Pinch
1 cup	chicken broth	250 mL
1 cup	soft breadcrumbs	250 mL
	Light Sour Cream Pastry for 2 crust 9-inch (23-cm) pie (recipe p. 162)	

▪ In large heavy saucepan, combine ground pork, ground chicken, garlic, onion, salt, sage, nutmeg, pepper, cloves, and allspice. Stir in broth. Cook over low heat, stirring and breaking up ground meats for about 15 minutes or until meat loses its pink color and half liquid evaporates. Reduce heat; simmer for 15 minutes.

▪ Stir breadcrumbs into meat mixture until well mixed. Set aside to cool for about 30 minutes.

▪ Meanwhile, prepare pastry. Divide pastry into two balls, one slightly larger than the other. Roll out larger one to fit 9-inch (23-cm) pie plate. Trim off at edge of pie plate. Fill pie shell with cooled meat mixture, smoothing top.

▪ Roll out remaining pastry to fit top of pie, allowing for ½-inch (1-cm) overhang. Place on top of filling. Tuck overhang under edge of bottom crust. Seal, pinch pastry into rim around pie and flute edge. Cut slashes in top for steam vents.

▪ Bake in 425°F (210°C) oven for 10 minutes. Reduce heat to 350°F (180°C); bake for about 35 minutes longer or until golden brown.

Makes 8 servings.

Pizza Primavera C.P.

Of all the various toppings for pizza, this one has become my favorite. It was created for lunch one day by my two assistants, Cathy Lewis and Patricia Spicer, when we were testing as many as a dozen different dishes a day.

1	unbaked Pizza Crust (recipe p. 168)	

TOPPING

1 Tbsp	tomato paste	15 mL
2 tsp	white wine vinegar	10 mL
1 tsp	olive oil	5 mL
1	large tomato, sliced	1
1	zucchini, sliced	1
4	large leaves basil, chopped	4
2	cloves garlic, minced	2
8	black olives, pitted and chopped	8
2	green onions	2
½ cup	feta cheese, crumbled	125 mL
4 Tbsp	Parmesan cheese	60 mL

▪ Shape Pizza Crust as directed in recipe on p. 168.

▪ Topping: In small bowl, combine tomato paste, vinegar, and oil. Brush over unbaked crust.

▪ Distribute tomato, zucchini, basil, and garlic evenly over surface of crust. Sprinkle olives and green onions over top, then feta and Parmesan cheeses.

▪ Bake in 425°F (210°C) oven for about 25 minutes or until edges of pizza are golden brown.

Makes one 12-inch pizza, 8 servings.

EACH SERVING
⅛ of recipe

1½ Starch
1 Vegetable
1 Fat

183 calories
5 g total fat
3 g saturated fat
16 mg cholesterol
7 g protein
25 g carbohydrate
478 mg sodium ✸
141 mg potassium

GOOD
Riboflavin, Niacin

MODERATE
Fiber

Latkes (Jewish)

Potato Pancakes

This potato mixture made into pancakes (latkes) and served with applesauce is a popular side dish served at Hanukkah. The same mixture is made by German cooks and becomes the German potato cake, katoffelkuchen, which is similar to Swiss roesti, when it is spread in a lightly greased 8-inch (20-cm) square nonstick pan and baked in a 425°F (210°C) oven for 40 minutes. These also resemble ratzelach (Polish potato cakes) and Irish boxty, which combines grated raw potato with mashed potatoes.

2	large potatoes, unpeeled and scrubbed	2
1	small onion, optional	1
2	egg whites	2
1 Tbsp	all-purpose flour	15 mL
1 tsp	salt	5 mL
½ tsp	baking powder	2 mL
4 tsp	canola oil	20 mL
½ cup	low-fat sour cream or yogurt	125 mL

▪ Finely shred potatoes and onion, if using. Place in sieve; press to remove excess moisture.

▪ In bowl, whisk together egg whites, flour, salt, and baking powder until smooth. Stir in potato mixture.

▪ In large nonstick skillet, heat 2 tsp (10 mL) oil over medium-high heat. When drop of water spatters on skillet, spoon potato mixture, about 2 Tbsp (25 mL) at a time onto skillet; form into 3-inch (7.5-cm) pancakes.

▪ Cook for 4 minutes on each side or until golden brown. Transfer to ovenproof plate. Keep warm in oven while remaining batch or batches cook, adding remaining oil as required.

▪ Serve with sour cream or yogurt.

Makes 12 latkes (pancakes), 6 servings.

EACH SERVING
⅙ of recipe

½   Starch
1   Fat

    90 calories
     4 g total fat
     0 g saturated fat
     6 mg cholesterol
     2 g protein
    10 g carbohydrate
425 mg sodium ✪
229 mg potassium

Falafel (Middle Eastern)

Falafel

Serve these meatless patties in a pocket of pita bread as they do on the street in Israel, with salad, a little low-fat yogurt, and a smidge of tahini for a nutty sesame flavor. Both these filled pitas and the patties, on their own, are known as falafels.

2 cups	cooked chickpeas	500 mL
2 Tbsp	chopped onion	25 mL
3	cloves garlic, chopped	3
¼ cup	fine breadcrumbs	50 mL
¼ cup	each chopped fresh parsley and cilantro or 1 Tbsp (15 mL) dried	50 mL
½ tsp	each ground cumin, coriander, and turmeric	2 mL
Pinch	cayenne	Pinch
	Salt and freshly ground black pepper	
¼ tsp	baking soda	1 mL
	Canola oil	

▪ In food processor, combine chickpeas, onion, and garlic. Process with on/off motion until finely chopped but not pureed. Transfer to mixing bowl.

▪ Stir in breadcrumbs, parsley, cilantro, cumin, coriander, turmeric, and cayenne. Season to taste with salt and pepper. Stir in baking soda.

▪ With damp hands, divide mixture into 24 pieces. Roll and flatten into small patties.

▪ Place on lightly oiled, nonstick baking sheet. Bake in 400°F (200°C) oven for 10 to 15 minutes or until golden brown.

Makes 24 patties, 8 servings (3 patties each).

EACH SERVING
⅛ of recipe

2   Starch
½   Fat

185   calories
3 g   total fat
0 g   saturated fat
0 mg   cholesterol
9 g   protein
31 g   carbohydrate
362 mg   sodium
392 mg   potassium

GOOD
Phosphorus, Iron, Zinc, Magnesium

EXCELLENT
Folate

Burritos (Mexican)

Beef Burritos

EACH SERVING
1/12 of recipe

1   Starch
1   Vegetable
1   Meat, lean

150 calories
4 g total fat
1 g saturated fat
13 mg cholesterol
8 g protein
19 g carbohydrate
34 mg sodium
216 mg potassium

GOOD
Folate, Vitamin B$_{12}$

Burritos could be called Mexican sandwiches. Tortillas are folded and rolled around fillings and then eaten out of hand. They can be made at the table. Place warm tortillas on a plate with bowls of fillings and have diners make their own.

½ lb	lean ground beef	250 g
2	cloves garlic, finely chopped	2
1	can (14 oz/398 mL) kidney beans	1
2 tsp	chopped pickled jalapeno peppers	10 mL
1 tsp	vinegar	5 mL
½ tsp	chili powder	2 mL
½ tsp	freshly ground black pepper	2 mL
Pinch	each ground cinnamon and salt	Pinch
12	Cornmeal Tortillas (recipe below)	12
1	tomato, finely chopped	1
2 cups	shredded lettuce	500 mL
⅓ cup	shredded mozzarella cheese	75 mL

▪ In nonstick skillet, cook meat and garlic over medium heat, stirring, until brown and no longer pink.

▪ Drain beans; rinse and drain well. Stir into meat with jalapeno peppers, vinegar, chili powder, pepper, cinnamon, and salt. Cook, mashing beans and stirring for 4 minutes or until mixture is like a thick spread.

▪ On each cornmeal tortilla place about ¼ cup (50 mL) meat filling just below center; add a little tomato, lettuce, and cheese. Fold over sides; roll up to secure ingredients. Eat out of hand like a sandwich.

Makes 12 burritos.

Tortillas (Mexican)

Cornmeal Tortillas

EACH SERVING
1/12 of recipe

½   Starch

38 calories
0 g total fat
0 g saturated fat
17 mg cholesterol
1 g protein
6 g carbohydrate
75 mg sodium
15 mg potassium

1	egg	1
1 cup	water	250 mL
½ cup	all-purpose flour	125 mL
⅓ cup	cornmeal	75 mL
½ tsp	each baking powder and salt	2 mL

▪ In a bowl, whisk egg and water. Beat in flour, cornmeal, baking powder, and salt. Set aside for 10 minutes.

▪ Heat nonstick 7-inch (17.5-cm) skillet over medium heat. Brush very lightly with vegetable oil.

▪ Stir batter, then pour batter, 2 Tbsp (25 mL) at a time, into skillet to make very thin pancakes. Cook just until dry on top. Do not turn. Stack until all pancakes are cooked. Stir batter as it is being used, since cornmeal settles to the bottom.

Makes 12 tortillas.

Pomodori Ripieni (Italian)

Basil & Lentil Stuffed Tomatoes

For a small meal with a chunk of crusty bread, these stuffed tomatoes are at the top of my list. They can be served as part of an antipasto (first course), as a contorno (side dish to a meat entrée), or as part of an all-vegetable meal with rice or pasta. Lentils supply impressive amounts of dietary fiber, besides being delicious.

2	firm tomatoes	2
2 Tbsp	finely chopped celery	25 mL
1 Tbsp	finely chopped onion	15 mL
1 Tbsp	chopped fresh basil	15 mL
	Salt and freshly ground pepper	
½ cup	cooked brown lentils	125 mL
2 tsp	freshly grated Parmesan cheese	10 mL

▪ Cut thin slice from stem end of each tomato; scoop pulp and juice into small saucepan. Place tomato shells, open end down, on paper towels to drain.

▪ To saucepan, add celery, onion, and basil. Cook over medium heat, stirring occasionally, for 5 minutes or until tender and most of liquid has evaporated. Season to taste with salt and pepper. Stir in lentils.

▪ Spoon mixture into tomato shells; place in small custard cups on baking sheet. Sprinkle each with Parmesan cheese.

▪ Bake in 350°F (180°C) oven for 10 minutes or until heated through and cheese begins to turn golden.

Makes 4 servings.

EACH SERVING
¼ **of recipe**

½   Starch

48   calories
0 g   total fat
0 g   saturated fat
0 mg   cholesterol
3 g   protein
8 g   carbohydrate
27 mg   sodium
225 mg   potassium

GOOD
Folate

MODERATE
Fiber

TIMELY TIP
Lentils are a quick-cooking legume, and they do not need presoaking. Also, canned ones are available for convenience; drain and use. For ½ cup (125 mL) cooked lentils, cook ¼ cup (50 mL) dried lentils in 1 cup (250 mL) lightly salted boiling water for 8 to 10 minutes or until lentils are tender and water is absorbed.

Toltott Paprika (Hungarian)

Stuffed Peppers

It seems every ethnic cuisine has some variation of the stuffed vegetable. Cooks with Ukrainian, Polish, and German backgrounds make cabbage rolls. Those from the Middle East and Mediterranean countries stuff grape leaves. Japanese cooks scoop out and fill squash. In East Indian kitchens, dum aloo, a wonderful steamed stuffed potato, is created. Similar to these stuffed peppers are the many versions of Mexican chiles rellenos. And, the list could go on and on!

8	medium-sized banana peppers	8
½ lb	ground chicken or lean pork	250 g
¼ lb	ground lean beef	125 g
1 cup	cooked brown rice	250 mL
1 tsp	paprika	5 mL
	Salt and freshly ground black pepper	
2 tsp	butter or canola oil	10 mL
¼ cup	all-purpose flour	50 mL
1 cup	water	250 mL
1	can (5½ oz/156 mL) tomato paste	1

▪ Wash peppers and cut in half lengthwise. Remove stalks, seeds, and inside ribs.

▪ In bowl, combine ground chicken and beef, cooked rice and paprika. Season to taste with salt and pepper. Stuff pepper halves with mixture.

▪ In saucepan, heat butter over medium heat. Stir in flour until lightly browned.

▪ Stir in water and tomato. Simmer, stirring, for 2 minutes or until thickened. Pour into shallow casserole.

▪ Arrange peppers in sauce. Cover and bake in 325°F (160°C) oven for 35 minutes or until meat is no longer pink.

▪ At serving time, spoon sauce over peppers.

Makes 8 stuffed peppers, 4 servings.

VARIATION

Courgettes à la Niçoise (French)
Stuffed Zucchini

Zucchini is one vegetable that it certainly easy to stuff.

▪ Substitute small zucchini for peppers. Cut in half lengthwise. Scoop out and discard seedy center.

▪ Subsitute 1 clove garlic, minced, for paprika.

▪ Fill and bake as directed above.

Hoisin Chicken in Crystal Fold
(Chinese, Vietnamese)

Chicken in Crystal Fold

The inspiration for creating these snappy snacks, which are quick and easy to prepare at home, came from similar ones that I have savored in Vietnamese, Thai, and Chinese restaurants.

½ lb	ground chicken	250 g
1 Tbsp	lite soy sauce	15 mL
1 Tbsp	each fresh lime juice and water	15 mL
2	cloves garlic, minced	2
1 Tbsp	finely chopped fresh ginger root	15 mL
2 tsp	oyster sauce	10 mL
¼ tsp	hot Oriental chili paste	1 mL
½ cup	chopped fresh cilantro	125 mL
2 tsp	sesame oil	10 mL
4	leaf or bibb lettuce leaves	4
4 tsp	hoisin sauce	20 mL

- In bowl, combine chicken, soy sauce, lime juice, water, garlic, ginger root, oyster sauce, and hot chili paste.
- In nonstick skillet, heat oil over medium-high heat. Cook chicken mixture, stirring, for 5 minutes or until just cooked through. Stir in cilantro and sesame oil.
- Spoon onto warm platter. Add lettuce leaves and small dish of hoisin sauce.
- To eat, have each diner spread a teaspoonful (5 mL) of hoisin sauce on one lettuce leaf, top it with ¼ chicken mixture, and roll it up (like a tortilla) to eat out of hand.

Makes 4 servings.

Five Spice Tomato Sauce (American/Chinese)

Five Spice Tomato Sauce

This is served with Egg Foo Yong (p. 62)

1 tsp	canola oil or butter	5 mL
1 tsp	finely chopped onion	5 mL
1	clove garlic, minced	1
¼ cup	tomato paste	50 mL
1 tsp	Chinese five spice powder	5 mL
¾ cup	chicken broth	175 mL
1 Tbsp	all-purpose flour	15 mL

- In small nonstick saucepan, heat butter over heat. Cook onion and garlic for 1 minute. Stir in tomato paste, five spice, and then broth; cook for 1 minute. Stir flour into 1 Tbsp (15 mL) cold water until smooth. Add to broth mixture. Cook, stirring, for 1½ minutes or until thickened.

Makes 1 cup (250 mL), 4 servings.

Egg Foo Yung

Fu yong hai today is different from the one known in classical Chinese cuisine, where it was served with brown gravy and rice. This version, with tomato sauce, is world-renowned and probably originated in North American Chinese restaurants.

½ cup	chopped, cooked chicken, pork, shrimp, or fish	125 mL
3	green onions, thinly sliced	3
1	zucchini, shredded	1
1	carrot, shredded	1
1 cup	bean sprouts, trimmed	250 mL
1	small clove garlic, minced	1
3	egg whites	3
1	egg	1
2 tsp	all-purpose flour	10 mL
1 tsp	lite soy sauce	5 mL
½ tsp	Worcestershire sauce	2 mL
Pinch	cayenne pepper	Pinch
	Salt and freshly ground black pepper	
	Five Spice Tomato Sauce (recipe p. 61)	
	Chopped fresh cilantro or green onions.	

■ In bowl, combine chicken, green onions, zucchini, carrot, bean sprouts, and garlic. Whisk together egg whites, egg, flour, soy sauce, Worcestershire, and cayenne. Stir into vegetable mixture.

■ Lightly brush large nonstick skillet with butter. Heat over medium-high heat. Spoon vegetable mixture, in 1/4 cup (50 mL) batches, on to skillet; flatten into pancakes. Cook for about 4 minutes or until set. Turn and cook for 2 minutes to brown other side. Transfer to heated platter.

■ Serve with Five Spice Tomato Sauce. Top with cilantro.

Makes 4 servings.

VARIATION

Eggah (Middle Eastern)

Lamb Omelette

The ingredients are similar, but it is the lamb and Middle Eastern herbs and spices (mint, cumin, and coriander) that change the ethnic character of these omelettes.

■ Substitute cooked lamb for chicken; use celery slices in place of bean sprouts. Add 1 Tbsp (15 mL) chopped fresh mint or 1 tsp (5 mL) dried to egg white mixture.

■ In the sauce, substitute ½ tsp (2 mL) each ground cumin and coriander for the Chinese five spice powder.

EACH SERVING
¼ of recipe

2 Vegetable
2 Meat, very lean

121 calories
2 g total fat
0 g saturated fat
79 mg cholesterol
15 g protein
8 g carbohydrate
177 mg sodium
322 mg potassium

GOOD
Riboflavin, Folate, Vitamin B$_6$

EXCELLENT
Vitamin A, Niacin

Calculations approximately the same as above.

Spanakopita (Greek)

Spanakopita

These spinach and cheese phyllo squares are thin and short on calories, but they are still full of the wonderful aroma and flavor of spinach and feta cheese, the main filling ingredients of traditional spanakopita.

½ lb	fresh spinach	250 g
¼ lb	feta cheese, crumbled	125 g
½ cup	light cottage cheese	125 mL
1	small onion, finely chopped	1
2 Tbsp	chopped fresh parsley	25 mL
1 Tbsp	chopped fresh dill or	15 mL
	1 tsp (5 mL) dried	
	Salt and white pepper	
1	egg	1
1	egg white	1
1 Tbsp	butter, melted	15 mL
8	sheets phyllo pastry	8

- Wash, drain, and chop spinach. Place in steamer or saucepan with only the rinsing water clinging to it. Cover and steam or cook for 3 minutes or until tender. In sieve, drain well and squeeze to remove excess moisture.

- In bowl, combine spinach, feta and cottage cheeses, onion, parsley, and dill. Season to taste with salt and pepper; mix well. Stir in egg and egg white until well mixed.

- Line 11 x 15 inch (28 x 38 cm) jelly roll pan with 1 sheet phyllo pastry. Lightly dab melted butter here and there with brush. Repeat with 4 additional sheets of phyllo.

- Spread spinach mixture evenly over top. Place 1 sheet of phyllo over filling, lightly dab with butter. Repeat with 2 remaining sheets of phyllo. With scissors, cut off any pastry hanging over edges of pan.

- With serrated knife, cut through top layers only into 24 squares.

- Bake in 350°F (180°C) oven for 20 minutes or until golden brown.

- Let stand for 10 minutes. Cut completely through top cuts to serve.

Makes 24 squares, 12 servings.

EACH SERVING
¹⁄₁₂ of recipe

½ Starch
1 Meat, lean

92 calories
4 g total fat
2 g saturated fat
28 mg cholesterol
5 g protein
9 g carbohydrate
278 mg sodium
144 mg potassium

Tortilla de Patatas (Spanish)

Potato Omelette

The Spanish call an omelette a tortilla, which has no resemblance whatsoever to a Mexican tortilla. Like the Italian frittata, it is a skillet-cooked egg pie that is cut into wedges before serving. It is delicious served cold and, for the Spanish, it is a favorite picnic dish.

2 tsp	olive oil	10 mL
2	medium potatoes, scrubbed and diced	2
1 cup	chopped Spanish or cooking onion	250 mL
1	small clove garlic, minced	1
1	egg	1
2	egg whites	2
½ tsp	salt	2 mL
¼ tsp	ground white pepper	1 mL

▪ In nonstick skillet, heat olive oil. Over medium heat, cook and stir potato, onion, and garlic for about 10 minutes or until potato is tender.

▪ Beat eggs and egg whites with salt and pepper. Pour over potatoes, allowing egg to run through potatoes to bottom of skillet.

▪ Cover and cook over low heat for about 10 minutes or until light brown on bottom and until eggs are set.

▪ Cut into wedges to serve.

Makes 4 servings.

VARIATION

Tortilla Española (Spanish)

Spanish Omelette

▪ Add 1 tomato, finely chopped and drained, and ½ red sweet pepper, diced, to the potato mixture.

Frittata di Spinaci e Capellini (Italian)

Capellini & Spinach Frittata

A frittata is the Italian equivalent of an omelette. It's always slipped out of the pan as a flat cake; it's never folded. Italian cooks find it's a great way to use up leftovers—pasta, vegetables, and bits of meat or fish. Serve it hot or at room temperature, as a starter or main course.

½ lb	fresh spinach, chopped	250 g
½ lb	angel hair pasta (capellini, capelli d'angelo)	250 g
2 tsp	olive oil	10 mL
⅓ cup	finely diced Asiago or feta cheese	75 mL
⅓ cup	grated Parmesan or Romano cheese Salt and freshly ground black pepper	75 mL
2	eggs	2
2	egg whites	2
2 tsp	butter	10 mL

■ Place spinach in steamer basket over boiling water, cover and steam for 1½ minutes or until wilted. Allow to drain in steamer until cool.

■ In saucepan of lightly salted boiling water, cook pasta for 3 minutes or until al dente (tender but firm); drain. In large bowl, toss pasta with 1 tsp (5 mL) olive oil, cheeses, and spinach. Season to taste with salt and pepper.

■ Lightly beat together eggs and egg whites. Stir into pasta mixture until well blended.

■ In large nonstick skillet, with ovenproof handle, heat remaining olive oil and butter over medium heat until foam disappears. Pour in pasta mixture, spreading evenly. Cook for 3 to 5 minutes or until egg is thickened throughout but still moist.

■ Bake in 350°F (180°C) oven for 3 minutes or until top is set.

■ With spatula, gently loosen edge and bottom, if necessary. Put heat-proof platter over skillet and invert frittata onto it.

■ Serve warm or at room temperature, cut into wedges.

Makes 6 servings.

EACH SERVING
⅙ of recipe

2   Starch
1   Meat, very lean
1   Fat

252 calories
8 g total fat
3 g saturated fat
86 mg cholesterol
13 g protein
30 g carbohydrate
318 mg sodium
290 mg potassium

GOOD
Calcium, Phosphorus, Magnesium, Riboflavin, Niacin, Vitamin B₁₂

EXCELLENT
Vitamin A, Folate

Blintzes (Jewish, Russian)
Cheese-Filled Pancake Rolls

Blintzes are sometimes mistaken for blini. Both begin as pancakes, but blini are small, with yeast used as the leavener. They are served as appetizers topped with caviar or smoked fish and sour cream. Classic blintzes are pancakes, as thin and tender as crepes, rolled around a fresh cheese filling.

PANCAKES

2	eggs	2
2	egg whites	2
¾ cup	all-purpose flour	175 mL
½ tsp	each granulated sugar and salt	2 mL
½ cup	each 1% milk and water	125 mL
1 tsp	vanilla	5 mL
2 tsp	melted butter	10 mL

FILLING

1 cup	1% cottage cheese, drained	250 mL
1 tsp	vanilla	5 mL
¼ tsp	each grated orange and lemon rind	1 mL
¼ cup	raisins, chopped	50 mL

SAUCE

1 cup	sliced fresh or frozen strawberries	250 mL
	Sugar substitute	

• In food processor or blender, combine eggs, egg whites, flour, sugar, and salt. Add milk, water, and vanilla. Process until smooth. Let stand for 30 minutes.

• In nonstick 6-inch (15-cm) omelette pan or skillet, heat butter over medium-high heat. Pour batter, 2 Tbsp (25 mL) at a time, into pan, swirl around and tilt to coat bottom of pan. Cook until top looks dry and bottom is golden. Slide onto plate. Repeat with remaining batter, stacking pancakes as they cook.

• Filling: In small bowl, mash together cottage cheese, vanilla, and orange and lemon rinds. Stir in raisins.

• Place pancakes brown side up on working surface. Divide filling among 12 pancakes, placing it close to the outside edge of each pancake. Fold edge up over filling, fold sides to center, and roll up into small log shapes.

• Sauce: In processor, puree strawberries and sweeten to taste with sugar substitute. Set aside.

• At serving time, lightly brush 10-inch (25-cm) nonstick skillet with butter. Arrange filled pancakes (blintzes), seam side down, in skillet over medium heat. Cook, turning occasionally, for 4 minutes or until golden.

• Place on serving plates. Spoon sauce over top.

Makes 12 servings.

EACH SERVING
¹/₁₂ **of recipe**

1   **Starch**

86 calories
1 g total fat
0 g saturated fat
38 mg cholesterol
5 g protein
11 g carbohydrate
175 mg sodium
92 mg potassium

Legumes, Grains, & Pasta

Favas à Sao Miguel - *Portuguese*

Feifoes Assados - *Portuguese*

Fèves au Lard - *French Canadian*

Moros Y Cristianos - *Canadian*

Louisiana Red Beans & Rice - *American South*

Dal - *East Indian*

Ceci alla Toscana - *Italian*

Arroz de Tomate cam Amêijoas - *Portuguese*

Wild Rice with Nuts - *Canadian Aboriginal*

Risi e Bisi - *Italian*

Risotto con Asparagi - *Italian*

Li Fan - *Chinese*

Polenta - *Italian*

Polenta con Funghi - *Italian*

Bulgur Pilavi - *Middle Eastern*

Pilau - *East Indian*

Saffron Couscous - *African*

Spaghetti Bolognese - *Italian*

Pasta al Pomodoro e Basilico - *Italian*

Tomato & Basil Sauce - *Italian*

Rotini all'Ortica - *Italian*

Creamy Mushroom Sauce - *Italian*

Fettucine alla Vongole Bianco - *Italian*

Orzo Riganati - *Greek*

Pasta Primavera - *North American/Italian*

Pasticcio Macaronia - *Greek*

Chow Mein - *Chinese-American*

Paad Thai - *Thai*

Favas à Sao Miguel (Portuguese)

Stewed Fava Beans

Fava beans (broad beans) are similar in shape to lima beans but larger. When cooking them at home, it is important to blanch them, after they have soaked, to remove the thick outer coating, which is bitter. Canned ones, of course, are ready to use as they are. Recipes using fava beans are still handed down from mother to daughter as they have been for generations in families who originated in Mediterranean and Middle Eastern countries where favas are popular.

1 Tbsp	olive or canola oil	15 mL
2	onions, finely chopped	2
2	cloves garlic, minced	2
½ cup	chopped, peeled tomatoes	125 mL
2 Tbsp	tomato paste	25 mL
1 Tbsp	white wine vinegar	15 mL
1 tsp	hot pepper sauce	5 mL
1	bay leaf	1
4 cups	cooked fava or broad beans	1 L
¼ cup	dry white wine or water	50 mL
	Salt and freshly ground black pepper	
½ cup	chopped fresh cilantro	125 mL

▪ In large heavy saucepan or Dutch oven, heat oil over medium heat. Cook onion and garlic for about 5 minutes or until onion is translucent.

▪ Stir in tomatoes, tomato paste, vinegar, hot pepper sauce, and bay leaf. Reduce heat and simmer, stirring occasionally, for 10 minutes or until thickened.

▪ Stir in beans until coated with sauce. Stir in wine. Bring to boil. Reduce heat, cover and simmer, stirring occasionally, for 20 minutes or until beans are well-seasoned.

▪ Remove from heat; discard bay leaf. Season to taste with salt and pepper. Stir in cilantro.

▪ Allow to cool to room temperature for flavors and sauce to permeate beans.

▪ Reheat to serve, or serve at room temperature.

Makes 6 servings.

Feifoes Assados (Portuguese)

Portuguese Baked Beans

All baked beans start out as dried beans, and they supply lots of fiber. The seasonings make these baked beans taste Portuguese and the ones in the following recipe taste French Canadian.

2 tsp	olive oil	10 mL
2	onions, chopped	2
2	cloves garlic, minced	2
4 cups	cooked white or red kidney beans	1 L
1 cup	chicken broth	250 mL
2 Tbsp	tomato paste	25 mL
2 tsp	hot pepper sauce	10 mL
1 tsp	hot paprika	5 mL
½ tsp	ground cinnamon	2 mL
3	bay leaves	3
4	slices back bacon, diced	4
	Salt and freshly ground black pepper	

▪ In Dutch oven or skillet, heat oil over medium heat. Cook onions and garlic for 5 minutes or until onion is translucent.

▪ Stir in beans, broth, tomato paste, hot pepper sauce, paprika, cinnamon, and bay leaves.

▪ Transfer bean mixture to a casserole, or bake in Dutch oven. Sprinkle bacon over beans.

▪ Bake in 300°F (150°C) oven for 15 minutes or until bacon is cooked. Stir bacon into beans. Season to taste with salt and pepper. Bake for another 20 minutes or until golden brown.

Makes 8 servings.

EACH SERVING
⅛ of recipe

1½ Starch
1   Meat, very lean

160 calories
2 g total fat
0 g saturated fat
6 mg cholesterol
11 g protein
23 g carbohydrate
279 mg sodium
453 mg potassium

GOOD
Phosphorus, Iron, Magnesium, Niacin

EXCELLENT
Folate

HIGH
Fiber

Fèves au Lard (French Canadian)

Old-Fashioned Baked Beans

Traditionally, chunks of salt pork were dispersed throughout good baked beans. However, in this recipe, the salt pork is buried in the beans as they bake, then it is removed, leaving only its subtle salty, smoky flavor. So, these baked beans have fewer calories than when the pork is left in the dish.

3 cups	navy beans, soaked and drained	750 mL
1	onion, chopped	1
¼ cup	packed brown sugar	50 mL
2 Tbsp	tomato paste	25 mL
1 Tbsp	cider vinegar	15 mL
1	bay leaf	1
2 tsp	dry mustard	10 mL
2 tsp	salt	10 mL
¼ tsp	freshly ground black pepper	1 mL
Pinch	ground cloves	Pinch
¼ lb	chunk salt pork	125 g

▪ In large saucepan, cover beans and onion generously with water (about 8 cups/2 L); bring to boil. Reduce heat and simmer for 20 minutes or until nearly tender, but with a little crunch. Pour into large 10-cup (2.5-L) bean pot or deep casserole.

▪ In small bowl, combine brown sugar, tomato paste, vinegar, bay leaf, dry mustard, salt, pepper, and cloves. Stir into beans. Cut chunk salt pork in half. Bury in beans.

▪ Pour on about 1 cup (250 mL) hot water just to cover beans.

▪ Bake, covered, in 275°F (140°C) oven, stirring occasionally and adding water if mixture seems dry, for 4½ hours.

▪ Uncover and bake for about 30 minutes or until tender.

▪ Remove and discard salt pork.

Makes 8 servings.

Moros Y Cristianos (Caribbean)

Cuban Black Beans & Rice

Black beans (turtle beans) are popular in Caribbean, Mexican, and South American cuisines. Like all combinations of rice and beans, this is a wholesome dish full of fiber and B-vitamins. When a grain (the rice) and a legume (the beans) are eaten together, they provide complete protein, making this a good substitute for meat.

1 tsp	canola oil	5 mL
3	cloves garlic, minced	3
2	onions, chopped	2
1	green sweet pepper, seeded and chopped	1
1	tomato, peeled, seeded, and chopped	1
1	stalk celery, chopped	1
1 Tbsp	vinegar	15 mL
¼ tsp	crushed red chili pepper	1 mL
1 cup	beef or vegetable broth	250 mL
2 cups	cooked black beans	500 mL
	Salt and freshly ground black pepper	
2 cups	hot cooked brown rice	500 mL
	Chopped green onion	
	Thin lemon wedges	

- In large nonstick saucepan, heat oil over medium heat; cook garlic, onions, green pepper, tomato, and celery, stirring often, for 7 minutes or until onion is translucent. Stir in vinegar and red chili pepper. Pour in broth.
- Add beans; bring to boil. Reduce heat and simmer, stirring occasionally, for about 20 minutes or until liquid is reduced. Season to taste with salt and pepper.
- Spoon rice onto serving plate or bowl. Spoon beans over top. Garnish with green onion and lemon wedges.

Makes 4 servings.

EACH SERVING
¼ of recipe

3 Starch
1 Vegetable

270 calories
2 g total fat
0 g saturated fat
0 mg cholesterol
11 g protein
51 g carbohydrate
575 mg sodium ❄
563 mg potassium

GOOD
Phosphorus, Iron, Zinc, Vitamin C, Thiamin, Niacin, Vitamin B_6

EXCELLENT
Magnesium, Folate

MODERATE
Fiber

VARIATIONS

Louisiana Red Beans & Rice (American South)

Red Beans & Rice

- Season vegetables in skillet with only 1 clove garlic, minced, ½ tsp (2 mL) paprika, and ¼ tsp (1 mL) each dried oregano and thyme leaves.
- Use red kidney beans in place of black beans.

Calculations approximately the same as above.

Dal (East Indian)

Lentil Puree

To East Indian cooks, dal is the term used to describe dozens of different legumes. However, the dish of the same name refers to a puree of flavored cooked lentils that has the consistency of spaghetti sauce. It is great served with rice, curries, and the same side dishes that go with curries—peanuts, coconut, sliced bananas, raisins, and chutney. Lentils are unlike other legumes; they cook quickly without presoaking.

1 cup	green or red lentils	250 mL
1	bay leaf	1
2 tsp	canola oil	10 mL
1	onion, chopped	1
1	clove garlic, minced	1
1 tsp	ground cumin	5 mL
1 tsp	turmeric	5 mL
½ tsp	salt	2 mL
¼ tsp	ground cardamom	1 mL
¼ tsp	ground ginger	1 mL
½ cup	water	125 mL

▪ In saucepan, cover lentils and bay leaf with 3 cups (750 mL) water; bring to boil. Reduce heat, cover and simmer for 25 minutes or until tender. Drain. Discard bay leaf.

▪ In nonstick skillet, heat oil over medium heat. Cook onion and garlic, stirring occasionally, for 5 minutes or until onion is translucent. Stir in cumin, turmeric, salt, cardamom, and ginger. Cook for 1 minute longer.

▪ Stir in lentils and ¼ cup (50 mL) water; bring to boil. Reduce heat and simmer for 5 minutes.

▪ Transfer to food processor or blender. Puree until sauce-like in consistency, adding a little water if desired. (If a coarser consistency is desired, puree only half of the lentil mixture and stir remaining lentils into pureed ones.)

Makes 6 servings.

Ceci alla Toscana (Italian)

Chickpeas with Rosemary & Garlic

Ceci are chickpeas, which are also known as garbanzos. They are often used in East Indian, Middle Eastern, and Mediterranean cooking. As dishes using chickpeas (such as hummus and couscous) have gained popularity in the Western world, their use in salads, soups, and stews has become more common.

1	can (19 oz/540 mL) chickpeas or 2 cups (500 mL) cooked	1
2	cloves garlic, peeled	2
2	sprigs fresh rosemary or 1 tsp (5 mL) dried	2
1 cup	chopped fresh or canned tomatoes, drained	250 mL
1 Tbsp	wine vinegar	15 mL
2 tsp	extra virgin olive oil	10 mL
	Salt and freshly ground black pepper	
	Chopped fresh Italian parsley	

▪ Empty can of chickpeas with their liquid into saucepan. Add ½ cup (125 mL) water, or add 1 cup (250 mL) water to home-cooked chickpeas. Add garlic and rosemary. Bring to boil. Reduce heat and simmer for 15 minutes.

▪ Drain, and discard rosemary and garlic. Stir in tomatoes. Bring to boil. Cook for 5 minutes to reduce slightly. Stir in vinegar and olive oil. Season to taste with salt and a generous amount of freshly ground black pepper.

▪ Garnish with parsley.

Makes 4 servings.

Arroz de Tomate cam Amêijoas (Portuguese)

Tomato Rice with Clams

Rice certainly has become an important ingredient for the global table. This one-pot meal, popular with Portuguese cooks, finds brown rice combined with chickpeas, clams, tomato, and flavorings indigenous to Portugal.

1 Tbsp	olive or canola oil	15 mL
1	onion, chopped	1
1	clove garlic, minced	1
¼ cup	chopped fresh parsley	50 mL
¼ cup	tomato paste	50 mL
1 tsp	hot pepper sauce or paste	5 mL
1	can (5 oz/142 g) clams	1
2 cups	hot cooked brown rice	500 mL
1 cup	cooked chickpeas	250 mL
½	green sweet pepper, seeded and diced	½
½	red sweet pepper, seeded and diced	½
6	pitted black olives, sliced	6

▪ In saucepan, heat oil over medium-high heat. Cook onions and garlic for 5 minutes or until onions are translucent.

▪ Stir in parsley, tomato paste, and hot pepper sauce. Stir in clams with their juice. Bring to a boil.

▪ Stir in brown rice, chickpeas, and green and red pepper. Bring to boil. Cook for 2 minutes.

▪ Transfer to serving platter. Garnish with olives.

Makes 6 servings.

Wild Rice with Nuts

Wild rice, known for its nutty taste and chewy texture, is not really a grain. It is the seed of a marsh grass, common in Canada and the northern part of the U.S. Local Indian natives still harvest it in those areas. Recently, the plant has been domesticated for commercial production, and wild rice is more readily available in supermarkets, as well as in specialty food shops.

1 cup	wild rice	250 mL
2 cups	chicken broth	500 mL
2 tsp	butter	10 mL
1	onion, finely chopped	1
¼ cup	chopped toasted walnuts	50 mL
½ tsp	crumbled sage	2 mL
	Salt and freshly ground black pepper	

▪ In sieve or colander, wash rice under cold running water.

▪ In saucepan, cover rice with boiling water; let stand for 5 minutes; drain and repeat. (This removes any weedy aroma or flavor.)

▪ Cover rice with chicken broth; bring to boil. Reduce heat, cover and simmer for 50 minutes or until rice splits and begins to curl.

▪ Meanwhile, in small nonstick skillet, melt butter over medium heat. Cook onion for 5 minutes or until translucent.

▪ Stir onion mixture into rice. Add nuts and sage; mix well. Season to taste with salt and pepper.

Makes 6 servings.

EACH SERVING
⅙ of recipe

1½ Starch
½ Fat

155 calories
5 g total fat
1 g saturated fat
3 mg cholesterol
6 g protein
22 g carbohydrate
273 mg sodium
202 mg potassium

GOOD
Zinc, Magnesium, Niacin

Risi e Bisi (Italian)

Italian Risotto with Peas

Here is proof that the Italian rice specialty, risotto, can vary depending on the addition of various herbs and flavorings, vegetables, and/or meats. This one, with peas and ham, is a Venetian classic. I like to use the top quality Parmesan cheese—Parmigiano-Reggiano—in it. It's expensive, but its flavor is vivid, especially when it is freshly grated from a chunk of the hard cheese.

1 Tbsp	butter	15 mL
1	onion, finely chopped	1
1	clove garlic, minced	1
1 cup	Arborio or short-grain pearl rice	250 mL
2¼ cups	simmering chicken broth	550 mL
1 cup	fresh or frozen green peas	250 mL
¼ cup	minced smoked ham (1 oz/30 g) (prosciutto preferred)	50 mL
	Salt and freshly ground black pepper	
½ cup	freshly grated Parmesan cheese	125 mL
¼ cup	chopped fresh parsley	50 mL

▪ In nonstick saucepan, melt half the butter over medium heat. Cook onion and garlic for about 4 minutes or until onion is translucent.

▪ Stir in rice; cook, stirring constantly for about 3 minutes, until golden. Add broth ½ cup (125 mL) at a time, cooking and stirring from the bottom up until broth disappears, then make the next addition. Continue until all broth is absorbed, for about 18 minutes or until mixture is creamy and rice is tender with a little crunch in the center.

▪ Cook peas in a small amount of water until tender.

▪ With fork, lightly toss peas, ham, Parmesan, and half the parsley into rice. Season to taste with salt and pepper.

▪ Transfer to serving dish and sprinkle with remaining parsley. Serve at once.

Makes 4 servings.

VARIATION

Risotto con Asparagi (Italian)

Risotto with Asparagus

Making risotto seems like a tedious process, but the results— a creamy mixture with the rice grains firm and separate from one another—are worth it.

▪ Substitute 1 cup (250 mL) asparagus pieces for the peas.

EACH SERVING
¼ of recipe

3 Starch
1 Vegetable
1 Meat, medium-fat

335 calories
8 g total fat
4 g saturated fat
21 mg cholesterol
15 g protein
48 g carbohydrate
831 mg sodium ✿
281 mg potassium

GOOD
Calcium, Phosphorus, Zinc, Folate, Vitamin B₁₂

EXCELLENT
Niacin

MODERATE
Fiber

Calculations approximately the same as above.

Li Fan (Chinese)

Chinese Fried Rice

The Chinese say that the secret to making good fried rice is to make sure the rice is cold before adding the other ingredients to it. So I recommend cooking it ahead or cooking extra when rice is called for in another meal and then refrigerating or freezing it to have on hand for fried rice. For a different presentation, roll up this variation in leaf lettuce to eat out of hand.

2 tsp	butter or canola oil	10 mL
1	egg	1
1	egg white	1
4	green onions, minced	4
1	stick celery, finely chopped	1
2 Tbsp	soy sauce	25 mL
¼ tsp	freshly ground black pepper	1 mL
2 cups	cooked short- or long-grain rice	500 mL
6	lettuce leaves	6
1 Tbsp	minced fresh cilantro or parsley or 1 tsp (5 mL) dried	15 mL

▪ In large nonstick skillet, heat butter over medium heat. Whisk together egg and egg white; pour into skillet and scramble. Remove and separate into small pieces; set aside.

▪ Add onions and celery to skillet. Stir-fry for 3 minutes or until limp. Stir in soy sauce and pepper. Add rice, toss to combine. Cook, lightly stirring, for 3 minutes or until heated through.

▪ Stir in scrambled egg. Remove from heat.

▪ Serve on lettuce leaves, garnished with cilantro.

Makes 6 servings.

EACH SERVING
⅙ of recipe

| 1 | Starch |
| ½ | Fat |

102	calories
2 g	total fat
0 g	saturated fat
35 mg	cholesterol
3 g	protein
15 g	carbohydrate
368 mg	sodium
87 mg	potassium

Polenta (Italian)

Polenta

When polenta is made following the traditional method of pouring dry cornmeal directly into boiling water, lumps sometimes form. Once formed, it is impossible to get rid of them. However, lumps will not develop if the cornmeal is mixed with cold water before being stirred into the boiling water.

1 cup	cornmeal (preferrably coarse)	250 mL
5 cups	water	1.25 L
1 tsp	salt	5 mL

- Gradually add cornmeal to 2 cups (500 mL) of cold water, stirring rapidly until smooth.
- In saucepan, heat remaining 3 cups (750 mL) water to boiling.
- Slowly pour the cornmeal mixture into the boiling water, all the time stirring with a wooden spoon. Stir in salt. Continue stirring, bringing mixture back to boil. Reduce heat and simmer, stirring frequently, for 30 minutes.
- Pour in mound on serving platter. Cool slightly then serve.

Makes 6 servings.

Polenta con Funghi (Italian)

Polenta with Mushrooms

Use Portabello mushrooms, if possible, for the sauce. Their rich, earthy flavor complements the creamy polenta.

Polenta (recipe above)
Creamy Mushroom Sauce (recipe p. 84)

- Prepare polenta following recipe directions. Spread out 2 inches (5 cm) thick on wooden board. Cool for ½ hour.
- Meanwhile, prepare Creamy Mushroom Sauce. Cut the cooled polenta into thin strips. Cover bottom of lightly buttered 8-inch (20-cm) baking dish with layer of strips. Spoon on layer of sauce. Continue layering. The top layer should be sauce.
- Bake in 400°F (200°C) oven for 15 minutes.

Makes 6 servings.

Bulgur Pilavi (Middle Eastern)

Bulgur Pilaf

There seem to be many spellings for bulgur—bulghur, burghul, bulgar. It looks like cracked wheat but it is not. Bulgur is the product created when whole wheat berries are steamed, dried, and broken up. That processing makes a product that cooks quickly. It is a staple for Middle Eastern cooks, and they use it in all sorts of pilafs, vegetable and meat dishes, and salads, such as tabbouleh. (For salad making, soaking bulgur in warm water for about half an hour and then draining it is enough to make it edible. Cooking is not needed.)

2 tsp	butter or olive oil	10 mL
1	onion, finely chopped	1
1	tomato, coarsely chopped	1
2 cups	chicken broth	500 mL
1 cup	bulgur	250 mL
	Salt and freshly ground black pepper	
2 Tbsp	chopped Italian (flat-leaf) parsley	25 mL

▪ In saucepan, heat butter over medium heat. Cook onion for 7 minutes or until golden brown. Add tomato, cook for 4 minutes. Stir in broth. Bring to boil.

▪ Stir in bulgur. Cover and cook for 5 minutes. Reduce heat and simmer, covered, for 12 minutes or until tender and all broth is absorbed. Remove from heat; let stand for 5 minutes.

▪ Fluff with fork. Season to taste with salt and pepper. Stir in parsley.

Makes 6 servings.

EACH SERVING
⅙ **of recipe**

1 Starch
1 Vegetable

115 calories
2 g total fat
0 g saturated fat
0 mg cholesterol
4 g protein
20 g carbohydrate
265 mg sodium
213 mg potassium

GOOD
Magnesium

HIGH
Fiber

Pilau (East Indian)

Mushroom Cashew Pilaf

Pilaf is to East Indians what fried rice is to the Chinese. In pilaf, the rice is cooked in butter or oil to brown it slightly—before it is cooked in liquid. Seasonings and added bits of meats or vegetables are the cooks' choice. Depending on the recipe and the intensity of the flavoring, pilaf can be a meal on its own or a great side dish with vindaloo or korma (curried dishes).

2 tsp	butter or canola oil	10 mL
1 cup	brown rice or pearl or pot barley	250 mL
1	onion, finely chopped	1
1 cup	chopped mushrooms	250 mL
¼ cup	cashew bits	50 mL
2 Tbsp	raisins or currants	25 mL
½ tsp	turmeric	2 mL
¼ tsp	dried thyme	1 mL
¼ tsp	each ground cardamom and cinnamon	1 mL
1 cup	shredded carrots	250 mL
2 cups	chicken broth	500 mL
	Salt and freshly ground black pepper	
	Chopped fresh parsley	

▪ In nonstick skillet, heat butter over medium heat. Cook rice, onion, mushrooms, cashews, and raisins for 7 minutes or until mushroom liquid evaporates. Stir in turmeric, thyme, cardamom, and cinnamon. Cook for 30 seconds. Stir in carrots and broth. Bring to boil.

▪ Reduce heat, cover and simmer, stirring occasionally, for 30 minutes or until tender.

▪ (Alternatively, transfer to casserole and cover. Bake in 350°F [180°C] oven, stirring once or twice, for 30 to 40 minutes or until tender.)

▪ Season to taste with salt and pepper. Sprinkle with parsley.

Makes 6 servings.

EACH SERVING
⅙ of recipe

2   Starch
1   Vegetable
½   Fat

202 calories
5 g total fat
0 g saturated fat
0 mg cholesterol
5 g protein
33 g carbohydrate
307 mg sodium
330 mg potassium

GOOD
Niacin

EXCELLENT
Magnesium, Vitamin A

Saffron Couscous (African)

Saffron Couscous with Currants

Couscous, like bulgur, is not a grain. It is a processed product. It is pasta, in tiny grain-like pieces, that is made from semolina (coarsely ground durum wheat) and water. This staple in the cuisine of North Africa is eaten as porridge, as a side dish, and as a dessert, sweetened and mixed with fruits.

1 tsp	canola oil	5 mL
1	onion, finely chopped	1
1	clove garlic, minced	1
½ tsp	each ground cumin, coriander, and ginger	2 mL
¼ tsp	saffron threads	1 mL
2 cups	chicken broth	500 mL
1 cup	couscous	250 mL
2 Tbsp	currants	25 mL
2 Tbsp	chopped fresh parsley	25 mL
	Salt and freshly ground black pepper	
1 Tbsp	toasted sesame seeds	15 mL

■ In heavy saucepan, heat oil over medium heat; cook onion and garlic, stirring, for 2 to 3 minutes or until softened. Add cumin, coriander, and ginger; cook, stirring for 1 minute or until fragrant.

■ Add saffron to broth. Stir into onion mixture. Bring to boil. Remove from heat. Stir in couscous and currants. Cover and let steam for 5 minutes; fluff with fork. Stir in parsley. Season to taste with salt and pepper.

■ Transfer to serving dish. Sprinkle with sesame seeds.

Makes 6 servings.

EACH SERVING
⅙ of recipe

2   Starch

156 calories
2 g total fat
0 g saturated fat
0 mg cholesterol
6 g protein
27 g carbohydrate
263 mg sodium
166 mg potassium

EACH SERVING
⅙ of recipe

4 Starch
1 Vegetable
1 Meat, lean
½ Fat

430 calories
9 g total fat
3 g saturated fat
23 mg cholesterol
20 g protein
66 g carbohydrate
272 mg sodium
587 mg potassium

GOOD
Phosphorus, Iron, Riboflavin, Folate, Vitamin B$_6$

EXCELLENT
Zinc, Magnesium, Vitamin A, Niacin, Vitamin B$_{12}$

HIGH
Fiber

Spaghetti Bolognese (Italian)

Spaghetti with Meat & Mushroom Sauce

Cooks from Bologna in Italy use mushrooms in their cooking. Here, the Bolognese sauce demonstrates how the fleshy aromatic fungi add their fragrant earthy touch to pasta.

1	package dried Italian mushrooms or ¼ lb (125 g) fresh mushrooms	1
1 tsp	olive oil	5 mL
½ lb	ground beef or pork	250 g
2	onions, chopped	2
2	cloves garlic, minced	2
2	stalks celery, finely chopped	2
2	carrots, finely chopped	2
1	can (19 oz/540 mL) tomatoes	1
	Salt and freshly ground pepper	
1 lb	spaghetti or spaghettini	500 g
¼ cup	grated Parmesan cheese	50 mL

▪ Soak dried mushrooms in lukewarm water for about 1 hour, drain and cut into small pieces. If fresh mushrooms are used, wipe with damp cloth (to preserve the flavor); chop.

▪ In nonstick skillet, heat oil over medium heat. Cook ground meat until no longer pink. Stir in onion, garlic, celery, carrot, and chopped mushrooms. Cook, stirring occasionally, for 15 minutes. Stir in tomatoes, breaking up with fork. Bring to boil. Reduce heat and simmer, uncovered, for 30 to 45 minutes or until sauce-like. Season to taste with salt and pepper.

▪ Meanwhile, in large pot of lightly salted boiling water, hold spaghetti upright in the water until the lower part is soft, then press down until all spaghetti is under water. Cook for about 12 minutes or until al dente (tender but firm); drain. Transfer to platter.

▪ Spoon meat sauce over spaghetti. Sprinkle with Parmesan cheese.

Makes 6 servings.

Pasta al Pomodoro e Basilico (Italian)
Pasta with Tomato & Basil Sauce

Among all the tomato-based pasta sauces I know, this one heads the list of favorites, especially when I make it in late summer with garden-fresh, juicy, crimson tomatoes and shiny basil leaves snipped from my country herb garden.

2 cups	Tomato & Basil Sauce (recipe below)	500 mL
1 lb	rigatoni or rotini	500 g
¼ cup	freshly grated Parmesan cheese	50 mL

▪ Prepare Tomato & Basil Sauce; keep warm.

▪ In large pot of lightly salted boiling water, cook rigatoni for 10 to 12 minutes or until al dente (tender but firm); drain and return to saucepan. Pour sauce over pasta. Toss well to coat. Sprinkle with Parmesan cheese.

Makes 6 servings.

EACH SERVING
⅙ of recipe

4 Starch
1 Vegetable

336 calories
3 g total fat
1 g saturated fat
3 mg cholesterol
12 g protein
62 g carbohydrate
259 mg sodium
473 mg potassium

GOOD
Calcium, Magnesium

EXCELLENT
Iron, Thiamin,
Riboflavin, Niacin

HIGH
Fiber

Tomato & Basil Sauce (Italian)
Tomato & Basil Sauce

2 tsp	olive oil or butter	10 mL
1	clove garlic, minced	1
1	can (19 oz/540 mL) tomatoes or 1 lb (500 g) fresh peeled plum tomatoes	1
¼ cup	chopped fresh basil or 1 Tbsp (15 mL) dried Salt and freshly ground black pepper	50 mL

▪ In nonstick skillet or saucepan, heat oil over medium heat. Cook garlic for 1 minute. Stir in tomatoes, breaking up with fork. Bring to boil. Cook, stirring frequently, for 5 minutes to reduce liquid. Stir in basil. Reduce heat and simmer, stirring occasionally, for 10 minutes or until sauce-like. Season to taste with salt and pepper.

Makes 2 cups (500 mL), 6 servings.

EACH SERVING
⅙ of recipe

1 Vegetable

31 calories
1 g total fat
0 g saturated fat
0 mg cholesterol
0 g protein
4 g carbohydrate
7 mg sodium
173 mg potassium

Rotini all'Ortica (Italian)

Rotini with Creamy Mushroom Sauce

This creamy sauce with an intense aroma of mushrooms has the flavor of a traditional Roman sauce, and spirals of pasta have a great affinity for it.

2 cups	Creamy Mushroom Sauce (recipe below)	500 mL
1 lb	rotini or fusilli Parsley sprigs	500 g

▪ Prepare Creamy Mushroom Sauce; keep warm.

▪ In large pot of lightly salted boiling water, cook rotini for 10 to 12 minutes or until al dente (tender but still firm); drain and return to saucepan.

▪ Pour sauce over pasta. Toss well to coat.

▪ Garnish with parsley sprigs.

Makes 6 servings.

Creamy Mushroom Sauce (Italian)

Creamy Mushroom Sauce

To exaggerate the mushroom flavor, take advantage of the full flavor of dried mushrooms. Soak about 6 dried Italian mushrooms in warm water for 10 minutes; remove stems; finely chop caps and add them to the fresh mushrooms in the skillet.

2 tsp	olive oil	10 mL
¾ lb	mushrooms, coarsely chopped	375 g
½ cup	2% evaporated milk	125 mL
½ cup	chicken broth	125 mL
¼ cup	chopped fresh parsley	50 mL
2 Tbsp	freshly grated Parmesan cheese Salt and freshly ground black pepper	25 mL

▪ In large nonstick skillet, heat oil over medium heat. Cook mushrooms for 10 minutes or until liquid nearly evaporates. Stir in evaporated milk, broth, and half the parsley; bring to boil. Reduce heat and simmer, uncovered, stirring occasionally, for about 10 minutes or until slightly thickened. Stir in Parmesan cheese. Season to taste with salt and pepper. Sprinkle with remaining parsley.

Makes 2 cups (500 mL), 6 servings.

EACH SERVING
⅙ of recipe

4 Starch
1 Vegetable

358 calories
4 g total fat
1 g saturated fat
4 mg cholesterol
15 g protein
64 g carbohydrate
150 mg sodium
449 mg potassium

GOOD
Phosphorus, Zinc,
Magnesium, Folate

EXCELLENT
Vitamin D,
Riboflavin, Niacin

EACH SERVING
⅙ of recipe

1 Vegetable
½ Fat

53 calories
2 g total fat
0 g saturated fat
2 mg cholesterol
3 g protein
4 g carbohydrate
120 mg sodium
208 mg potassium

GOOD
Vitamin D

Fettucine alla Vongole Bianco (Italian)

Fettucine with White Clam Sauce

Canned baby clams are a good substitute for vongole, which are the small clams of the Mediterranean. They stay tender if they are set aside and added to the sauce just before serving. Both fettucine and linguine, which are like flat narrow ribbons of pasta, have a great affinity for this sauce.

WHITE CLAM SAUCE

2	cans (5 oz/142 g each) baby clams	2
2 tsp	canola oil	10 mL
1	large clove garlic, slivered	1
1 Tbsp	all-purpose flour	15 mL
1 tsp	dehydrated chicken broth mix	5 mL
2 Tbsp	chopped fresh parsley	25 mL
	Salt and freshly ground black pepper	

PASTA

1 lb	fettucine or linguine	500 g
2 Tbsp	chopped fresh basil	25 mL

▪ White Clam Sauce: Drain clams, reserving clams and juice. In nonstick skillet, heat oil over medium heat. Cook garlic for 1 minute or until fragrant. Stir in flour and chicken broth mix until blended; cook for 1 minute. Slowly stir in clam juice until smooth. Cook, stirring, for about 2 minutes or until thickened.

▪ Reduce heat and simmer, stirring occasionally, for 5 minutes to reduce slightly. Stir in clams and parsley; cook for 1 minute to heat through. Season to taste with salt and pepper.

▪ In large pot of lightly salted boiling water, cook fettucine for 10 to 12 minutes or until al dente (tender but still firm); drain and return to saucepan.

▪ Pour clam sauce onto hot fettucine; add basil and toss.

Makes 4 servings.

EACH SERVING
¼ of recipe

4½ Starch

368 calories
6 g total fat
0 g saturated fat
84 mg cholesterol
13 g protein
64 g carbohydrate
338 mg sodium
253 mg potassium

GOOD
Phosphorus, Iron, Zinc, Magnesium, Thiamin, Niacin

EXCELLENT
Vitamin B$_{12}$

Orzo Riganati (Greek)

Herb-Scented Orzo & Beans

Orzo is one of the many different pasta shapes available in our markets today. It is shaped like long-grain rice or barley. Manestra is pasta that is about the size of cantaloupe seeds. After these pasta are cooked, they are denser than most other pasta.

2 cups	water	500 mL
2 cups	chicken broth	500 mL
1 cup	orzo or manestra	250 mL
1 tsp	olive oil	5 mL
1	onion, finely chopped	1
1 Tbsp	finely chopped fresh parsley or 1 tsp (5 mL) dried	15 mL
1½ tsp	each fresh chopped thyme and oregano or ½ tsp (2 mL) dried	7 mL
1 cup	cooked white or red kidney beans	250 mL
1 Tbsp	low-fat plain yogurt	15 mL
1 Tbsp	lemon juice	15 mL
	Chopped fresh mint or parsley	

▪ In saucepan, bring water and broth to a boil. Add orzo; cook for about 10 minutes or until tender but firm. Drain; set aside.

▪ Meanwhile, in nonstick skillet, heat oil over medium heat. Cook onion, parsley, thyme, and oregano for about 3 minutes or until onion is tender. Stir in drained orzo and beans; cook until heated through.

▪ Combine yogurt and lemon juice. Stir into hot mixture just before serving.

▪ Garnish with mint.

Makes 6 servings.

Pasta Primavera

Primavera means "spring style." To the Italian cook, it means garden-fresh vegetables. When they are steamed, sauced, and combined with thin spaghetti, they are transformed into a meatless dish full of vitamins and minerals.

	Tomato & Basil Sauce (recipe p. 83)	
12	snow peas	12
8	spears asparagus	8
1	zucchini	1
1	yellow summer squash	1
2 cups	broccoli florets	500 mL
½ cup	fresh or frozen peas	125 mL
2 tsp	olive oil	10 mL
2 tsp	butter	10 mL
2	cloves garlic, finely chopped	2
½ tsp	crushed red chili pepper	2 mL
¼ lb	fresh mushrooms, sliced	125 g
½ cup	hot chicken broth	125 mL
½ cup	1% milk	125 mL
	Salt and freshly grated black pepper	
1 lb	angel hair pasta or spaghettini	500 g
¼ cup	grated Parmesan cheese	50 mL

▪ Prepare Tomato & Basil Sauce; set aside.

▪ Cut snow peas and asparagus spears diagonally in thirds. Place in steamer basket. Cut zucchini and squash into ¼-inch (6-mm) slices; add to steamer basket. Top with broccoli and peas. Cover steamer basket. Set over boiling water; steam for 10 to 12 minutes or until tender but crisp.

▪ In large nonstick skillet, heat olive oil and butter over medium heat. Cook pepper flakes for 1 minute.

▪ Add mushrooms. Cook, stirring occasionally, for 6 minutes or until mushroom liquid evaporates. Stir in broth and milk; bring to boil. Reduce heat and simmer for 5 minutes or until reduced slightly. Season to taste with salt and pepper. Stir in steamed vegetables.

▪ Meanwhile, in large pot of lightly salted boiling water, cook pasta for 10 to 12 minutes or until al dente (tender but firm); drain and return to saucepan. Pour vegetable mixture over pasta and toss. Spoon into serving bowl.

▪ Meanwhile, reheat Tomato & Basil Sauce; spoon over pasta mixture. Sprinkle with Parmesan cheese.

Makes 6 servings.

EACH SERVING
⅙ of recipe

4 Starch
2 Vegetable
½ Fat

405 calories
7 g total fat
2 g saturated fat
7 mg cholesterol
16 g protein
68 g carbohydrate
187 mg sodium
586 mg potassium

GOOD
Phosphorus, Iron, Zinc, Vitamin A, Riboflavin, Vitamin B6

EXCELLENT
Magnesium, Vitamin C, Niacin, Folate

HIGH
Fiber

Macaroni & Meat Casserole

There are quite a few ingredients in this recipe. However, like lasagne, you end up with dinner all in one dish.

1½ cups	macaroni	375 mL
¼ cup	low-fat yogurt	50 mL
2 Tbsp	grated Parmesan cheese	25 mL
¾ lb	lean ground beef, lamb, or veal	375 g
1	onion, finely chopped	1
1	clove garlic, minced	1
1	can (19 oz/540 mL) tomatoes	1
1	can (5½ oz/156 mL) tomato paste	1
1 cup	beef broth	250 mL
1 Tbsp	chopped fresh mint or	15 mL
	1 tsp (5 mL) dried	
½ tsp	dried oregano	2 mL
¼ tsp	ground cinnamon	1 mL
Pinch	ground nutmeg	Pinch
	Salt and freshly ground black pepper	

SAUCE

1 cup	1% milk	250 mL
2 Tbsp	all-purpose flour	25 mL
1 tsp	Dijon mustard	5 mL

TOPPING

¼ cup	grated Parmesan cheese	50 mL
	Freshly grated nutmeg	

- In large saucepan of lightly salted boiling water, cook macaroni for 15 minutes or until tender but still firm. Drain; stir in yogurt and Parmesan cheese. Set aside.

- Meanwhile, in nonstick skillet, cook ground beef over medium heat, stirring to break up into small pieces. Add onion and garlic and cook for 7 minutes or until meat is no longer pink. Drain off excess fat.

- Stir in tomatoes, breaking up with fork, tomato paste, beef broth, mint, oregano, cinnamon, and nutmeg. Bring to boil. Reduce heat and simmer for 7 minutes or until sauce thickens. Season to taste with salt and pepper.

- To assemble: Layer half macaroni mixture in bottom of 8-inch (20-cm) square baking dish. Top with half meat mixture. Repeat layers.

- In saucepan, combine milk, flour, and mustard until smooth. Cook over medium heat, stirring, until thickened. Pour over top of last layer. Sprinkle with Parmesan and grated nutmeg.

- Bake in 350°F (180°C) oven for 40 to 45 minutes or until heated through and Parmesan cheese turns golden brown.

Makes 6 servings.

EACH SERVING
⅙ of recipe

2 Starch
1 Vegetable
2 Meat, medium-fat

329 calories
11 g total fat
5 g saturated fat
38 mg cholesterol
20 g protein
35 g carbohydrate
581 mg sodium ✹
720 mg potassium

GOOD
Calcium, Phosphorus, Iron, Magnesium, Riboflavin, Vitamin B₆

EXCELLENT
Zinc, Niacin, Vitamin B₁₂

MODERATE
Fiber

Chow Mein (Chinese-American)

Chinese Noodles

The noodles that are most authentic for Chinese combinations, such as this, are noodles made from rice flour. They are white but become translucent as they cook.

½ lb	rice vermicelli or thin rice stick noodles	250 g
¼ lb	raw medium shrimp, peeled and deveined	125 g
2 Tbsp	rice vinegar	25 mL
1 Tbsp	minced fresh ginger root	15 mL
1 tsp	sesame oil	5 mL
⅓ lb	cooked smoked or barbecued pork	150 g
½ cup	chicken broth	125 mL
2 Tbsp	lite soy sauce	25 mL
2 tsp	canola oil	10 mL
2 tsp	curry powder	10 mL
6	green onions, thinly and diagonally sliced	6
2 cups	bean sprouts	500 mL

▪ In bowl, cover vermicelli with cold water. Let stand for 20 minutes; drain well. Set aside.

▪ Cut shrimps in half lengthwise. Place in bowl. Combine vinegar, ginger root, and sesame oil. Pour over shrimp. Let stand for 20 minutes.

▪ Cut pork into thin strips. Set aside.

▪ Combine chicken broth and soy sauce; set aside.

▪ In nonstick wok or skillet, heat oil over high heat. Add curry powder, stir-fry for 10 seconds. Add onions, stir-fry for 1 minute; add bean sprouts, stir-fry for a few seconds.

▪ Add pork, shrimp and marinade, drained vermicelli, and chicken broth mixture. Stir-fry for 3 minutes or until vermicelli is heated through and shrimp are pink.

Makes 6 servings.

EACH SERVING
⅙ of recipe

2½ Starch
1   Meat, very lean

232 calories
4 g total fat
0 g saturated fat
42 mg cholesterol
13 g protein
34 g carbohydrate
250 mg sodium
252 mg potassium

GOOD
Zinc, Niacin,
Vitamin B$_{12}$

Paad Thai (Thai)

Thai Noodles
with Chicken & Shrimp

This rendition of the Thai rice noodle dish displays the spicy-salty-sweet-sour taste so typical of the popular Asian cuisine. It is surprisingly easy to duplicate it in our kitchens.

½ lb	flat rice noodles or spaghetti	250 g
9	raw shrimp, peeled and deveined	9
¼ cup	dried lemon grass	50 mL
	or 1-inch (2.5-cm) strip lemon peel	
¼ lb	boneless, skinless chicken	125 g
2 oz	bean sprouts	60 g
2	carrots	2
2 Tbsp	lime juice	25 mL
2 Tbsp	lite soy sauce or nam pla	25 mL
1 Tbsp	grated fresh ginger root	15 mL
1 tsp	shrimp paste	5 mL
½ tsp	hot Oriental chili paste	2 mL
2 tsp	canola oil	10 mL
2	cloves garlic, minced	2
3	green onions, diagonally sliced	3
2 Tbsp	chopped fresh cilantro or parsley	25 mL
1 Tbsp	chopped toasted peanuts	15 mL
	Lime wedges	

■ Soak noodles in warm water for 20 minutes. Or, if using spaghetti, cook spaghetti in lightly salted boiling water until just tender but firm. Drain and reserve.

■ Cut shrimps in half lengthwise. Cut chicken into thin strips. Trim bean sprouts. Julienne carrots. Set aside.

■ Soak lemon grass in ⅓ cup (75 mL) boiling water; let stand for 15 minutes. Strain through sieve into bowl; discard grass. Stir in lime juice, soy sauce, ginger root, shrimp paste, and hot chili paste; set this sauce aside.

■ In large nonstick skillet or wok, heat oil over high heat. Stir-fry garlic for 10 seconds; add shrimp, chicken, and carrots. Stir-fry for 4 minutes or until shrimp is pink and chicken is no longer pink.

■ Add noodles and half of reserved sauce; mix well. Stir-cook until noodles are heated through.

■ Stir in bean sprouts, green onions, and remaining sauce; cook for 1 minute or until heated through.

■ Garnish with fresh cilantro, peanuts, and lime wedges.

Makes 6 servings.

EACH SERVING
⅙ of recipe

2   Starch
1   Vegetable
1   Meat, very lean

  217 calories
    3 g total fat
    0 g saturated fat
 26 mg cholesterol
 12 g protein
 34 g carbohydrate
213 mg sodium
263 mg potassium

GOOD
Magnesium, Niacin

EXCELLENT
Vitamin A

MODERATE
Fiber

Poultry

Blueberry Glazed Wild Duck Breast - *Canadian Aboriginal*

Jerk Chicken - *Carribbean*

Gai Yaang Sawaan - *Thai*

Tandoori Murghi - *East Indian*

Yakitori - *Japanese*

Gimisti Kotta - *Greek*

Wu Hsiang Chi - *Chinese*

Pollo Sevilla - *Spanish*

Oven-Crisp Chicken - *Canadian/American*

Rouxinol - *Portuguese*

Csirke Paprikás - *Hungarian*

Pollo alla Cacciatore - *Italian*

Jaffa Chicken - *Israeli*

Korma - *East Indian*

Asopao de Pollo - *Caribbean*

Mole Poblano - *Mexican*

Hu Nan Ji - *Chinese*

Hsing Jen Chi Ting - *Chinese*

Cotletki Pojarski - *Russian*

Kufta Izmir - *Middle Eastern*

Matsukaze-yaki - *Japanese*

Toriniku Dango - *Japanese*

Iridofu - *Japanese*

Szechuan Bang Bangi - *Chinese*

Coronation Chicken - *British*

Blueberry Glazed Wild Duck Breast

It is the breast of the wild duck that has the choicest meat. Finishing it with a glaze created with blueberries, particularly if they are wild ones, makes it a specialty that will please any hunter of game birds.

6	wild duck breasts	6
1 cup	wild blueberries	250 mL
2 Tbsp	white vinegar	25 mL
1 tsp	canola oil	5 mL
¼ tsp	each ground cloves and nutmeg	1 mL
	Salt and freshly ground black pepper	

- Bone and skin duck breasts. Place in glass bowl.
- In bowl or small food processor, mash together or puree blueberries, vinegar, oil, cloves, and nutmeg. Season to taste with salt and pepper.
- Pour over duck breasts, completely coating each one. Cover and marinate for 30 minutes.
- Arrange on lightly greased rack in shallow roasting pan.
- Roast in 350°F (180°C) oven, basting once or twice with any remaining marinade, for 30 minutes or until duck breasts are glazed and no longer pink.

Makes 6 servings.

EACH SERVING
⅙ of recipe

5 Meat, very lean
1 Fat

225 calories
7 g total fat
2 g saturated fat
127 mg cholesterol
33 g protein
3 g carbohydrate
96 mg sodium
422 mg potassium

GOOD
Magnesium, Folate

EXCELLENT
Phosphorus, Iron, Thiamin, Riboflavin, Niacin, Vitamin B$_6$, Vitamin B$_{12}$

Jerk Chicken (Caribbean)

Jamaican Jerk Chicken

Typically, this marinade calls for Scotch bonnet pepper. It's too hot for me, so I use jalapeno pepper, which is a little less fiery.

2 lbs	chicken pieces, skinned	1 kg
2 tsp	each ground allspice and dried thyme	10 mL
½ tsp	each ground nutmeg and cinnamon	2 mL
	Salt	
3	green onions, finely chopped	3
2	cloves garlic, minced	2
1	fresh jalapeno pepper, seeded and minced, or 1 Tbsp (15 mL) minced pickled jalapeno	1
¼ cup	orange juice	50 mL
2 tsp	red wine vinegar	10 mL

- Remove and discard any fat from chicken. Place chicken pieces in glass dish.
- In small bowl, combine allspice, thyme, nutmeg, cinnamon, and salt to taste. Stir in green onions, garlic, jalapeno pepper, orange juice, and vinegar. Pour over chicken, turning to coat well. Cover and marinate in refrigerator, turning occasionally, for at least 4 hours or overnight.
- Remove chicken from marinade. Place on lightly greased barbecue grill or broiler pan.
- Barbecue or broil at medium-high heat for about 20 minutes on each side or until no longer pink. Or place on rack in shallow pan and bake in 325°F (160°C) oven for 45 minutes or until no longer pink.

Makes 6 servings.

VARIATION

Gai Yaang Sawaan (Thai)
Thai Barbecued Chicken

The nam pla (fish sauce) gives a salty, fishy taste that is ever present in Thai cuisine. It is worth having for duplicating as close as possible the taste of Thai, and it can be purchased in specialty shops selling Asian and Oriental ingredients.

- In place of the above marinade, crush 1 Tbsp (15 mL) peppercorns in mortar. Add 5 cloves garlic, 1 Tbsp (15 mL) chopped cilantro roots and stems, and 2 tsp (10 mL) fish sauce (nam pla). Pound until coarse paste forms.
- Barbecue or broil as directed above.
- Garnish with cilantro leaves.

EACH SERVING
⅙ of recipe

4   Meat, very lean

159 calories
3 g total fat
1 g saturated fat
92 mg cholesterol
26 g protein
2 g carbohydrate
122 mg sodium
315 mg potassium

GOOD
Phosphorus, Zinc, Vitamin B$_{12}$

EXCELLENT
Niacin, Vitamin B$_6$

Calculations approximately the same as above

Tandoori Murghi (East Indian)

Tandoori Chicken

Tandoori is the name of the brick and clay oven that is used throughout India to cook foods over intense smoky heat, almost like a barbecue. The turmeric and saffron, popular in East Indian cooking, contribute to the deep, golden marinade that stains the chicken the same rich color.

1 tsp	saffron	5 mL
2 Tbsp	boiling water	25 mL
2 lbs	chicken pieces, skinned	1 kg
2 Tbsp	lemon juice	25 mL
½ cup	low-fat yogurt	125 mL
1	clove garlic, minced	1
1 Tbsp	grated fresh ginger root	15 mL
½ tsp	each ground cardamom, coriander, cumin, and turmeric	2 mL
¼ tsp	freshly ground pepper	1 mL
Pinch	cayenne	Pinch
	Paprika	
	Lemon wedges	

- Soak saffron in boiling water for 5 minutes.
- With sharp knife, slash chicken pieces in several places. Brush all over with lemon juice then with saffron water. Place in glass dish.
- Combine yogurt, garlic, ginger root, cardamom, coriander, cumin, turmeric, pepper, and cayenne.
- Pour over chicken, turning to coat well. Cover and marinate in refrigerator, turning occasionally, for at least 4 hours or overnight.
- Remove chicken from marinade. Place on lightly greased barbecue grill or broiler pan.
- Barbecue or broil over or under medium-high heat for about 20 minutes each side or until chicken is no longer pink.
- Or place on rack in shallow pan and bake in 325°F (160°C) oven for 45 minutes or until no longer pink.
- Sprinkle with paprika. Garnish with lemon wedges.

Makes 6 servings.

EACH SERVING
⅙ of recipe

4 Meat, very lean

143 calories
1 g total fat
0 g saturated fat
68 mg cholesterol
28 g protein
2 g carbohydrate
91 mg sodium
334 mg potassium

GOOD
**Phosphorus,
Magnesium**

EXCELLENT
**Niacin, Vitamin B$_6$,
Vitamin B$_{12}$**

Yakitori (Japanese)
Grilled Chicken Japanese-Style

Translated, "yaki" means grilled and "tori" means chicken. This clearly is the Japanese version of kebabs—skewered chicken and vegetables. Basting with the marinade gives them a golden brown savory glaze.

	Bamboo skewers	
2	skinless, boneless chicken breasts (½ lb/250 g)	2
¼ lb	chicken livers	125 g
½ cup	cooking sherry	125 mL
¼ cup	lite soy sauce	50 mL
1 Tbsp	minced fresh ginger root	15 mL
1	clove garlic, minced	1
12	medium mushrooms, cut in half	12
8	green onions, cut diagonally into 1-inch (2.5-cm) lengths	8

- Soak bamboo skewers in hot water while preparing ingredients.
- Cut chicken and livers into approximately 1-inch (2.5-cm) squares.
- In small saucepan, combine cooking sherry, soy sauce, ginger root, and garlic. Bring to boil. Cook for 2 minutes or until reduced by half.
- Alternately thread chicken, mushroom, chicken liver, and onion onto skewers (8 pieces on each one).
- Place on lightly greased barbecue grill over medium-hot coals.
- Barbecue, brushing frequently with sherry sauce, for 4 minutes on each side or until chicken is no longer pink.

Makes 3 servings.

EACH SERVING
⅓ of recipe

1   Vegetable
4   Meat, very lean

212 calories
2 g total fat
0 g saturated fat
213 mg cholesterol
27 g protein
7 g carbohydrate
665 mg sodium ✪
472 mg potassium

GOOD
Zinc, Magnesium

EXCELLENT
Phosphorus, Iron, Vitamin A, Riboflavin, Niacin, Folate, Vitamin B$_6$, Vitamin B$_{12}$

Gimisti Kotta (Greek)

Roast Chicken with Lemon

Cooks of many different ethnic origins have their own special touch with a whole chicken. Since the final flavor depends on seasonings that are indigenous to their homeland, there is no end to the variations.

1	small roasting chicken, 3 lbs/1.5 kg	1
1	lemon	1
1 tsp	dried oregano	5 mL
	Salt and freshly ground black pepper	
1	clove garlic, cut in half	1
1	celery stalk, sliced	1
1 tsp	butter, melted	5 mL
½ cup	chicken broth	125 mL

▪ Rinse bird inside and out; pat dry.

▪ Grate lemon rind and reserve. Cut lemon in half. Rub inside and skin of bird with cut edge. Squeeze lemon and reserve juice. Sprinkle chicken inside and out with oregano, and salt and pepper to taste. Place lemon peel, garlic halves, and celery in cavity. Truss bird by tucking wings back and tying legs close to body. Brush chicken with butter. Place on rack in roasting pan.

▪ Roast, uncovered, in 350°F (180°C) oven, basting occasionally, for 1½ hours or until golden brown and juice runs clear. Transfer to warm platter.

▪ Skim fat from pan and discard. Mix together broth and lemon juice and pour into roasting pan. Scrape down brown bits; strain into small saucepan. Boil for 1 minute to reduce slightly. Serve with chicken.

Makes 6 servings.

VARIATIONS
Wu Hsiang Chi (Chinese)
Five Spice Chicken

▪ Substitute 1 Tbsp (15 mL) grated fresh ginger root and 1 tsp (5 mL) five spice powder for oregano, and canola oil for butter.

Pollo Sevilla (Spanish)
Sherried Chicken with Orange

▪ Substitute 1 tsp (5 mL) ground cumin for oregano, rind and juice of half orange and 2 Tbsp (25 mL) sherry for lemon and its juice, and olive oil for butter.

Oven-Crisp Chicken

This provides the crunchy fried chicken experience without the frying. Add a pinch or two of dried herbs and spices, typical of your country of origin, to the breadcrumbs. That will give the scrumptious pieces a specific flavor, just as rouxinal (below) has the taste of Portuguese cooking.

8	small chicken thighs, skinned	8
¼ cup	1% milk	50 mL
1	egg white	1
½ cup	dry breadcrumbs	125 mL
1 Tbsp	slivered almonds	15 mL
1 tsp	butter	5 mL
	Salt and freshly ground pepper	

- Remove all visible fat from thighs and discard.
- Whisk together milk and egg white.
- In small processor or in mortar and pestle, grind together crumbs, almonds, and butter until fine crumb forms. Season to taste with salt and pepper. Place in shallow plate. Dip each thigh into milk mixture and then coat with crumb mixture.
- Place on rack in shallow pan. Let stand for 10 minutes.
- Bake in 400°F (200°C) oven for 35 minutes or until golden brown and juice runs clear.

Makes 4 servings.

VARIATION

Rouxinal (Portuguese)
Crunchy Almond Chicken
- Add ½ tsp (2 mL) each chili powder and paprika and a pinch of cayenne to crumb mixture before grinding.

EACH SERVING
¼ of recipe

½ Starch
4 Meat, very lean
1 Fat

238 calories
7 g total fat
2 g saturated fat
117 mg cholesterol
29 g protein
10 g carbohydrate
236 mg sodium
331 mg potassium

GOOD
Phosphorus, Magnesium, Riboflavin, Vitamin B$_6$, Vitamin B$_{12}$

EXCELLENT
Zinc, Niacin

Calculations approximately the same as above.

sirke Paprikás (Hungarian)

Chicken Paprikash

Any dish with paprikas or paprikash in its title indicates paprika is a key player in the team of seasonings. Hungarian paprikas are among the best. Supermarkets carry mild versions of the spice and, fortunately, specialty food shops, along with some supermarkets, now carry more pungent and hot varieties. Choose the one that best suits the family's palate or try a combination. This close cousin of the gulyás (goulash) always has sour cream or cream stirred into the pan sauce to make reddish pink gravy.

1	chicken, 3 lbs/1.5 kg, cut into 8 pieces and skinned	1
2 tsp	butter or canola oil	10 mL
2	large onions, finely chopped	2
1 Tbsp	Hungarian paprika	15 mL
1	can (19 oz/540 mL) tomatoes	1
1	green pepper, seeded and sliced	1
½ cup	low-fat sour cream	125 mL

▪ Skin and rinse chicken pieces; pat dry.

▪ In large nonstick skillet, heat oil over medium heat. Cook onion for 7 minutes or until golden. Stir in paprika.

▪ Add chicken pieces. Cook, turning, until golden on all sides.

▪ Stir in tomatoes, breaking up with fork, and green pepper slices. Bring to boil. Reduce heat, cover and simmer for 35 minutes or until juice of chicken pieces is no longer pink.

▪ Reduce heat to medium-low. Whisk sour cream until smooth, and stir into tomato mixture until well blended and just heated through. Do not boil again, or cream will separate.

Makes 8 servings.

EACH SERVING
⅛ of recipe

1 Vegetable
4 Meat, very lean
½ Fat

189 calories
5 g total fat
1 g saturated fat
92 mg cholesterol
27 g protein
6 g carbohydrate
220 mg sodium
473 mg potassium

GOOD
Phosphorus, Zinc, Magnesium, Vitamin B$_{12}$

EXCELLENT
Niacin, Vitamin B$_6$

Pollo alla Cacciatore (Italian)

Hunters' Chicken Cacciatore

According to folklore, Italian hunters cooked their venison with wine and wine vinegar, then added rosemary and a hint of garlic to flavor the sauce. Today, there are many versions of the stew, using chicken embellished with mushrooms, more garlic, additional herbs, and bay leaf. The most popular ones also use tomatoes, and that is what I do.

3 lb	chicken pieces	1.5 kg
1 Tbsp	olive oil	15 mL
1	onion, chopped	1
1	stalk celery, chopped	1
1	clove garlic, minced	1
2 tsp	dried rosemary	10 mL
1 tsp	dried basil	5 mL
	Salt and freshly ground black pepper	
½ cup	dry white wine	125 mL
2 Tbsp	white wine vinegar	25 mL
1	can (19 oz/540 mL) tomatoes or 8 plum tomatoes, peeled and chopped Chopped Italian parsley or green pepper	1

- Skin chicken pieces, rinse, and pat dry.

- In large nonstick skillet, heat oil over medium heat. Cook onion, celery, and garlic, stirring occasionally, for 5 minutes or until onion is translucent. Push to the side of the pan.

- Add chicken pieces; cook for 4 minutes or until golden brown. Turn, cook for 3 minutes or until other side is browned.

- Sprinkle with rosemary, basil, and salt and pepper to taste. Add wine and vinegar; simmer for 1 minute to reduce slightly.

- Stir in tomatoes, breaking up with fork. Reduce heat to low. Cook at slow simmer, partly covered, turning and basting occasionally, for about 35 minutes or until tender and meat comes away from the bone. (Add water, a little at a time, if the liquid evaporates too quickly.)

- Transfer chicken pieces to warm platter.

- Spoon sauce over chicken. Sprinkle with parsley.

Makes 8 servings.

EACH SERVING
⅛ of recipe

1	Vegetable
4	Meat, very lean
½	Fat

195	calories
4 g	total fat
1 g	saturated fat
86 mg	cholesterol
27 g	protein
4 g	carbohydrate
210 mg	sodium
447 mg	potassium

GOOD
Phosphorus, Zinc, Magnesium, Vitamin B_{12}

EXCELLENT
Niacin, Vitamin B_6

EACH SERVING
1/6 of recipe

1 Fruit
3 Meat, very lean
1/2 Fat

200 calories
4 g total fat
0 g saturated fat
76 mg cholesterol
23 g protein
13 g carbohydrate
92 mg sodium
428 mg potassium

GOOD
Phosphorus, Zinc,
Magnesium,
Vitamin B$_{12}$

EXCELLENT
Vitamin A, Niacin,
Vitamin B$_6$

Jaffa Chicken (Israeli)
Chicken with Orange

Chicken is basic to Jewish cuisine. One creative Jewish cook combined chicken with the sweet and sour combination of raisins and oranges, no doubt the Jaffa variety, and punctuated it with Middle Eastern herbs and spices for this tasty chicken dish.

2 lbs	skinless chicken pieces	1 kg
1/2 cup	orange juice	125 mL
1/4 cup	dry white wine	50 mL
1	onion, chopped	1
1	carrot, sliced	1
1 tsp	paprika	5 mL
1 tsp	ground cumin	5 mL
	Salt and freshly ground black pepper	
2 tsp	canola oil	10 mL
1	orange	1
1/4 cup	raisins	50 mL
	Fresh thyme or parsley sprigs	

▪ Wipe chicken pieces. Arrange in shallow roasting pan.

▪ Combine orange juice, wine, onion, carrot, paprika, and cumin. Pour over chicken, turning pieces to coat all sides. Marinate for 1 hour. Remove chicken, and reserve marinade in pan. Pat chicken dry.

▪ In nonstick skillet, heat oil over medium heat. Brown chicken on all sides. Return to marinade. Season to taste with salt and pepper.

▪ Wash and grate orange, reserving grated rind. Peel off white pith and section orange. Place orange sections and raisins over chicken.

▪ Bake, covered, in 350°F (180°C) oven for 35 minutes. Remove cover; turn chicken. Bake uncovered for 30 minutes or until browned.

▪ Transfer chicken, orange sections, and raisins to heated serving platter.

▪ Strain pan juice into small saucepan. Stir in grated orange rind. Bring to boil and cook for about 2 minutes or until reduced and slightly thickened. Pour over chicken.

▪ Garnish with sprigs of thyme.

Makes 6 servings.

Korma (East Indian)

Curried Chicken

Korma is a braised meat or chicken snappily seasoned with the spices that are blended to make curry powder. The uniqueness of the resulting seasoned sauce is a good example of how East Indian cooks make their own curried dishes to taste, some hotter than others.

2 tsp	butter	10 mL
1	onion, chopped	1
2	cloves garlic, minced	2
2 tsp	each ground coriander and turmeric	10 mL
1 tsp	each ground cumin, ginger, and dry mustard	5 mL
½ tsp	dried fennel seed, crushed	2 mL
¼ tsp	freshly ground black pepper	1 mL
Pinch	cayenne	Pinch
½ cup	chicken broth	125 mL
2 Tbsp	cider vinegar	25 mL
1 Tbsp	tomato paste	15 mL
2	skinless chicken breasts, cut into 4 pieces	2
2	zucchini	2
1 cup	low-fat yogurt or sour cream	250 mL
¼ cup	finely chopped red sweet pepper or carrot	50 mL

OR substitute 2 Tbsp (25 mL) curry powder for coriander, turmeric, cumin, ginger, dry mustard, and fennel seed.

▪ In large nonstick skillet, heat butter over medium heat. Cook onion and garlic for 4 minutes. Stir in coriander, turmeric, cumin, ginger, dry mustard, fennel seed, pepper, and cayenne; cook 1 minute or until fragrant. Stir in chicken broth, vinegar, and tomato paste.

▪ Add chicken pieces; coat well with seasoning mixture. Cover and simmer for 35 minutes, adding water, if necessary, to prevent scorching.

▪ Cut zucchini into thin slices. Stir into chicken and sauce. Cover and cook for 5 minutes or until tender-crisp. Stir in yogurt until well blended.

▪ Garnish with chopped red pepper.

Makes 6 servings.

EACH SERVING
⅙ of recipe

1   Vegetable
3   Meat, very lean

147 calories
2 g total fat
1 g saturated fat
49 mg cholesterol
21 g protein
8 g carbohydrate
161 mg sodium
454 mg potassium

GOOD
Phosphorus,
Magnesium,
Vitamin B$_{12}$

EXCELLENT
Niacin, Vitamin B$_6$

Asopao de Pollo (Caribbean)

Caribbean Chicken Stew

The not-too-hot, not-too-mild unique flavor of Caribbean stews comes from sofrito—a unique blend of herbs, spices, and aromatic vegetables. The combination of ingredients for this adaptation copies the taste and can be found in your favorite market. Asopao is a Spanish word meaning "soupy" rice dish.

6	chicken legs, skinned	6
1 tsp	salt	5 mL
½ tsp	ground oregano	2 mL
½ tsp	ground coriander	2 mL
Pinch	freshly ground pepper	Pinch
1	can (14 oz/398 mL) tomatoes	1
1 cup	water	250 mL
2	cloves garlic, minced	2
1	onion, chopped	1
1 cup	long-grain brown rice	250 mL
1	green sweet pepper, diced	1
1 cup	fresh or frozen green peas	250 mL
½ cup	cubed cooked ham	125 mL
6	pimento-stuffed green olives, cut in half	6
1 Tbsp	chopped pickled jalapeno peppers	15 mL
2 Tbsp	chopped fresh cilantro or parsley	25 mL

- Disjoint each chicken leg by cracking and cutting between drumstick and thigh.
- Combine salt, oregano, coriander, and a generous pinch of pepper. Sprinkle over chicken pieces. Allow to marinate for 15 minutes.
- In 12-inch (30-cm) skillet, combine tomatoes, water, garlic, and onion. Heat to boiling over medium heat; cook for 2 minutes.
- Bury chicken pieces in tomato mixture. Bring to boil. Reduce heat; cover and simmer for 20 minutes.
- Stir in rice. Cover and simmer for about 20 minutes or until thickest pieces of chicken are done (no longer pink when pierced) and rice is tender.
- Add green pepper, peas, ham, olives, and jalapeno peppers. Cover and simmer for 5 minutes until heated through and peas are cooked.
- Sprinkle with cilantro. Serve from skillet into bowls or deep plates.

Makes 6 servings.

EACH SERVING
⅙ of recipe

2 Starch
1 Vegetable
4 Meat, very lean
½ Fat

356 calories
8 g total fat
2 g saturated fat
113 mg cholesterol
34 g protein
33 g carbohydrate
1047 mg sodium ✤
617 mg potassium

GOOD
Iron, Vitamin C, Thiamin, Riboflavin, Folate

EXCELLENT
Phosphorus, Zinc, Magnesium, Niacin, Vitamin B$_6$, Vitamin B$_{12}$

MODERATE
Fiber

Mole Poblano (Mexican)

Mexican Chicken Stew

*Of all the moles, this one seems the most exotic. Poblano
stands for the town of Puebla, where, apparently, this dish
was first created by a group of nuns who had to prepare for
a special guest with what was on hand. Now, it is known as
Mexico's national dish.*

4 lbs	chicken or turkey pieces	2 kg
1 Tbsp	canola oil	15 mL
2	onions, chopped	2
2	cloves garlic, minced	2
½ cup	raisins	125 mL
¼ cup	slivered almonds	50 mL
¼ cup	salted peanuts	50 mL
2 Tbsp	sesame seeds	25 mL
½ tsp	each ground anise, coriander, cumin, and cloves	2 mL
1	can (5½ oz/156 mL) tomato paste	1
1 Tbsp	chopped pickled jalapeno peppers	15 mL
1 oz	bittersweet chocolate (1 square)	30 g
½ tsp	hot pepper sauce	2 mL
	Salt and freshly ground pepper	
	Chopped fresh cilantro or parsley	

- In large saucepan, combine chicken and lightly salted
water to cover. Bring to boil over medium-high heat.
Reduce heat, cover and simmer for 40 minutes or until
chicken is nearly done. Drain and reserve stock.

- Bone chicken; arrange boneless pieces in large casserole.

- Return bones to stock and simmer until stock is reduced
to about half. Strain and reserve stock.

- In nonstick saucepan, heat oil over medium heat. Cook
onions and garlic for 5 minutes or until onion is tender.

- In skillet over medium heat, toast almonds, peanuts, and
sesame seeds until golden brown. Add to onion mixture.
Stir in anise, coriander, cumin, and cloves. Cook for
1 minute. Stir in tomato paste, jalapeno peppers,
chocolate, hot pepper sauce, and 2 cups (500 mL)
reserved stock. Cook, stirring, for 3 minutes or until
chocolate melts.

- Transfer to food processor. Process until pureed. Season to
taste with salt and pepper. Pour over chicken.

- Cover and cook in 325°F (160°C) oven for 45 minutes or
until chicken is tender.

- Garnish with cilantro.

Makes 10 servings.

Lemon Chicken

Hot chili peppers make a big impact on the food cooked by the Chinese from Szechuan and Hunan. With the added lemon, this stir-fry dish has the hot and sour taste characteristic of food from those regions.

1 lb	skinless, boneless chicken	500 g
1 Tbsp	cornstarch	15 mL
1 Tbsp	cooking sherry	15 mL
2 tsp	minced ginger root	10 mL
½ tsp	sesame oil	2 mL
¼ tsp	hot Oriental chili paste	1 mL
	or pepper sauce	
2 tsp	canola oil	10 mL
4	green onions, thickly sliced	4
½ cup	chicken broth	125 mL
1 Tbsp	fresh lemon juice	15 mL
4	thin lemon slices, cut in half	4
	Salt and white pepper	
	Chopped fresh cilantro or parsley	

■ Trim visible fat from chicken. Cut chicken into 1-inch (2.5-cm) pieces. In glass bowl, combine cornstarch, cooking sherry, ginger root, sesame oil, and chili paste until smooth. Pour over chicken; toss to coat pieces with marinade. Marinate for 30 minutes.

■ With slotted spoon, transfer chicken to plate; reserve marinade.

■ In nonstick wok or skillet, heat oil over high heat. Stir-fry chicken 2 minutes. Stir in onions, chicken broth, and lemon juice. Reduce heat to low, cover and simmer for 2 minutes.

■ Add lemon slices. Simmer for 1 minute or until chicken is no longer pink.

■ Stir reserved marinade and 2 Tbsp (25 mL) water into juices in wok. Cook for 1 minute or until thickened. Season to taste with salt and white pepper.

■ Garnish with cilantro.

Makes 4 servings.

EACH SERVING
¼ of recipe

1   Vegetable
4   Meat, very lean

173 calories
4 g total fat
0 g saturated fat
65 mg cholesterol
27 g protein
4 g carbohydrate
174 mg sodium
345 mg potassium

GOOD
**Phosphorus,
Vitamin B$_{12}$**

EXCELLENT
Niacin, Vitamin B$_6$

Hsing Jen Chi Ting (Chinese)

Cantonese Chicken with Almonds

This stir-fry combination is a good example of the milder, lightly seasoned cooking of Cantonese cooks. It is more typical of the Chinese food prepared in the first Chinese restaurants that sprang up in the small towns of Canada and the U.S.

½ lb	skinless, boneless chicken	250 g
2 tsp	cornstarch	10 mL
2 tsp	lite soy sauce	10 mL
2 tsp	cooking sherry	10 mL
2 tsp	grated fresh ginger root	10 mL
½ tsp	Chinese five spice powder	2 mL
	Salt and freshly ground black pepper	
2 tsp	canola oil	10 mL
1	clove garlic, sliced	1
½ cup	slivered almonds or walnut pieces	125 mL
2	stalks celery, diagonally sliced	2
2 cups	broccoli florets	500 mL
½ cup	chicken broth	125 mL
2 tsp	oyster sauce	10 mL

∎ Trim visible fat from chicken. Cut into 1-inch (2.5-cm) pieces.

∎ In bowl, combine cornstarch, soy sauce, sherry, ginger root, five spice, and salt and pepper to taste. Add chicken; stir to coat.

∎ In nonstick wok or skillet, heat oil over high heat. Cook garlic for 30 seconds to flavor oil; discard garlic. Add chicken in two batches. Stir-fry for 2 minutes, transfer to warm plate.

∎ Cook almonds for 1 to 2 minutes or until golden. Add celery and broccoli; stir-fry for 2 minutes. Combine chicken broth and oyster sauce; stir into celery mixture; bring to boil. Return chicken to wok. Stir to coat all ingredients with sauce.

∎ Serve immediately.

Makes 4 servings.

EACH SERVING
¼ of recipe

½ Starch
2 Meat, medium-fat

188 calories
10 g total fat
1 g saturated fat
31 mg cholesterol
17 g protein
7 g carbohydrate
358 mg sodium
418 mg potassium

GOOD
Phosphorus, Folate, Vitamin B$_6$

EXCELLENT
Magnesium, Vitamin C, Niacin

MODERATE
Fiber

Cotletki Pojarski (Russian)

Chicken Cutlets

Apparently, this ground chicken cutlet is named for Prince Dimitri Pozharsky, who headed an army that drove the Poles out of Russia in the early 17th century. Some cookbooks refer to it as Pozharskiye Kotlety. It uses only the finest ground chicken breast, fresh breadcrumbs, cream, and butter. This version, even though it's not oozing with cream and butter, is still special.

¾ lb	ground chicken	375 g
1½ cups	fresh breadcrumbs	375 mL
1	egg white, lightly beaten	1
¼ cup	2% evaporated milk	50 mL
1 Tbsp	butter, softened	15 mL
½ tsp	salt	2 mL
⅛ tsp	freshly ground black pepper	0.5 mL
Pinch	ground nutmeg	Pinch

▪ In bowl, break apart ground chicken. Stir in 1 cup (250 mL) breadcrumbs, egg white, milk, 1 tsp (5 mL) butter, salt, pepper, and nutmeg until well blended.

▪ Divide into 4 evenly shaped flat cutlets (patties).

▪ Coat all sides with remaining breadcrumbs, lightly pressing to adhere to cutlets.

▪ In nonstick skillet, heat remaining butter over medium heat. Cook patties for about 10 minutes on each side or until golden brown.

Makes 4 servings.

VARIATION

Kufta Izmir (Middle Eastern)
Chicken Meatballs

The seasonings are different, but this mixture is basically the same as for the cotletki. Instead of being shaped into cutlets, it is formed into balls. Traditionally, kufta or kofta were deep fried. But not these; they are baked.

▪ Substitute 1 tsp (5 mL) curry powder, ½ tsp (2 mL) ground cumin for the nutmeg, and add ¼ cup (50 mL) chopped fresh parsley.

▪ Shape mixture into 12 round balls. Roll in remaining breadcrumbs.

▪ Place slices from 1 small onion on bottom of 8-inch (20-cm) baking pan. Arrange meatballs on top. Sprinkle with 2 Tbsp (25 mL) lemon juice.

▪ Bake in 350°F (180°C) oven for 30 minutes or until chicken is no longer pink and almost all liquid is absorbed.

Matsukaze-yaki (Japanese)

Flat Chicken Loaf

This is more like a big pancake or omelette than a meatloaf as we know it. For counterpoint of flavor, serve with lite soy sauce and wasabi (Japanese horseradish).

1 lb	ground chicken	500 g
1	leek or 2 green onions, white only, finely chopped	1
1	egg white	1
1 Tbsp	miso (bean paste)	15 mL
2 tsp	minced fresh ginger root	10 mL
1 tsp	rice vinegar	5 mL
2 tsp	canola oil	10 mL
1 Tbsp	poppy or sesame seeds, toasted	15 mL
	Fresh watercress or parsley	

▪ In bowl, combine chicken, leek, egg white, miso, ginger root, and vinegar; mix until well blended.

▪ In 10-inch (25-cm) nonstick skillet, heat oil over medium heat. Put in chicken mixture and spread evenly until about ½ inch (1 cm) thick. Cook for 4 minutes.

▪ Sprinkle with poppy seeds. Turn carefully. (Or cut into 4 wedges and turn.) Cook for 3 minutes or until golden and no longer pink.

▪ (Alternatively, the ground chicken mixture for this thin loaf can be spread in a lightly greased 9-inch [23-cm] pie plate, sprinkled with poppy seeds, and baked in a 350°F [180°C] oven for 12 minutes or until no longer pink.)

▪ Cut into wedges to serve. Garnish with watercress.

Makes 4 servings.

VARIATION

Toriniku Dango (Japanese)

Chicken Balls

▪ Shape ground chicken mixture into 12 balls. Roll lightly in sesame seeds. Bake on rack in 350°F (180°C) oven for 25 minutes or until no longer pink.

EACH SERVING
¼ of recipe

| 4 | Meat, very lean |
| ½ | Fat |

168	calories
4 g	total fat
0 g	saturated fat
65 mg	cholesterol
27 g	protein
2 g	carbohydrate
91 mg	sodium
313 mg	potassium

GOOD
Phosphorus, Magnesium, Vitamin B$_{12}$

EXCELLENT
Niacin, Vitamin B$_6$

Calculations approximately the same as above.

Tofu with Chicken and Vegetables

I love food. It is my vocation and avocation. However, it has taken a little while for me to get used to and use tofu. This is a good example of home-style tofu cooking (the chicken can be thought of as only a garnish). I like it, and it is wonderful spooned over sticky or fluffy rice.

4	dried Chinese mushrooms	4
½ lb	firm tofu	250 g
3	carrots	3
2	green onions	2
2 tsp	canola oil	10 mL
¼ lb	ground chicken or lean pork	125 g
2 Tbsp	grated fresh ginger root	25 mL
1 Tbsp	lite soy sauce	15 mL
1 Tbsp	rice vinegar	15 mL
1	egg, beaten	1

▪ In bowl, cover mushrooms with warm water; soak for 10 minutes or until soft. Remove stems; cut caps into fine strips; set aside.

▪ With chopsticks or fork, break tofu into small chunks; set aside.

▪ Cut carrot into julienne strips 1½ inches (4 cm) long, and cut green onions, including greens, into ½-inch (1-cm) slices.

▪ In nonstick skillet, heat oil over high heat. Stir-fry chicken and ginger root, stirring to break up lumps, for 3 minutes or until no longer pink. Add carrots; cook for 3 minutes or until tender-crisp. Stir in mushrooms and tofu, taking care not to mush it. Cook only until heated through.

▪ Whisk together soy sauce and vinegar. Pour over chicken mixture. Fold in green onions.

▪ Stir in beaten egg until scrambled, and immediately remove from heat.

▪ Serve hot or at room temperature.

Makes 4 servings.

EACH SERVING
¼ of recipe

½   Starch
1   Vegetable
2   Meat, lean
½   Fat

190 calories
8 g total fat
1 g saturated fat
69 mg cholesterol
17 g protein
12 g carbohydrate
178 mg sodium
449 mg potassium

GOOD
Phosphorus, Zinc, Magnesium, Folate, Vitamin B$_6$

EXCELLENT
Calcium, Iron, Vitamin D, Vitamin A, Niacin

MODERATE
Fiber

Szechuan Bang Bangi (Chinese)

Cold Chicken, Cucumbers, & Rice Sticks

The addition of hot Oriental chili paste to the poaching liquid gives this chicken a little heat. The slivers of tender chicken complement the crisp cucumbers. The dressing clings to the rice noodles, coating them with fabulous flavor in this cold salad that makes a satisfying cool summer meal.

2	whole chicken breasts, skinned (2 lb/1 kg)	2
6	green onions, sliced	6
1 Tbsp	chopped fresh ginger root	15 mL
½ tsp	hot Oriental chili paste	2 mL
	Salt	
¼ lb	uncooked rice sticks or rice vermicelli	125 g
2	English cucumbers	2
2 Tbsp	each rice vinegar and chicken broth	25 mL
1 Tbsp	hoisin sauce	15 mL
1 Tbsp	sesame oil	15 mL
1 Tbsp	lite soy sauce	15 mL
1 Tbsp	toasted sesame seeds	15 mL

- In large saucepan, combine chicken breasts, half green onions, ginger root, chili paste, and salt to taste. Add just enough water to cover; bring to boiling. Reduce heat, cover and simmer for about 30 minutes or until chicken is tender and no longer pink.

- Cool in broth. Bone chicken; cut into ½-inch (1-cm) strips. Place in bowl with remaining green onions.

- In lightly salted boiling water, cook rice sticks for about 8 minutes or until tender. Drain, rinse with cold water, and drain again.

- Cut cucumbers into halves lengthwise; scoop out seeds. Cut each half evenly into 3 pieces and then into thin lengthwise strips.

- Arrange cucumbers on serving platter. Top with rice sticks.

- Combine vinegar, chicken broth, hoisin sauce, sesame oil, and soy sauce; mix well. Pour over chicken, toss to coat. Spoon over rice sticks. Sprinkle with sesame seeds.

- Cover and chill for up to 4 hours.

Makes 6 servings.

EACH SERVING
⅙ of recipe

1	Starch
1	Vegetable
2	Meat, very lean
½	Fat

203 calories
4 g total fat
0 g saturated fat
45 mg cholesterol
20 g protein
19 g carbohydrate
470 mg sodium ✪
293 mg potassium

GOOD
Phosphorus,
Magnesium

EXCELLENT
Niacin, Vitamin B$_6$

Coronation Chicken (British)

Cold Chicken with Fruit & Curry Mayonnaise

*Cold chicken with curry mayonnaise is just another
example of the influence that the flavorings of East India
cooking have had on the cuisine of the British. For this
version of the salad, which was apparently served to Queen
Elizabeth II on her coronation day, the dressing is low-fat.*

2 lbs	chicken pieces	1 kg
SAUCE		
1 tsp	olive oil	5 mL
1	small onion, finely chopped	1
1	small clove garlic, chopped	1
2 tsp	curry powder	10 mL
½ cup	chicken broth or water	125 mL
1 Tbsp	lemon juice	15 mL
1 tsp	tomato paste	5 mL
2	dried apricots, chopped	2
1	bay leaf	1
½ cup	light mayonnaise	125 mL
½ cup	low-fat sour cream	125 mL
	Bunch watercress	
½	small sweet red pepper	½

- Roast or poach chicken at least 8 hours ahead to allow it to thoroughly cool in refrigerator.
- Sauce: In small saucepan, heat oil over medium heat. Cook onion and garlic for 4 minutes or until tender.
- Stir in curry powder; cook and stir for 1 minute. Stir in broth, lemon juice, tomato paste, apricots, and bay leaf. Simmer for about 8 minutes or until apricots are soft. Discard bay leaf.
- In food processor, puree apricot mixture or mash with fork and press through sieve. Stir into mayonnaise and sour cream.
- Cut chicken into even pieces. Reserve about ¾ cup (175 mL) sauce; mix remainder with chicken.
- Arrange chicken in center of serving dish. Coat with reserved sauce. Surround with watercress.
- Cut red pepper into thin slivers. Scatter over top.
- Serve cold or at room temperature.

Makes 8 servings.

Meats

Moose Burgers - *Canadian Aboriginal*

Roast Venison - *Canadian Aboriginal*

Grilled Rabbit - *Canadian Aboriginal*

Ho Yow Ngow Yuke - *Chinese*

Moo Waan - *Thai*

Cha Shao Rou - *Chinese*

Bifes de Cebolada - *Portuguese*

Spuntature al Sugo - *Italian*

Rouladen - *German*

Stroganov - *Russian*

Schnitzel - *Austrian/German*

Piccata di Vitello al Limone - *Italian*

Porco Alentejana - *Portuguese*

Shami Kebob - *East Indian*

Seekh Kabob - *Middle Eastern*

Frikadeller - *Scandinavian*

Albodigintos - *Latin American*

Ragoût de Boulettes - *French Canadian*

Zhen Zhu Wan Zi - *Chinese*

Picadillo - *Mexican*

Shashlik - *Middle Eastern*

Souvlaki - *Greek*

Choucroute à l'Alsacienne - *French*

Gulyás - *Hungarian*

Vindaloo - *East Indian*

Couscous - *African*

Moose Burgers (Canadian Aboriginal)

Moose or Venison Burgers

Hunters with aboriginal backgrounds still follow their cardinal rule when hunting, and they teach it to their youth: on any outing, kill only what is going to be used for food, and no more.

1 lb	ground moose or venison	500 g
1 cup	water	250 mL
¼ cup	tomato paste	50 mL
2	onions, chopped	2
1 tsp	curry powder	5 mL
½ tsp	horseradish	2 mL
½ tsp	salt	2 mL

▪ Shape meat into 4 flat patties.

▪ In nonstick skillet over medium heat, brown patties on both sides.

▪ Combine water, tomato paste, onions, curry powder, horseradish, and salt. Pour over patties. Bring to boil.

▪ Reduce heat, cover and simmer, turning patties once, for 10 minutes or until meat is no longer pink and onions are tender.

▪ Serve with sauce from skillet.

Makes 4 servings.

Roast Venison

Venison's protein content is higher and its fat content is lower, cut for cut, than most other meats. Slow cooking at low temperatures helps to keep the meat tender. Higher temperatures tighten and toughen the protein.

3 lb	venison roast	1.5 kg

MARINADE

1 cup	apple juice	250 mL
½ cup	cider vinegar	125 mL
1 Tbsp	canola oil	15 mL
2	bay leaves	2
1	small onion, thinly sliced	1
1	clove garlic, minced	1
½ tsp	salt	2 mL
¼ tsp	freshly ground black pepper	1 mL
2	slices side bacon	2
1 Tbsp	all-purpose flour	15 mL
1 Tbsp	crabapple or red currant jelly	15 mL

- Rinse venison with cold water; pat dry.
- Marinade: In large glass bowl or heavy plastic bag, combine apple juice, vinegar, oil, bay leaves, onion, garlic, salt, and pepper. Place venison in marinade, turning several times to coat well. (If using plastic bag, close bag around roast and marinade, twist and secure top. Place in bowl.) Marinate in refrigerator, turning occasionally, for 24 to 30 hours.
- Place roast on rack in shallow roasting pan. Reserve marinade. Criss-cross bacon over top of roast. Brush with marinade.
- Roast in 300°F (150°C) oven for 2 hours or until no longer pink.
- Transfer to serving platter; keep warm
- Remove all but 1 Tbsp (15 mL) of drippings. Stir flour into pan until combined with drippings. Add water to remaining marinade to make 1 cup (250 mL). Stir into flour mixture; discard bay leaves. Stir and bring to boil for 1 minute or until slightly thickened. Stir in jelly until melted. Pour into sauce or gravy dish.
- Carve venison into thin slices. Serve with sauce.

Makes 14 servings.

EACH SERVING
1/14 of recipe

½ Starch
3 Meat, very lean
½ Fat

159 calories
5 g total fat
1 g saturated fat
84 mg cholesterol
22 g protein
5 g carbohydrate
129 mg sodium
317 mg potassium

GOOD
Phosphorus, Iron, Zinc

EXCELLENT
Riboflavin, Niacin

Grilled Rabbit

Rabbit is actually more similar to chicken than to pork or beef. Its flesh is almost all white meat, and its fat content is low compared to other meats. It can be prepared in the same ways as chicken. Younger, smaller rabbits are best grilled or roasted. Larger ones are best braised and stewed as in German hassenpfeffer and French lapin dijonnaise.

1	young rabbit (about 2 lbs /1 kg)	1

MARINADE

¾ cup	apple juice or white wine	175 mL
2	bay leaves, crumbled	2
1	clove garlic, minced	1
1 Tbsp	lemon juice	15 mL
1 tsp	salt	5 mL
½ tsp	freshly ground black pepper	2 mL

- Disjoint and cut rabbit into pieces.
- Marinade: In baking dish, combine apple juice, bay leaves, garlic, lemon juice, salt, and pepper. Place rabbit pieces in marinade, and turn to coat well. Cover and refrigerate, turning occasionally, for 3 to 4 hours.
- Remove rabbit pieces; reserve marinade. Place on lightly greased barbecue grill.
- Grill about 5 inches (12.5 cm) from medium-hot coals, turning often and basting with marinade, for 20 to 30 minutes or until well done and meat is no longer pink.

Makes 8 servings.

EACH SERVING
⅛ of recipe

4 Meat, very lean

141 calories
3 g total fat
1 g saturated fat
91 mg cholesterol
25 g protein
3 g carbohydrate
347 mg sodium
413 mg potassium

GOOD
Phosphorus

EXCELLENT
Iron, Niacin

Ho Yow Ngow Yuke (Chinese)

Oyster Sauce Beef

This Chinese way of preparing strips of meat or chicken in a marinade that includes cornstarch always results in wonderfully moist and tender morsels. The juices seem to be sealed in as the coating of marinade cooks.

1	beef strip loin steak (8 oz/250 g)	1
1 Tbsp	cornstarch	15 mL
2 tsp	lite soy sauce	10 mL
2	drops hot pepper sauce	2
1 Tbsp	canola oil	15 mL
6	green onions, sliced	6
½ cup	water	125 mL
2 Tbsp	oyster sauce	25 mL

▪ Cut steak into thin strips.

▪ In bowl, combine 1 tsp (5 mL) cornstarch, soy sauce, and hot pepper sauce. Add steak strips, and toss to coat each piece with soy sauce mixture. Marinate for 15 minutes.

▪ In nonstick skillet, heat oil over high heat. Stir-fry steak strips for 2 minutes. Add onions; stir-fry for 1 minute.

▪ Stir together water, oyster sauce, and remaining cornstarch until smooth. Add to skillet, stirring, for about 1 minute or until thickened.

Makes 2 servings.

EACH SERVING
½ of recipe

½ Starch
3 Meat, medium-fat
½ Fat

292 calories
17 g total fat
4 g saturated fat
61 mg cholesterol
25 g protein
7 g carbohydrate
512 mg sodium ✿
519 mg potassium

GOOD
Phosphorus, Iron, Magnesium, Riboflavin

EXCELLENT
Zinc, Niacin, Vitamin B$_6$, Vitamin B$_{12}$

Moo Waan (Thai)

Thai Tenderloins

When I can find it, I like to use chopped fresh lemon grass in this marinade in place of the lemon rind. If only dry is available, I soak it in twice its volume of boiling water for 10 minutes then add it to the marinade. Still, the strip of lemon rind nearly duplicates the subtle lemony notes that ring through authentic Thai dishes using lemon grass.

| 2 | pork tenderloins or 1 boneless pork loin (1½ lb / 750 g) | 2 |

MARINADE

⅓ cup	chicken broth	75 mL
2 Tbsp	lime juice	25 mL
1 Tbsp	fish sauce (nam pla) or lite soy sauce	15 mL
1 Tbsp	freshly grated ginger root (or 1 tsp/5 mL, ground)	15 mL
2	cloves garlic, minced	2
1	2-inch (5-cm) strip lemon rind	1
1 tsp	hot Oriental chili paste	5 mL

▪ Place pork in heavy plastic bag or glass bowl.

▪ Marinade: In bowl, whisk together 2 Tbsp (25 mL) chicken broth, lime juice, fish sauce, ginger root, garlic, lemon rind, and chili paste. Pour over pork. Close bag, secure, and set in bowl. Marinate overnight in the refrigerator or at room temperature for 1 hour. Remove pork. Strain marinade into small saucepan.

▪ Barbecue pork over medium-hot coals, turning once or twice, for 25 to 35 minutes or until juices run clear.

▪ Or, place pork on rack in shallow roasting pan. Roast in 350°F (180°C) oven for 30 to 45 minutes or until juice runs clear. To serve, cut into thin slices.

▪ Add remaining chicken broth to reserved marinade. Bring to boil for 2 minutes. Brush over cooked pork.

Makes 6 servings.

VARIATION

Cha Shao Rou (Chinese)

Oriental Barbecued Pork

Marinating gives the pork a more robust flavor.

▪ Substitute the following marinade for the one above: Whisk together 2 Tbsp (25 mL) rice vinegar, 1 Tbsp (15 mL) hoisin sauce, 1 Tbsp (15 mL) lite soy sauce, 1 Tbsp (15 mL) freshly grated ginger root, 2 cloves garlic, minced, and 2 tsp (10 mL) Chinese five spice powder.

Bifes de Cebolada (Portuguese)

Portuguese Beef & Onions

Both Portuguese and Spanish cooks have always used olive oil extensively in their cooking. When as little is used as in this recipe, which helps cut down the fat, I recommend using top quality extra virgin olive oil. Its flavor makes a difference.

1 lb	beef tenderloin, cut into thin slices	500 g
2 tsp	olive oil or butter	10 mL
3	onions, thinly sliced	3
2	garlic cloves, minced	2
1 lb	tomatoes, peeled, seeded, & chopped	500 g
1 tsp	finely chopped parsley	5 mL
1	bay leaf	1
	Salt and freshly ground black pepper	
	Chopped fresh cilantro or parsley	

▪ In nonstick skillet, heat olive oil over medium-high heat. Sauté beef slices for 2 minutes. Add onion slices, garlic, tomatoes, parsley, and bay leaf. Season to taste with salt and pepper. Heat to simmering. Cover and cook for 30 minutes.

▪ When too much liquid from the tomatoes builds up, remove the lid and allow it to evaporate.

▪ Garnish with cilantro.

Makes 6 servings.

EACH SERVING
⅙ of recipe

1 Vegetable
2 Meat, lean

156 calories
7 g total fat
3 g saturated fat
41 mg cholesterol
17 g protein
7 g carbohydrate
61 mg sodium
457 mg potassium

GOOD
Phosphorus, Iron, Niacin, Vitamin B_6

EXCELLENT
Zinc, Vitamin B_{12}

Spuntature al Sugo (Italian)

Spareribs in Sauce

The tomato sauce created while the ribs cook is great with pasta as a first course. Following that, the ribs make a delicious second course with steamed green beans or broccoli. However, it is more traditional to serve the ribs with their rich red sauce as a one-dish meal with polenta (recipe p. 78).

1½ lbs	pork back ribs	750 g
1 Tbsp	olive oil	15 mL
½ tsp	crushed red chili pepper	2 mL
	Salt and freshly ground black pepper	
1 cup	chicken broth	250 mL
1	can (19 oz/540 mL) tomatoes	1
1 Tbsp	red wine vinegar	15 mL

▪ Cut strip of ribs into 2 rib portions.

▪ In large nonstick skillet, heat oil over medium-high heat. Cook chili pepper for 30 seconds. Add ribs. Cook, turning, until browned on all sides. Season to taste with salt and pepper.

▪ Stir in broth, tomatoes, breaking them up with fork, and vinegar. Bring to boil. Reduce heat and cook, stirring occasionally, for 1 hour or until meat is tender and no longer pink close to the bone. (The sauce will be reduced by about half. If it becomes drier during cooking, stir in a bit of water to maintain a sauce-like consistency.)

▪ Skim any visible fat from surface of sauce.

Makes 6 servings.

Rouladen (German)
Braised Stuffed Beef Rolls

These tasty beef rolls are permeated with the unusual flavor of the bacon and dill pickle filling. A German cook's potato dish is the perfect accompaniment.

1½ lbs	minute steak	750 g
	(6 pieces about ¼ in/5 mm thick)	
2 Tbsp	prepared mustard,	25 mL
	preferably German style	
4	slices back bacon, chopped	4
1	onion, chopped	1
¼ cup	chopped fresh parsley	50 mL
2	dill pickles, quartered lengthwise	2
1 Tbsp	canola oil	15 mL
1 cup	beef broth	250 mL
½ cup	dry red wine or beef broth	125 mL
	Salt and freshly ground black pepper	
2 Tbsp	water	25 mL
1 Tbsp	all-purpose flour	15 mL

■ Place steak slices between 2 pieces of waxed paper and pound beef to half its thickness. Pieces should be about 7 x 4 inches (18 x 10 cm).

■ Spread mustard on each piece and sprinkle with bacon, onion, and parsley. Place pickle quarter on narrow end of each piece; roll up. Fasten with wooden toothpicks or tie with string.

■ In nonstick skillet, heat oil over medium heat. Cook rolls until brown on all sides. Add broth, wine, salt, and pepper. Bring to boil. Reduce heat, cover and simmer on top of stove or braise in 325°F (160°C) oven for 1 hour or until tender.

■ Transfer rolls to warm platter and keep warm.

■ Add enough water to pan juices to make 1 cup (250 mL).

■ In jar with screw top, shake 2 Tbsp (25 mL) cold water and flour together until smooth. Stir gradually into broth. Heat to boiling, stirring constantly, and boil for 1 minute until gravy thickens. Spoon over rolls and serve.

Makes 6 servings.

EACH SERVING
⅙ of recipe

| 1 | Vegetable |
| 3 | Meat, lean |

202 calories
5 g total fat
1 g saturated fat
49 mg cholesterol
26 g protein
4 g carbohydrate
897 mg sodium ✿
538 mg potassium

GOOD
Phosphorus, Iron

EXCELLENT
**Zinc, Niacin,
Vitamin B₆,
Vitamin B₁₂**

Beef Stroganoff

The story goes that a French chef created beef stroganov for Count Stroganov, a merchant-nobleman of prerevolutionary Russia who had a passion for things French. It blends the preparation style of French cooking with the taste of Russian cooking in the sour cream sauce. Here is my low-fat version of the classic.

1 lb	tenderloin or strip loin beef	500 g
	Flour for dredging	
1 Tbsp	butter	15 mL
8	mushrooms, sliced	8
1	onion, thinly sliced	1
1	clove garlic, minced	1
1 cup	beef broth	250 mL
1 Tbsp	tomato paste	15 mL
1 tsp	Worcestershire sauce	5 mL
½ tsp	Dijon mustard	2 mL
½ tsp	salt	2 mL
Pinch	freshly ground black pepper	Pinch
¼ cup	all-purpose flour	50 mL
1 cup	low-fat sour cream	250 mL
	Chopped fresh parsley	

■ With sharp knife, cut beef across the grain into 2 x ¼ inch (5 cm x 5 mm) strips. Dredge with flour.

■ In large nonstick skillet, heat butter over medium-high heat. Cook mushrooms, onion, and garlic for 5 minutes or until tender. Transfer to warm plate and set aside.

■ In same skillet, stir-fry steak in 3 batches until lightly browned. Transfer to plate of onion mixture as batches brown. To the last batch, add reserved onion mixture and browned beef.

■ Reserve ¼ cup (50 mL) beef broth. Stir remainder into beef mixture with tomato paste, Worcestershire sauce, mustard, salt, and pepper. Cook for 3 minutes or just until beef is no longer pink.

■ Blend flour into reserved broth. Stir into beef mixture. Heat to boiling, stirring constantly for 1½ minutes or until thickened.

■ Whisk sour cream until smooth. Stir into beef mixture. Heat through and do not boil again (or sauce will curdle).

■ Garnish with parsley.

Makes 4 servings.

EACH SERVING
¼ of recipe

1	Starch
3	Meat, lean
1	Fat

288 calories
14 g total fat
4 g saturated fat
74 mg cholesterol
23 g protein
15 g carbohydrate
660 mg sodium ✿
480 mg potassium

GOOD
Phosphorus, Iron, Riboflavin, Vitamin B$_6$

EXCELLENT
Zinc, Magnesium, Niacin, Vitamin B$_{12}$

Schnitzel (Austrian/German)

Pork Schnitzel

Some resources say Wiener schnitzel originated in Vienna. Others indicate it is an offshoot of the Italian costolette alla Milanese that has been renamed. Italian cooks made it with veal chops that were pounded thin. Now, both versions are made with thin scallops of veal. Lean pork, turkey, and chicken also make wonderful schnitzel. This version uses less fat than the original ones.

6	thin slices boneless pork (¼ in/5 mm thick) from leg, shoulder, or loin (1 lb/ 500 g)	6
¼ cup	all-purpose flour	50 mL
1	egg white, lightly beaten with 2 tsp (10 mL) water	1
½ cup	dry breadcrumbs	125 mL
½ tsp	salt	2 mL
⅛ tsp	freshly ground black pepper	0.5 mL
1 Tbsp	butter	15 mL
2 Tbsp	capers, chopped Chopped parsley	25 mL

- Pound each slice of pork lightly with mallet to flatten. Dredge thoroughly with flour.
- Dip floured slices into egg white mixture, then coat with crumbs seasoned with salt and pepper.
- Place pork on wire rack. Let stand for 15 minutes to dry crumb coating. (This prevents coating from falling off during cooking.)
- In nonstick skillet, heat butter over medium-high heat. Sauté pork slices quickly, turning once or twice, until golden brown on both sides.
- Combine chopped capers and parsley. Sprinkle over Schnitzel.

Makes 6 servings.

VARIATION

Piccata di Vitello al Limone (Italian)

Veal Piccata

- Substitute veal for pork, and flour for breadcrumbs.
- As soon as veal is golden brown, push to one side in skillet. Add 2 Tbsp (25 mL) each lemon juice and white wine. Scrape up brown bits. Stir in ¼ cup (50 mL) water. Simmer for 5 minutes. Season to taste with salt and pepper. Spoon over veal.
- Delete the capers and garnish veal with parsley and thin lemon slices.

EACH SERVING
⅙ of recipe

1   Starch
2   Meat, lean

187 calories
7 g total fat
2 g saturated fat
45 mg cholesterol
18 g protein
10 g carbohydrate
268 mg sodium
329 mg potassium

GOOD
Phosphorus, Zinc, Riboflavin, Vitamin B$_6$, Vitamin B$_{12}$

EXCELLENT
Thiamin, Niacin

Calculations approximately the same as above.

Porco Alentejana (Portuguese)
Pork with Clams

The surprising combination of pork and clams may have developed as a bold way for Portuguese cooks to emphasize their Christian enthusiasm. It proscribes Jewish and Moorish dietary laws, but more importantly, the stew is delicious.

1 lb	well-trimmed boneless lean pork	500 g

MARINADE

1	clove garlic, minced	1
1 Tbsp	paprika	15 mL
1	bay leaf, broken	1
¼ tsp	freshly ground black pepper	1 mL
½ cup	water	125 mL
24	small hard-shelled clams or 1 can (5 oz/142 g) baby clams	24
1 Tbsp	olive oil	15 mL
1	onion, coarsely chopped	1
2	tomatoes, peeled, seeded, and chopped	2
6	drops hot pepper sauce	6
½ tsp	salt	2 mL
¼ tsp	freshly ground black pepper	1 mL
4	slices bread, toasted	4
1 Tbsp	chopped fresh cilantro or parsley	15 mL
4	lemon wedges	4

- Cut pork into ¾-inch (1-cm) cubes.
- Marinade: In glass bowl, stir together garlic, paprika, bay leaf, pepper, and water until well blended. Toss pork cubes in marinade mixture. Cover and let stand, turning the cubes occasionally, for ½ to 1 hour at room temperature or as long as overnight in the refrigerator.
- Scrub clams under cold running water. Place them in nonstick skillet; cover and cook over low heat for 5 minutes or until clams open, discarding any whose shells do not open. Discard all shells; strain and reserve any pan juices along with clams.
- Drain pork cubes; place on paper towels and pat dry. In nonstick skillet, heat olive oil. Cook pork over medium heat, stirring occasionally, for about 7 minutes or until browned on all sides. Add onion; cook for 5 minutes longer. Add tomatoes, hot pepper sauce, salt, and pepper. Cook for 5 minutes.
- Stir in clams and juice. (Discard half the juice when canned clams are used.) Simmer, stirring once or twice, for 3 minutes or until tomato mixture is sauce-like.
- Spoon over toast. Garnish with cilantro and lemon.

Makes 6 servings.

EACH SERVING
⅙ of recipe

1 Starch
2 Meat, very lean
½ Fat

172 calories
4 g total fat
1 g saturated fat
43 mg cholesterol
18 g protein
14 g carbohydrate
318 mg sodium
433 mg potassium

GOOD
Phosphorus, Iron, Zinc, Riboflavin, Vitamin B$_6$

EXCELLENT
Thiamin, Niacin, Vitamin B$_{12}$

Shami Kebob (East Indian)

Spicy Meat Patties

Cumin and hot peppers give their distinct flavors to these Hindu-style meat patties, which are always made with lamb by Hindus. Most East Indian cooks will have their own version, with the hot and spicy notes tuned to the likes and dislikes of their family.

1 Tbsp	canola oil	15 mL
2	onions, finely chopped	2
2	cloves garlic, minced	2
2 tsp	chopped pickled jalapeno peppers	10 mL
¼ tsp	hot red pepper flakes	1 mL
1 tsp	ground cumin	5 mL
1 Tbsp	chopped fresh cilantro or parsley	15 mL
1 lb	lean ground lamb, beef, or chicken, or mixture of meats	500 g
¼ cup	whole-bean or split-pea flour	50 mL
1 tsp	salt	5 mL
1	onion, thinly sliced	1
1	lime, cut into wedges	1

▪ In nonstick skillet over medium heat, combine oil, onion, garlic, jalapeno and red pepper, cumin, and cilantro leaves. Cook, stirring, for about 2 minutes. Cool.

▪ In bowl, combine ground meat, bean flour, salt, and onion mixture until well mixed. Form into 12 small patties.

▪ Cook in nonstick skillet over medium heat for 4 to 5 minutes on each side or until meat is no longer pink. Transfer to paper towels to drain.

▪ Serve garnished with onion rings and lime wedges.

Makes 6 servings.

VARIATIONS

Seekh Kabob (Middle Eastern)

Shish Kebob

In Israel, shish kebob is served on the meze table. On the street, the grilled meat is put into pitas with tahini and salad, like falafels, to be eaten out of hand.

▪ Substitute chopped fresh mint for the cilantro and add ½ tsp (2 mL) each ground coriander and cardamom and a pinch of allspice to the meat mixture.

▪ Form mixture into 2-inch (5-cm) rolls like sausages. Slip onto skewers. Place on barbecue grill over hot coals. Barbecue, turning once, for 4 minutes on each side or until no longer pink (or broil 4 inches [10 cm] from heat).

EACH SERVING
⅙ of recipe

1   Vegetable
1   Meat, medium-fat

104 calories
4 g total fat
0 g saturated fat
27 mg cholesterol
8 g protein
5 g carbohydrate
423 mg sodium ✖
213 mg potassium

GOOD
Niacin

EXCELLENT
Vitamin B₁₂

MODERATE
Fiber

Calculations approximately the same as above.

Frikadeller (Scandinavian)

Danish Meatballs

Through the years, many variations of these meatballs have been passed on from generation to generation in Danish, Finnish, Swedish, and Norwegian families.

2 tsp	butter	10 mL
1	onion, finely chopped	1
½ cup	minced fresh dill	125 mL
2	slices white bread, crusts removed	2
¼ cup	milk	50 mL
1	egg white	1
Pinch	each ground allspice and nutmeg	Pinch
½ lb	ground chicken	250 g
½ lb	lean ground beef or lamb	250 g
½ lb	lean ground pork	250 g
	Salt and freshly ground black pepper	

SAUCE
1 cup	chicken broth	500 mL
½ cup	low-fat sour cream or yogurt	125 mL
1 Tbsp	all-purpose flour	15 mL
1 Tbsp	chopped fresh dill or	15 mL
	1 tsp (5 mL) dried dill sprigs	

▪ In nonstick skillet, heat butter over medium heat. Cook onion for 5 minutes. Stir in dill. Set aside.

▪ Crumble bread into bowl; soak with milk and beat in egg white. Stir in allspice and nutmeg. Crumble meats into bread mixture and add onion mixture; stir well. Season to taste with salt and pepper. Shape into 35 meatballs, about 1½ inches (4 cm) thick. Arrange on rack in shallow roasting pan.

▪ Bake in 325°F (160°C) oven for 15 minutes or until no longer pink.

▪ Sauce: In saucepan, bring broth to boil for 2 minutes. Whisk sour cream and flour until smooth. Whisk into hot broth. Cook for 2 minutes or until thickened. Reduce heat. Stir in remaining dill and meatballs. Season to taste with pepper. Simmer for 5 minutes to heat through.

▪ Transfer to chafing dish or bowl. Garnish with dill sprigs.

Makes 7 servings.

VARIATION

Albodigintos (Latin American)

Piquant Meatballs

▪ Substitute 2 Tbsp (25 mL) chopped pickled jalapeno peppers for the dill. In place of the broth-based sauce, serve meatballs with Salsa Picante (recipe p. 160).

Ragoût de Boulettes (French Canadian)

Meatball Stew

The gelatinous quality of the stock and the meaty nuggets from the pork hock add to this style of meatballs, popular with French Canadian cooks.

1	pork hock (1 lb / 500 g), rinsed	1
3	whole cloves garlic	3
¼ tsp	freshly ground black pepper	1 mL

BOULETTES (MEATBALLS)

½ lb	lean ground pork	250 g
½ lb	lean ground beef	250 g
2 oz	back bacon, finely chopped	60 g
1	onion, finely chopped	1
½ cup	dry breadcrumbs	125 mL
½ cup	1% milk	125 mL
1 tsp	salt	5 mL
¼ tsp	freshly ground black pepper	1 mL
¼ tsp	each mustard, ground cloves, cinnamon, and nutmeg	1 mL
¼ cup	all-purpose flour	50 mL
¼ cup	browned flour*	50 mL
	Chopped fresh parsley	

▪ Place pork hock in saucepan. Cover with water; add garlic and pepper. Bring to boil. Reduce heat, cover and simmer for 2 hours or until meat separates easily from bone. Remove and cool. Strain and reserve stock. Discard bone, skin, and excess fat; reserve meat.

▪ Meatballs: In bowl, combine ground pork and beef, bacon, onion, and breadcrumbs. With fork, beat together milk, salt, pepper, mustard, cloves, cinnamon, and nutmeg. Stir into meat mixture until well blended.

▪ Shape into 1½-inch (4-cm) meatballs. Roll in flour to coat. Arrange on wire rack in shallow baking pan.

▪ Bake in 350°F (180°C) oven for 20 minutes or until golden brown.

▪ Bring reserved stock to boil. Add meatballs. Reduce heat and simmer, partly covered, for 30 minutes. Add meat from pork hock.

▪ In jar with tight-fitting lid, combine ½ cup (125 mL) cold water and browned flour; shake until well blended. Stir slowly into stock, stirring constantly for 1 to 2 minutes or until thickened. Simmer for 5 minutes. Season to taste with salt and pepper.

▪ Transfer to serving dish. Garnish with parsley.

Makes 8 servings.

EACH SERVING
⅛ of recipe

| 1 | Starch |
| 3 | Meat, medium-fat |

303 calories
15 g total fat
5 g saturated fat
99 mg cholesterol
28 g protein
13 g carbohydrate
511 mg sodium ✪
353 mg potassium

GOOD
Phosphorus, Thiamin, Vitamin B6

EXCELLENT
Zinc, Niacin, Vitamin B12

*TIMELY TIP
To brown flour, sprinkle flour into small nonstick skillet over medium heat; stir until golden brown or caramel color.

Zhen Zhu Wan Zi (Chinese)
Pearl Balls

Back in the days of home economics classes, we called these "little pocupines." Since then, I have discovered it is best to use sticky glutenous rice for the balls. As the rice coating steams with the meatballs, it swells, adhering to the meat and forming a pearl-like covering. Hot or cold, these balls make grand little finger foods for the dim sum table, or they can be served as a main course with sauce.

4	dried Chinese mushrooms	4
	Warm water	
½ cup	short-grain pearl rice	125 mL
½ lb	ground lean pork	250 g
½ lb	ground chicken	250 g
8	water chestnuts, finely chopped	8
3	slices fresh ginger root, finely chopped	3
2	green onions, finely chopped	2
2 Tbsp	lite soy sauce	25 mL
1 Tbsp	hoisin sauce	15 mL
2 tsp	sesame oil	10 mL
2 tsp	cornstarch	10 mL

▪ Soak mushrooms in lukewarm water for 20 minutes or until soft. Drain and chop finely.

▪ Wash rice. Cover with water and let soak for 15 minutes.

▪ In bowl, combine pork, chicken, water chestnuts, ginger root, onions, soy sauce, hoisin sauce, and sesame oil; mix well. Stir in cornstarch until blended.

▪ Shape about 1 Tbsp (15 mL) at a time into round ball.

▪ Drain rice; roll meatball in it to coat. Roll in hands to press rice in place. Continue forming balls and rolling in rice until all filling is used.

▪ Line bottom of steamer basket with damp cloth or cheese-cloth. Arrange meatballs on top. Place basket in steamer. Cover and steam for 25 minutes or until meat is no longer pink.

Makes 36 to 40 balls, 8 servings.

EACH SERVING
⅛ of recipe

1   Starch
1½ Meat, very lean

144 calories
2 g total fat
0 g saturated fat
35 mg cholesterol
15 g protein
14 g carbohydrate
223 mg sodium
265 mg potassium

GOOD
Vitamin D, Thiamin,
Vitamin B$_6$,
Vitamin B$_{12}$

EXCELLENT
Niacin

Picadillo (Mexican)

Picadillo (Meat Hash)

Beef and/or pork and/or veal, onion, garlic, and tomatoes, plus seasonings indigenous to the locale are found in picadillo. Picadillo is something like a hash with Spanish beginnings. In Mexican homes, it often becomes a stuffing for peppers. In Caribbean homes, it is often an accompaniment for beans and rice.

1 lb	ground beef	500 g
1	onion, chopped	1
3	cloves garlic, minced	3
1	can (14 oz/398 mL) tomatoes	1
2	potatoes, peeled and diced	2
1	carrot, minced	1
2 tsp	raisins, chopped	10 mL
1	jalapeno pepper, seeded and minced	1
	or 1 Tbsp (15 mL) chopped pickled jalapeno	
2 tsp	chili powder	10 mL
1 tsp	each dried oregano and cumin	5 mL
¼ tsp	allspice	1 mL

▪ In nonstick skillet, cook beef, onions, and garlic over medium heat, breaking up beef with the back of spoon, for 10 minutes or until beef is no longer pink.

▪ Stir in tomatoes, potatoes, carrot, raisins, jalapeno pepper, chili powder, oregano, cumin, and allspice. Bring to boil. Reduce heat, cover and cook, stirring occasionally, for about 15 minutes or until potatoes are tender.

▪ Uncover, cook for a few minutes longer or until liquid evaporates.

Makes 6 servings.

EACH SERVING
⅙ of recipe

½ Starch
1   Vegetable
2   Meat, lean
1   Fat

226 calories
11 g total fat
4 g saturated fat
42 mg cholesterol
16 g protein
14 g carbohydrate
195 mg sodium
602 mg potassium

GOOD
Iron, Magnesium, Vitamin B₆

EXCELLENT
Zinc, Vitamin A, Niacin, Vitamin B₁₂

MODERATE
Fiber

Lamb Kabobs

Shashlik, souvlaki, kebabs, and shish kebab are terms for meat cubes that are marinated then skewered and cooked over an open fire. Nomads did this for centuries throughout the Middle East and Eastern Europe, when they used their swords as skewers. Lamb is usually the meat of choice; however, beef, pork, and also chicken or turkey are suitable alternatives.

2 lbs	boneless lamb, well trimmed	1 kg
MARINADE		
½ cup	lemon juice	125 mL
¼ cup	chopped fresh rosemary	50 mL
	or 1 Tbsp (15 mL) dried	
3	cloves garlic, minced	3
1 tsp	hot red pepper flakes	5 mL
	Salt and freshly ground black pepper	
2 Tbsp	olive oil	25 mL
2	zucchini	2
2	small onions	2
1	red or yellow sweet pepper	1

- Cut lamb into 2-inch (5-cm) chunks; place in bowl.
- Marinade: Combine lemon juice and seasonings. Whisk in oil. Pour marinade over lamb, stirring to coat well. Cover and marinate in refrigerator for at least 6 hours or overnight.
- Cut zucchini in 1-inch (2.5-cm) slices. Cut each onion into 8 wedges. Cut pepper into bite-size pieces.
- On skewers, alternately thread meat, onion, zucchini, and pepper chunks. Brush with marinade.
- Barbecue on lightly oiled grill over medium-high heat or broil 5 inches (12.5 cm) under preheated broiler, turning once or twice, for 12 to 15 minutes or until medium done. Brush with marinade before last 5 minutes of cooking, then discard marinade.

Makes 8 skewers, 8 servings.

VARIATIONS

Souvlaki (Greek)
Skewered Meat

- Prepare lamb, pork, beef, or chicken, as above. Marinate and thread meat only on skewers. Place vegetables on separate skewers.

EACH SERVING
⅛ of recipe

1   Vegetable
3   Meat, lean

201 calories
9 g total fat
2 g saturated fat
73 mg cholesterol
23 g protein
5 g carbohydrate
76 mg sodium
410 mg potassium

GOOD
Phosphorus, Iron, Magnesium, Vitamin C, Riboflavin, Folate

EXCELLENT
Zinc, Niacin, Vitamin B$_{12}$

Calculations approximately the same as above.

Choucroute à l'Alsacienne (French)

Alsatian Sauerkraut Stew

To the French from Alsace, where sauerkraut reached perfection, this stew is a classic. Some traditional cooks left it to stew all night, but the general rule was to cook it for the duration of the church service.

2	slices back bacon, diced	1
1	onion, chopped	1
1	can (19 oz/540 mL) sauerkraut, drained	1
2	carrots, cut in chunks	2
2	potatoes, peeled and quartered	2
1	tart apple, sliced	1
8	whole juniper berries	8
8	whole peppercorns	8
4	sprigs parsley	4
1	bay leaf	1
1 cup	chicken broth	250 mL
½ cup	white wine	125 mL
1 lb	lean pork loin, cubed	500 g
½ lb	bratwurst, sliced	250 g
1 tsp	caraway seeds, crushed	5 mL
	Chopped fresh parsley	

- In Dutch oven over medium heat, cook bacon and onion for 5 minutes or until translucent but not brown.

- Rinse sauerkraut; drain. Stir into onion mixture.

- Stir in carrots, potatoes, and apple. In cheesecloth, tie juniper berries, peppercorns, parsley, and bay leaf or place them in a teaball. Add to sauerkraut mixture. Pour on broth and wine; bring to boil. Reduce heat and cook gently for 10 minutes.

- Add pork, bratwurst, and caraway seeds. Cook for 40 minutes or until pork is no longer pink. Remove spice bag.

- Or transfer to casserole. Cover and cook in 325°F (160°C) oven for 40 to 45 minutes or until tender.

- With slotted spoon, transfer sauerkraut, carrots, potatoes, and apples to heated platter. Top with pork cubes and bratwurst. Garnish with parsley.

Makes 6 servings.

EACH SERVING
⅙ of recipe

1	Starch
1	Vegetable
3	Meat, medium-fat

341 calories
15 g total fat
5 g saturated fat
69 mg cholesterol
25 g protein
19 g carbohydrate
660 mg sodium ✴
878 mg potassium

GOOD
Iron, Magnesium, Vitamin C, Riboflavin, Folate

EXCELLENT
Phosphorus, Zinc, Vitamin A, Thiamin, Niacin, Vitamin B$_6$, Vitamin B$_{12}$

HIGH
Fiber

Gulyás (Hungarian)
Beef Paprikash

Goulash is probably the more commonly used name for this country-style stew. It originated on the Hungarian plains, where cattle-raising people found that tough cuts (less expensive ones today) cooked slowly with assorted vegetables and fragrant paprika turn into a sumptuous one-pot meal.

1 lb	lean stewing beef	500 g
2 tsp	canola oil	10 mL
1	red onion, chopped	1
2 tsp	paprika	10 mL
1 tsp	salt	5 mL
1 tsp	red pepper paste or hot pepper sauce	5 mL
6 cups	water	1.5 L
2	carrots, diced	2
2	parsnips, diced	2
1	large potato, diced	1

DUMPLINGS (SPAEZLE)

1	egg	1
½ tsp	salt	2 mL
½ cup	all-purpose flour	125 mL

- Remove any visible fat from beef; cut into 1-inch (2.5-cm) cubes.

- In large saucepan or soup kettle, heat oil over medium-high heat. Cook onion for about 4 minutes or until light golden color. Add beef; brown on all sides. Stir in paprika, salt, red pepper paste, and water. Bring to boil. Reduce heat, cover and simmer for 1 hour.

- Stir in carrots, parsnips, potato, and remaining water. Cook, covered, for 20 minutes or until meat and vegetables are tender.

- Dumplings: In bowl, beat eggs with salt. Stir in flour until smooth and sticky paste forms. With tip of spoon, take up bit of dough and push it off spoon into boiling soup.

- Allow soup to boil for 1 minute or until dumplings are cooked.

Makes 6 cups (1.5 L), 6 servings.

EACH SERVING
⅙ of recipe

1   Starch
2   Meat, lean
½   Fat

210 calories
8 g total fat
2 g saturated fat
72 mg cholesterol
19 g protein
14 g carbohydrate
584 mg sodium ✪
492 mg potassium

GOOD
Phosphorus, Iron,
Riboflavin, Vitamin B6

EXCELLENT
Zinc, Vitamin A,
Niacin, Vitamin B12

Vindaloo (East Indian)

Curried Lamb

Curry powder originated in India, where housewives still prepare it themselves with a combination of herbs and spices to suit their family's tastes. Curries from Madras, for instance, are much hotter that those from northern India. During the English imperial expansion, when English officials and soldiers brought it home with them, at once it began adding more pungency to some English cooking.

1 lb	lean stewing lamb or beef	500 g
2 tsp	butter or canola oil	10 mL
2	onions, chopped	2
1	stalk celery, chopped	1
1	clove garlic, minced	1
1 Tbsp	curry powder	15 mL
Pinch	each ground cloves and cinnamon	Pinch
1	apple, peeled and finely chopped	1
1 cup	chicken broth	250 mL
2 Tbsp	tomato paste	25 mL
¼ cup	low-fat yogurt	50 mL
2 tsp	all-purpose flour	10 mL
	Raita (recipe p. 160)	

■ Cut the meat into 1-inch (2.5-cm) cubes.

■ In nonstick skillet or large saucepan, heat butter over medium heat. Cook onion, celery, and garlic for 5 minutes or until onion is translucent. Stir in curry powder, cloves, and cinnamon until mixture is golden. Add meat and apple. Cook, stirring, until all sides of meat are colored. Stir in broth and tomato paste. Bring to boil. Reduce heat, cover and simmer for about 2 hours or until meat is tender and almost all liquid has evaporated.

■ In small bowl, stir together yogurt and flour until smooth. Stir into broth mixture. Simmer for 5 minutes or until thickened.

■ Serve with Raita

Makes 6 servings.

EACH SERVING
⅙ of recipe

½ Starch
2 Meat, lean

157 calories
5 g total fat
2 g saturated fat
52 mg cholesterol
17 g protein
8 g carbohydrate
204 mg sodium
362 mg potassium

GOOD
Phosphorus

EXCELLENT
Zinc, Niacin, Vitamin B$_{12}$

Couscous

Both the granular semolina pasta used in this stew and the dish itself are called couscous. Most African homes have a special pot called a couscoussiere for cooking it. The pot has a perforated top part that allows the couscous to cook in the steam created by the meat and vegetables simmering in the lower part. In my kitchen, a colander, sieve, or steam basket set over the stew pot does the same job.

1 cup	couscous	250 mL
1 Tbsp	butter or canola oil	15 mL
1	onion, chopped	1
1	clove garlic, minced	1
1 lb	lamb shoulder, cut into 1-inch (2.5-cm) cubes	500 g
1½ lbs	chicken legs (8), skinned	750 g
1	stalk celery, sliced	1
1	carrot, sliced	1
½	red sweet pepper, chopped	½
1	can (19 oz/540 mL) tomatoes	1
1	can (19 oz/540 mL) chickpeas, drained	1
2 Tbsp	raisins	25 mL
1 tsp	paprika	5 mL
½ tsp	turmeric	2 mL
½ tsp	ground cinnamon	2 mL
Pinch	each cayenne and ground cloves	Pinch
1 cup	fresh or frozen peas	250 mL
	Salt and freshly ground pepper	

- Place couscous in fine sieve, and rinse with cold water. Rub between the hands to separate the grains. Set aside.
- In Dutch oven or large saucepan, heat 1 tsp (5 mL) butter over medium heat. Cook onions and garlic until limp. Add lamb and chicken legs. Cook until golden on all sides.
- Add celery, carrot, and red pepper. Cook for 2 minutes. Stir in tomatoes, chickpeas, raisins, paprika, turmeric, cinnamon, cayenne, and cloves. Bring to boil. Reduce heat, cover and simmer for 25 minutes.
- Fluff couscous in sieve. Place sieve over stew using edge of Dutch oven for support. Place double tea towel over top, then cover with lid. Steam for 15 minutes.
- Mound couscous into a cone in center of warm serving platter. Dab remaining butter on top. Keep warm.
- Add peas to stew. Cook for 3 minutes until tender. Season to taste with salt and pepper.
- Spoon stew around couscous.

Makes 12 servings.

EACH SERVING
1/12 of recipe

1½ Starch
1 Vegetable
4 Meat, very lean
½ Fat

310 calories
7 g total fat
2 g saturated fat
96 mg cholesterol
30 g protein
28 g carbohydrate
327 mg sodium
540 mg potassium

GOOD
Iron, Magnesium, Riboflavin, Vitamin C

EXCELLENT
Phosphorus, Zinc, Vitamin A, Niacin, Folate, Vitamin B$_6$, Vitamin B$_{12}$

Fish & Seafood

Poisson Florentine - *French*

Bacalhoa à Portuguesa - *Portuguese*

Paella Valenciana - *Spanish*

Coquilles Saint-Jacques - *French*

Zheng Yu - *Chinese*

Pâté aux Patates et au Saumon - *French Canadian*

Hu Nan Yu - *Chinese*

Kedgeree - *British/East Indian*

Patéis de Bacalhoa - *Portuguese*

Stamp and Go - *Caribbean*

Sauce Tartare - *French*

Tien Shuen Yu - *Chinese*

Sweet & Sour Tomato Sauce - *Chinese*

Gan Shao Ming Xia - *Chinese*

Paad Priew Wan Goong - *Thai*

Abura-yakidofu - *Japanese*

Psari Plaki - *Middle Eastern*

Bacalhoa al Ajo Arriero - *Portuguese*

Stuffed Fish - *Canadian*

Poisson Florentine (French)

Fish & Spinach Foldovers

French cooks have a way with fish. Oven steaming these fillets or microwaving them, with their spinach stuffing, keeps them moist and delicate. Overcooking always makes the fish flakes feel dry.

2	fish fillets (sole) (½ lb/250 g)	2
½ lb	spinach, steamed	250 g
2 Tbsp	grated Parmesan cheese	25 mL
Pinch	nutmeg	Pinch
1 tsp	lemon juice	5 mL
1 tsp	chopped fresh parsley	5 mL
	Salt and white pepper	

CAPER AND RED PEPPER SAUCE

1	small red sweet pepper, seeded and chopped	1
1 Tbsp	drained capers	15 mL
½ cup	2% yogurt	125 mL
Pinch	white pepper	Pinch

▪ Lightly butter small shallow casserole dish. Lay fish fillets out flat.

▪ In piece of cheesecloth or light clean cloth, squeeze spinach to remove excess juice. Chop spinach.

▪ In bowl, combine spinach, Parmesan cheese, and nutmeg. Divide spinach mixture and spread evenly on one end of each fish fillet. Fold other end over spinach. Sprinkle with lemon juice and parsley. Season to taste with salt and pepper.

▪ Cover with lid or foil if cooking in an oven, or with plastic wrap (with an edge turned back) if cooking in a microwave oven.

▪ Bake at 400°F (200°C) for 20 minutes, or microwave on high for 8 minutes (rotating dish ½ turn after 4 minutes) or until fish just flakes easily with a fork.

▪ Sauce: In a food processor or blender, combine red pepper, capers, yogurt, and white pepper. Process until very finely chopped and sauce-like. Or, finely chop pepper and capers, then combine with yogurt and pepper; mix well.

▪ Spoon sauce onto plates; place stuffed fillet on top.

Makes 2 servings.

Bacalhoa a Portuguesa (Portuguese)

Portuguese Fish & Potatoes

Codfish is a favorite food of the Portuguese. It's like the faithful friend who never lets you down. It's been said that a girl's chances at marriage depend partly on her knowing at least 10 different codfish recipes!

1 lb	dried salt codfish fillets	500 g
1 Tbsp	olive oil	15 mL
2	onions, sliced	2
1	leek, sliced	1
1	clove garlic, minced	1
1 Tbsp	chopped fresh thyme (1 tsp/5 mL dried)	15 mL
¼ tsp	crushed fennel seeds	1 mL
1	can (19 oz/540 mL) tomatoes	1
	Freshly ground black pepper	
1 lb	potatoes (3)	500 g
	Chopped fresh parsley	

▪ In glass, enamel, or stainless steel bowl, soak codfish for about 12 hours, changing water twice. Drain and rinse well under running water. Remove skin and bones and cut fish into small pieces. Drain.

▪ In saucepan, cover codfish with cold water, and bring to boil. Cook for 10 minutes to remove more salt. Drain; rinse with cold water.

▪ In nonstick skillet, heat olive oil over medium heat. Cook onions, leek, garlic, and thyme for 6 minutes or until onions are golden. Add crushed fennel seeds, tomatoes, and codfish. Pour about 1 cup (250 mL) water over the fish to cover it by 1 inch (2.5 cm). Bring to boil. Reduce heat and simmer, uncovered, for 10 minutes or until fish is nearly tender. Season to taste with pepper.

▪ Cut potatoes into thick slices; add to skillet. Cook, covered, for 20 to 25 minutes or until both fish and potatoes are tender.

▪ Serve sprinkled with parsley.

Makes 4 servings.

EACH SERVING
¼ of recipe

2   Starch
3   Meat, very lean

272 calories
5 g total fat
0 g saturated fat
54 mg cholesterol
25 g protein
31 g carbohydrate
326 mg sodium
1275 mg potassium

GOOD
Iron, Vitamin C, Folate

EXCELLENT
Phosphorus, Magnesium, Vitamin D, Niacin, Vitamin B$_6$, Vitamin B$_{12}$

MODERATE
Fiber

Paella Valenciana (Spanish)
Spanish Paella

Most Spanish cooks will prepare this in the traditional large shallow two-handled pan, which, like the dish, is also called paella. My large skillet (with its cover) is put to use when I prepare this light version. Variations abound, but three ingredients are common and necessary: chicken, shellfish of some kind, and rice.

2 tsp	olive oil	10 mL
½ lb	raw shrimp, peeled, deveined, and cut in small pieces	250 g
12	small fresh clams	12
¼ lb	boneless, skinless chicken breast, cut into 1-inch (2.5-cm) pieces	125 g
¼ lb	cooked, smoked sausage, sliced	125 g
2	onions, chopped	2
1	clove garlic, minced	1
1	medium red sweet pepper, julienned	1
½ tsp	saffron threads, soaked in ¼ cup (50 mL) water	2 mL
1 Tbsp	sweet paprika	15 mL
1 Tbsp	chopped fresh rosemary or 1 tsp (5mL) dried	15 mL
1	can (19 oz/540 mL) tomatoes, drained	1
2 cups	chicken broth	500 mL
1 cup	short-grain (Arborio) rice	250 mL
1 cup	fresh or frozen peas	250 mL
1	lemon, cut in wedges	1

▪ In large nonstick skillet, heat oil over medium heat. Cook shrimp, clams, chicken, and sausage for 6 minutes or until lightly browned. Transfer to warm plate.

▪ Cook onions and garlic for 5 minutes or until onion is translucent. Stir in red pepper, saffron, paprika, and rosemary.

▪ Stir in tomatoes. Return shrimp and meat mixture to skillet. Cover with chicken broth. Sprinkle rice over all.

▪ Bring to boil, reduce heat, cover and simmer for 20 minutes or until rice is tender and liquid absorbed. Stir in peas. Cook for 3 minutes or until tender.

▪ Transfer to platter or plates. Garnish with lemon wedges.

Makes 4 servings.

EACH SERVING
¼ of recipe

4   Starch
3   Meat, lean

   500 calories
    13 g total fat
     3 g saturated fat
131 mg cholesterol
    35 g protein
    58 g carbohydrate
   5.5g fiber
1069 mg sodium ✥
937 mg potassium

GOOD
Thiamin, Riboflavin

EXCELLENT
Phosphorus, Iron, Zinc, Magnesium, Vitamin D, Vitamin A, Vitamin C, Niacin, Folate, Vitamin B$_6$, Vitamin B$_{12}$

HIGH
Fiber

Coquilles Saint-Jacques (French)

Scallops Gratinée with Mushrooms

Baked scallops show up in the cuisine of people from Mediterranean countries. Vieras guisadas, a Portuguese specialty, is similar to this one, except onions replace the mushrooms and pinches of ground cloves and nutmeg add spiciness. In Italian kitchens, scallops are broiled then drizzled with olive oil and minced garlic.

½ lb	mushrooms, quartered	250 g
¼ cup	white wine	50 mL
1 tsp	fresh thyme leaves	5 mL
	or ¼ tsp (1 mL) dried	
1 Tbsp	butter	15 mL
1	clove garlic	1
1 Tbsp	all-purpose flour	15 mL
¾ cup	1% milk	175 mL
¼ cup	grated Parmesan cheese	50 mL
¾ lb	bay scallops, rinsed	375 g
1 Tbsp	snipped chives	15 mL
¼ cup	dry breadcrumbs	50 mL
	Salt and freshly ground black pepper	

▪ In nonstick skillet over medium-high heat, stir-cook mushrooms in white wine. When liquid evaporates, stir in thyme. Set aside.

▪ In small saucepan, heat 2 tsp (10 mL) butter and garlic over medium heat. Whisk in flour until blended. Cook for 1 minute. Whisk in milk, and cook, whisking constantly, until sauce thickens. Stir in Parmesan cheese. Add mushrooms and scallops; cook for 4 minutes or until scallops are opaque. Stir in chives.

▪ Spoon into individual ovenproof serving dishes or shells.

▪ Combine breadcrumbs and remaining butter. Season to taste with salt and pepper. Sprinkle evenly on top of each serving. Place dishes on baking sheet.

▪ Broil for about 1 minute or until golden.

Makes 4 servings.

EACH SERVING
¼ of recipe

1   Starch
3   Meat, very lean
½   Fat

213 calories
6 g total fat
3 g saturated fat
41 mg cholesterol
20 g protein
14 g carbohydrate
356 mg sodium
535 mg potassium

GOOD
Calcium, Zinc

EXCELLENT
Phosphorus, Magnesium, Vitamin D, Riboflavin, Niacin, Vitamin B$_{12}$

Zheng Yu (Chinese)

Steamed Sea Bass

Nuttiness from the sesame oil, heat from the Oriental chili sauce, and a little acid from the vinegar complement the flavor of bass. Steaming it preserves its moist texture.

MARINADE

2 Tbsp	lite soy sauce	25 mL
2 tsp	sesame oil	10 mL
2 tsp	white wine vinegar	10 mL
½ tsp	hot Oriental chili paste	2 mL
½ lb	sea bass fillets, or swordfish, shark, or tuna	250 g
4	green onions, sliced	4
2 tsp	sesame seeds	10 mL

▪ In small bowl, combine soy sauce, sesame oil, wine vinegar, and chili paste.

▪ Cut bass into two pieces; rub each piece all over with soy sauce mixture, reserving any remaining marinade. Marinate for 15 minutes.

▪ Place fish in steamer basket. Sprinkle half of green onions over fish. Cover and steam for 20 minutes or until bass is opaque and just flakes when touched with a fork.

▪ In small skillet, toast sesame seeds over medium heat for 2 minutes or until golden. Remove from heat and quickly stir in remaining green onions and marinade.

▪ Transfer fish from steamer to plate; discard steamed green onions. Reheat sesame seed mixture; pour over fish.

Makes 2 servings.

TIMELY TIP
Line steamer basket with wet cheesecloth, overlapping edge, to prevent sticking and for easier removal of fish from steamer basket.

Pâté aux Patates et au Saumon
(French Canadian)

Salmon Potato Pie

When fish every Friday was the routine, this easy-to-make savory pie, featuring Canada's top quality canned salmon, became popular among French Canadian cooks.

	Light Sour Cream Pastry for one-crust (9-inch/23-cm) pie (recipe p. 162)	
3	potatoes, peeled and quartered	3
½ cup	1% milk	125 mL
	Salt and freshly ground black pepper	
2 tsp	butter	10 mL
1	onion, finely chopped	1
1½ tsp	chopped fresh summer savory or ½ tsp (2 mL) dried	7 mL
1	can (7½ oz/213 g) salmon, flaked	1
1 Tbsp	chopped fresh parsley	15 mL
¼ cup	dry breadcrumbs	50 mL
2 Tbsp	grated Parmesan cheese	25 mL

- Line 9-inch (23-cm) pie plate with pastry. Form rim around edge; crimp.

- In lightly salted boiling water, cook potatoes for about 20 minutes or until tender. Drain well. Add milk; mash until smooth. Season to taste with salt and pepper. Set aside.

- In nonstick skillet, heat butter over medium heat. Cook onions for 5 minutes or until translucent. Add savory; mix well. Stir into potatoes. Fold in salmon and parsley; mix well.

- Spoon into pastry shell, smoothing top.

- Mix together breadcrumbs and Parmesan cheese. Sprinkle evenly over top potato mixture.

- Bake in 400°F (200°C) oven for 25 minutes or until golden.

Makes 8 servings.

EACH SERVING
⅛ of recipe

1½ Starch
1   Meat, lean
½   Fat

197 calories
9 g total fat
2 g saturated fat
13 mg cholesterol
8 g protein
20 g carbohydrate
277 mg sodium
346 mg potassium

GOOD
Niacin

EXCELLENT
Phosphorus, Vitamin D, Vitamin B$_{12}$

Hoisin Salmon with Green Onion & Peas

Salmon is superb steamed. This Chinese method of cooking, also used for vegetables, dumplings, and poultry, is one of the healthiest. No added fat is called for in the preparation.

1 lb	fresh salmon fillets (whole or cut into 4)	500 mL
2 Tbsp	orange juice	25 mL
1 Tbsp	hoisin sauce	15 mL
2 tsp	each lite soy sauce and sesame oil	10 mL
2 tsp	each grated orange rind and ginger root	10 mL
½ tsp	Chinese five spice powder	2 mL
4	green onions	4
1⅓ cups	fresh or frozen green peas Orange twists*	325 mL

- Rinse salmon and pat dry.
- In shallow dish, whisk together orange juice, hoisin sauce, soy sauce, sesame oil, orange rind, ginger root, and five spice powder. Roll salmon in mixture to coat completely; marinate for 15 minutes.
- Arrange in cheesecloth-lined steamer basket.
- Cut green onions into 1-inch (2.5-cm) pieces. Sprinkle over salmon. Add peas to steamer. Sprinkle a little marinade over all.
- Place over boiling water. Cover and steam for 15 minutes or until fish just flakes when touched.
- Transfer to platter or dinner plates. Garnish with orange twists.

Makes 4 servings.

EACH SERVING
¼ of recipe

½ Starch
3 Meat, lean
½ Fat

236 calories
9 g total fat
1 g saturated fat
62 mg cholesterol
25 g protein
10 g carbohydrate
313 mg sodium
677 mg potassium

GOOD
Iron, Zinc, Magnesium, Thiamin, Vitamin C

EXCELLENT
Phosphorus, Riboflavin, Niacin, Folate, Vitamin B$_6$, Vitamin B$_{12}$

MODERATE
Fiber

*TIMELY TIP
To make orange twists, cut orange into thin slices. Make 1 cut from edge to center of orange. Twist 1 cut edge away from the other. Stand slice up on these edges.

Kedgeree (British/East Indian)

Kedgeree

This popular English breakfast and brunch dish originated in Britain by way of India, hence the touch of curry and cayenne pepper.

2	hard cooked eggs, separated	2
1 lb	smoked haddock or cod	500 g
2 tsp	butter	10 mL
1	onion, finely chopped	1
½ tsp	curry powder	2 mL
2 cups	hot cooked rice	500 mL
	Salt and cayenne pepper	
	Chopped fresh parsley	

▪ Chop egg whites. With fork, mash 1 yolk. Set aside. Discard second yolk.

▪ Place fish in single layer in skillet. Cover with cold water and bring to boil. Reduce heat, cover and poach for 10 minutes or until fish is opaque. Drain and break fish into chunks, discarding any bones and skin.

▪ In nonstick skillet, melt butter. Cook onion and curry powder for 5 minutes or until onion is translucent. Stir in chopped egg white and rice. Season to taste with salt and the amount of cayenne desired.

▪ Carefully fold in fish. Mound on serving platter. Sprinkle with egg yolk and parsley.

Makes 6 servings.

Patéis de Bacalhoa (Portuguese)

Codfish Cakes

Cod, fresh or dried, and potatoes—popular mainstays of the Portuguese diet—blend well in these savory patties. For an appetizer or a main course, serve them with Salsa Picante (recipe p. 160) or light mayonnaise perked up with a few dashes of hot pepper sauce, such as Portuguese piri piri.

1 lb	salt codfish fillets	500 g
3	potatoes (1 lb/500 g), peeled	3
2 tsp	olive oil	10 mL
1	onion, finely chopped	1
1	egg	1
2 Tbsp	minced red sweet pepper	25 mL
2 Tbsp	chopped fresh parsley	25 mL
	Freshly ground black pepper	
1 cup	dry breadcrumbs	250 mL

▪ In glass, enamel, or stainless steel bowl, cover fish with cold water. Soak for 24 hours, changing water 3 times at regular intervals. Drain.

▪ In saucepan, cover cod with fresh water; bring to boil. Reduce heat and simmer, uncovered, for 15 minutes or until tender. Drain well. When cool enough to handle, remove skin and bones. Coarsely shred cod into bowl.

▪ Meanwhile, in saucepan, in lightly salted boiling water, cook potatoes, cut in half, for 18 minutes or until tender. Drain. When cool enough to handle, coarsely shred. Stir into cod.

▪ In nonstick skillet, heat 1 tsp (5 mL) oil over medium heat. Cook onion for 5 minutes or until tender. Stir into cod mixture.

▪ Beat in egg until well blended. Stir in red pepper, parsley, and pepper to taste. Form into 12 small patties. (Mixture will be moist.) Roll in breadcrumbs to coat. Place on wire rack for 15 minutes to dry coating.

▪ In nonstick skillet, heat remaining oil over medium heat. Cook patties in batches for 2 to 3 minutes on each side or until golden brown.

Makes 12 servings.

Stamp and Go (Caribbean)

Jamaican Codfish Fritters

These fritters are take-out food for Jamaicans, just as fish and chips are take-out food for the British. The fat used in this homemade version is reduced to the bare minimum, making this an acceptable low-fat alternative.

½ lb	cod fillets	250 g
4 tsp	canola oil	20 mL
1	onion, chopped	1
½ cup	all-purpose flour	125 mL
¼ cup	whole-wheat flour	50 mL
1 tsp	baking powder	5 mL
½ tsp	salt	2 mL
¼ tsp	crushed red chili pepper flakes	1 mL
½ cup	1% milk	125 mL
1	egg	1
	Tartar Sauce (recipe below)	
	Lemon wedges	

- In steamer or in saucepan covered with simmering water, cover and cook fish for 5 to 7 minutes or until fish just flakes. Remove fish. Flake and set aside to cool.
- In nonstick skillet, heat 1 tsp (5 mL) oil over medium heat. Cook onion for 5 minutes or until tender.
- In bowl, combine all-purpose and whole-wheat flours, baking powder, salt, and chili pepper flakes.
- Whisk together milk and egg. Beat into flour mixture until smooth. Stir in fish and onions.
- In nonstick skillet used to cook onions, heat 1 tsp (5 mL) oil over medium-high heat.
- Drop fish batter, 1 Tbsp (15 mL) at a time, onto skillet. Cook until bubbles form on top; turn and cook for 2 minutes or until golden. Repeat with remaining fish batter, adding remaining oil, as required.
- Serve with Tartar Sauce and lemon wedges.

Makes 30 fritters, 6 servings.

Sauce Tartare (French)

Tartar Sauce

| ⅓ cup | light mayonnaise | 75 mL |
| ⅓ cup | sweet pickle relish | 75 mL |

- In small bowl, combine mayonnaise and relish; mix well. Spoon into small dish.

Makes 6 servings.

Sweet & Sour Fish

Stir-frying marinated nuggets of fish with the addition of very little fat is possible when a good quality nonstick skillet is used.

	Sweet & Sour Tomato Sauce (recipe below)	
1½ lbs	fish fillets (sea bass, halibut, cod)	750 g
2 tsp	rice vinegar	10 mL
1	egg white	1
2 tsp	oyster sauce or soy sauce	10 mL
2 tsp	grated fresh ginger root	10 mL
¼ tsp	hot Oriental chili paste	1 mL
2 Tbsp	cornstarch	25 mL
2 tsp	canola oil	10 mL
1	stalk celery, thinly sliced	1
½	green pepper, cut into ½-inch (1-cm) pieces	½

▪ Cut fish into 1-inch (2.5-cm) pieces. Set aside.

▪ In bowl, whisk together vinegar, egg white, oyster sauce, ginger root, and chili paste. Whisk in cornstarch until well blended. Add fish pieces. Stir to coat well.

▪ In large nonstick skillet or wok, heat oil over medium-high heat. Cook fish, about 8 pieces at a time, turning once or twice, for 5 minutes or until golden brown on all sides. Transfer to warm platter. Cook remaining fish. Add celery and green pepper to skillet. Stir-fry for 2 minutes or until tender-crisp. Stir in sauce until just heated through. Pour over fish.

Makes 6 servings.

Sweet & Sour Tomato Sauce

For a hotter sauce, stir in ¼ to ½ tsp (1 to 2 mL) hot Oriental chili paste.

½ cup	water	125 mL
¼ cup	each ketchup and rice vinegar	50 mL
1 tsp	sesame oil	5 mL
1 Tbsp	cornstarch	15 mL
	Sugar substitute equivalent to 2 Tbsp (25 mL) sugar	

▪ In saucepan, combine water, ketchup, vinegar, and sesame oil. Whisk in cornstarch until smooth. Bring to boil, stirring constantly, over medium heat for 2 minutes or until thickened. Remove from heat. Cool, and sweeten to taste with sugar substitute.

Makes 1 cup (250 mL).

EACH SERVING
⅙ of recipe

½   Starch
3   Meat, very lean

159   calories
3 g   total fat
0 g   saturated fat
53 mg   cholesterol
23 g   protein
9 g   carbohydrate
273 mg   sodium
561 mg   potassium

GOOD
Phosphorus, Magnesium, Vitamin B₆

EXCELLENT
Vitamin D, Niacin, Vitamin B₁₂

EACH SERVING
⅙ of recipe

1   Vegetable

27   calories
0 g   total fat
0 g   saturated fat
0 mg   cholesterol
0 g   protein
5 g   carbohydrate
134 mg   sodium
50 mg   potassium

Gan Shao Ming Xia (Chinese)

Shrimp with Tomato Sauce

Shrimp shows up as a specialty in many ethnic kitchens. The seasonings in the marinade and the sauce determine whether the recipe originated in a Chinese, Thai, or Portuguese kitchen.

1½ lb	raw shrimp, shelled and deveined	750 g
MARINADE		
2 Tbsp	cooking sherry	25 mL
1 Tbsp	grated fresh ginger root	15 mL
2 tsp	hoisin sauce	10 mL
1 tsp	sesame oil	5 mL
½ tsp	hot Oriental chili paste	2 mL
2	green onions, minced	2
1	clove garlic, minced	1
1 cup	Sweet & Sour Tomato Sauce (recipe p. 144)	250 mL

- Place shrimp in heavy plastic bag; set in bowl.
- Marinade: In small bowl, combine cooking sherry, ginger root, hoisin sauce, sesame oil, chili paste, green onions, and garlic; mix well. Pour over shrimp, secure bag well. Refrigerate for 4 hours or overnight. Allow to stand at room temperature for 30 minutes before cooking.
- In baking dish, arrange shrimp in single layer. Pour marinade over shrimp.
- Broil, about 4 inches (10 cm) from heat, for 5 minutes. Turn shrimp; broil for 2 to 3 minutes or until pink.
- Serve with sauce—hot or at room temperature.

Makes 6 servings.

VARIATIONS
Paad Priew Wan Goong (Thai)
Thai Shrimp

- Use the following for marinade: Combine 2 Tbsp (25 mL) each lime juice and white wine; ¼ cup (50 mL) chopped fresh or dry lemon grass; 1 Tbsp (15 mL) each chopped fresh ginger root and cilantro root; 1 clove garlic, minced; and 1 tsp (5 mL) hot Oriental chili paste. Serve with Lemon Cilantro Dipping Sauce (recipe p. 19).

EACH SERVING
⅙ of recipe

1	Vegetable
3	Meat, very lean
½	Fat

161 calories
3 g total fat
1 g saturated fat
172 mg cholesterol
24 g protein
7 g carbohydrate
380 mg sodium
268 mg potassium

GOOD
Phosphorus, Iron, Magnesium

EXCELLENT
Vitamin D, Niacin, Vitamin B$_{12}$

Calculations approximately the same as above.

Abura-yakidofu (Japanese)

Tofu, Shrimp, & Vegetable Patties

Just a bit of shrimp flavors the tofu to make these tasty pancake-like patties.

4	dried Chinese mushrooms	4
1 cup	crumbled firm tofu	250 mL
¼ lb	raw shrimp, peeled, deveined, and finely chopped	125 g
2	green onions, thinly sliced	2
1	carrot, shredded	1
⅓ cup	chopped water chestnuts	75 mL
¼ cup	finely chopped green sweet pepper	50 mL
2	egg whites	2
1 tsp	lite soy sauce	5 mL
1 tsp	rice vinegar	5 mL
1 tsp	sesame oil	5 mL
2 Tbsp	cornstarch	25 mL
2 tsp	canola oil	10 mL
	Wasabi (Japanese horseradish)	

- In bowl, cover mushrooms with hot water; soak for 10 minutes or until soft. Drain; remove and discard stems, and finely chop caps. Set aside.
- In bowl, combine tofu, shrimp, green onions, carrot, water chestnuts, sweet pepper, and chopped mushrooms.
- Whisk together egg white, soy sauce, vinegar, and sesame oil; whisk in cornstarch until smooth. Stir into shrimp/vegetable mixture until well mixed.
- In large nonstick skillet, heat oil over medium-high heat.
- Divide tofu mixture into 8 portions. Spoon each portion into skillet, and form into flat patty. Cook for 4 minutes on each side or until golden brown.
- Serve patties hot, with Wasabi for dipping, remembering that even a tiny bit is fiery hot.

Makes 8 servings.

Psari Plaki (Middle Eastern)

Baked Fish Aegean-Style

Like so many fish dishes, this one originated with people who lived by the sea, in this case the Aegean. To make it more Italian, omit the cumin, replace the black olives with green ones, and add a couple teaspoonful of capers.

1 lb	fish fillets (perch, flounder, halibut)	500 g
1 Tbsp	dry breadcrumbs	15 mL
2 Tbsp	lemon juice	25 mL
¼ cup	tomato paste	50 mL
¼ cup	water	50 mL
2 tsp	extra virgin olive oil	10 mL
1	clove garlic, minced	1
1½ tsp	chopped fresh herbs, such as oregano, thyme, rosemary, dill, and cilantro, or ½ tsp (2 mL) dried	7 mL
½ tsp	ground cumin	2 mL
¼ tsp	crushed red chili pepper flakes	1 mL
	Salt and freshly ground black pepper	
4	black pitted olives, sliced	4
	Lemon wedges	

▪ Pat fish dry with paper towels.

▪ Sprinkle 8-inch (20-cm) square baking dish with breadcrumbs. Arrange fish in single layer on top. Sprinkle with lemon juice.

▪ In bowl, combine tomato paste, water, olive oil, garlic, herbs, cumin, and chili pepper flakes. Season to taste with salt and pepper. Pour over fish.

▪ Bake, uncovered, in 400°F (200°C) oven for 20 minutes or until fish just flakes when touched with fork.

▪ Spoon pan juice over fish. Garnish with olive slices and lemon wedges.

Makes 4 servings.

VARIATIONS

Bacalhoa al Ajo Arriero (Portuguese)
Portuguese Baked Fish

▪ In place of tomato paste mixture, sprinkle fish with ½ tsp (2 mL) paprika and top with 1 sliced green pepper, 1 sliced tomato, 1 sliced small onion, and 1 minced clove garlic. Drizzle with 2 tsp (10 mL) extra virgin olive oil and season to taste with salt and pepper. Garnish with lemon slices.

EACH SERVING
¼ of recipe

1   Vegetable
3   Meat, very lean
1   Fat

184 calories
7 g total fat
1 g saturated fat
77 mg cholesterol
22 g protein
7 g carbohydrate
169 mg sodium
546 mg potassium

GOOD
Phosphorus, Iron, Magnesium

EXCELLENT
Niacin, Vitamin B$_{12}$

Calculations approximately the same as above.

Stuffed Fish (Canadian)

Stuffed Fish

Russian, Ukrainian, and other cooks whose families originated in Eastern Europe bake stuffed fish similar to this for celebrations, such as Christmas Eve, during which a meatless meal is the custom.

| 1 | whole fish—sea bass, whitefish, pickerel, or salmon (3 lb/1.5 kg) | 1 |

STUFFING

1 Tbsp	butter	15 mL
1	onion, chopped	1
1 cup	finely chopped celery	250 mL
1½ cup	dry breadcrumbs	375 mL
1 tsp	ground sage	5 mL
½ tsp	dried savory	2 mL
¼ tsp	dried thyme	1 mL
	Salt and freshly ground black pepper	
	Lemon wedges and red sweet pepper slivers	
	Fresh parsley	

▪ Scale and clean fish. Rinse well and pat dry.

▪ In large nonstick skillet, heat butter over medium heat. Cook onion and celery for 5 minutes or until translucent.

▪ Stir in 1¼ cup (300 mL) breadcrumbs, sage, savory, and thyme. Season to taste with salt and pepper. Moisten with ¼ to ½ cup (50 to 125 mL) water.

▪ Stuff fish and loosely sew up opening. Brush outside lightly with a little butter. Sprinkle with remaining ¼ cup (50 mL) breadcrumbs. Place on rack in shallow roasting pan.

▪ Bake in 400°F (200°C) oven for 10 minutes per inch (2.5 cm) of thickness (measured at the thickest point).

▪ Serve on hot platter, garnished with lemon wedges, red pepper slivers, and parsley.

Makes 10 servings.

*Stuffed Fish,
Pyrohy*

Vegetables

Peperonata - *Italian*

Parmigiana di Broccoli - *Italian*

Cavolfiore alla Milanese - *Italian*

Creamed Greens - *Canadian Aboriginal*

Horta - *Greek*

Feijao Verde Guizado - *Portuguese*

Courgettes à la Provençale - *French*

Ratatouille - *French*

Imam Bayeldi - *Middle Eastern*

Chinese Stir-Fried Vegetables - *Chinese*

Sesame Snow Peas & Bean Sprouts - *Japanese*

Grilled Vegetables - *Italian /Canadian*

Tzimmes - *Jewish*

Oven-Crisp Chips - *American/Canadian*

Gratin Dauphinois - *French*

Jansson's Temptation - *Scandinavian*

Raita - *East Indian*

Salsa Picante - *Mexican*

*Peperonata
(Roasted Peppers,
Onions, and Tomatoes),
Parmigiana de Broccoli*

Roasted Peppers, Onions, & Tomatoes

EACH SERVING
⅙ of recipe

2 Vegetable
½ Fat

 65 calories
 2 g total fat
 0 g saturated fat
 0 mg cholesterol
 2 g protein
 11 g carbohydrate
154 mg sodium
408 mg potassium

EXCELLENT
Vitamin A, Vitamin C

MODERATE
Fiber

There are about as many versions of this dish as there are Italian cooks. Green peppers are included in some; fewer or more onions and tomatoes may be used, and some have capers, olives, and/or anchovies added. Peperonata is good hot or cold, particularly for lunch with crusty Italian bread or as a sandwich filling, or as antipasto or a side dish with pasta, risotto, or with meat, fish, or poultry entrées.

2	red sweet peppers	2
2	yellow sweet peppers	2
2 tsp	olive oil	10 mL
2	onions, sliced	2
2	ripe tomatoes, seeded and chopped or 1 can (19 oz/540 mL) tomatoes	2
1 tsp	red wine vinegar	5 mL
¼ cup	chopped fresh basil or 1 Tbsp (15 mL) dried	50 mL
	Salt and freshly ground black pepper	

▪ To roast peppers, place them on grill over hot coals. Turn frequently until skins become blackened and blistered. (Alternatively, spear peppers with fork and toast over gas flame or broil under oven broiler.) Set aside under clean, dry tea towel until cool enough to handle. Cut in half and drain liquid. Discard seeds and stems. With fingers, rub, peel, and discard skin. Cut lengthwise into strips. Set aside.

▪ In large nonstick skillet, heat oil over medium heat. Cook onions for 4 minutes or until soft. Add tomatoes and vinegar. Bring to boil. Reduce heat and simmer for 10 minutes. Add basil and peppers; mix well. Season to taste with salt and pepper.

▪ Cover and simmer for 4 minutes, or until peppers are just tender.

▪ Serve hot or at room temperature.

Makes 6 servings.

Parmigiana di Broccoli (Italian)

Steamed Broccoli with Parmesan

Steaming vegetables brings out their true flavor, and, happily, no added fat is necessary for the cooking process. All vegetables lend themselves to this method of cooking. Using an automatic electrical steamer certainly helps control the steaming time and takes the guesswork out of the job.

4 cups	broccoli florets	1 L
2 tsp	grated lemon rind	10 mL
1	small clove garlic, minced	1
	Salt and freshly ground black pepper	
2 Tbsp	freshly grated Parmesan cheese	25 mL

▪ Arrange broccoli in steamer basket. Sprinkle with lemon rind and garlic.

▪ Place steamer basket over base of steamer with water as recommended in manufacturer's directions, or over pan of boiling water.

▪ Cover and steam for 8 to 10 minutes or until tender-crisp and still bright green. Season to taste with salt and pepper.

▪ Serve immediately, sprinkled with Parmesan cheese.

Makes 4 servings.

VARIATION

Cavolfiore alla Milanese (Italian)

Cauliflower Milanese

▪ Substitute cauliflower for broccoli. After sprinkling with Parmesan cheese, garnish with sprinkling of chopped fresh parsley.

EACH SERVING
¼ of recipe

1 **Vegetable**

  37 **calories**
  1 g **total fat**
  0 g **saturated fat**
  1 mg **cholesterol**
  3 g **protein**
  5 g **carbohydrate**
 70 mg **sodium**
263 mg **potassium**

EXCELLENT
Vitamin C, Folate

MODERATE
Fiber

Calculations approximately the same as above.

Creamed Greens

Spring is the best time to forage for wild greens. That is when they are the most succulent and tender. Wild greens and other leafy green vegetables are best when they are steamed until just limp. Cooking them in boiling water makes them more watery and not nearly as palatable as when they are steamed. And they also won't have the same affinity for a light cream sauce.

6 cups	watercress, dandelion, nettle, or lamb's quarters leaves	1.5 L
1 Tbsp	butter or canola oil	15 mL
1 Tbsp	all-purpose flour	15 mL
½ tsp	salt	2 mL
¼ tsp	white pepper	1 mL
¼ tsp	ground nutmeg	1 mL
1 cup	1% milk	250 mL

▪ In steamer or saucepan, with only the rinse water clinging to greens, steam or cook greens for 5 minutes or until partly wilted; drain.

▪ In saucepan, melt butter over medium-low heat. Stir in flour, salt, pepper, and nutmeg until smooth. Slowly add milk, stirring constantly, for 2 minutes or until sauce is thick and smooth.

▪ Chop drained greens. Stir into sauce; cook only until heated through.

Makes 4 servings.

Sidebar

EACH SERVING
¼ **of recipe**

2   Vegetable
½   Fat

80 calories
3 g total fat
2 g saturated fat
10 mg cholesterol
3 g protein
8 g carbohydrate
295 mg sodium
314 mg potassium

GOOD
Calcium, Vitamin C

EXCELLENT
Vitamin A

MODERATE
Fiber

Calculations approximately the same as above.

Variation

VARIATION
Horta (Greek)
Spinach with Lemon

For Greek families, horta means greens, and they eat lots of them. Greek markets are known for their great assortment of both wild and cultivated greens. Spinach is mild compared to the bitter and sour mustard, kale, or dandelion greens. Some cooks mix them to come up with the taste they prefer for combinations like this or for fillings for their cheese-and-greens phyllo squares, spanakopita, or horopita.

▪ Substitute extra virgin olive oil for butter, and then add 1 Tbsp (15 mL) fresh lemon juice to sauce.

Feijao Verde Guizado (Portuguese)

Green Beans in Tomato Sauce

This dish is great with fish, which is always popular and important in the food plans of Portuguese families. Be careful not to overcook the beans; once they change from a lovely fresh green color to a dull yellowy green, they are past the point of no return.

1 lb	green beans	500 g
1 Tbsp	olive oil	15 mL
2	onions, finely chopped	2
1	clove garlic, minced	1
1	can (19 oz/540 mL) tomatoes	1
	Salt and freshly ground black pepper	

■ Cut beans into 1½-inch (4-cm) pieces.

■ In saucepan, heat oil over medium heat. Cook onions and garlic for about 5 minutes or until onion is translucent.

■ Quickly stir in green beans. Pour tomatoes over all, breaking up large pieces with a fork. Bring to boil.

■ Reduce heat and simmer for about 10 minutes or until beans are just tender.

■ Season to taste with salt and pepper.

Makes 6 servings.

VARIATION

Courgettes à la Provençale (French)
Zucchini in Tomato Sauce

Count on this green and red vegetable medley to add a splash of color and a burst of flavor to a plate of food that may otherwise seem monochromatic and plain, such as poached chicken with steamed rice.

■ Substitute 4 sliced zucchini for beans and add 1½ tsp (7 mL) chopped fresh thyme leaves or ½ tsp (2 mL) dried with the tomatoes.

EACH SERVING
⅙ of recipe

2   Vegetable
½   Fat

69 calories
2 g total fat
0 g saturated fat
0 mg cholesterol
2 g protein
11 g carbohydrate
153 mg sodium
353 mg potassium

GOOD
Folate

MODERATE
Fiber

Calculations approximately the same as above.

Ratatouille (French)

Vegetable Medley

This dish from Provence is made from a wonderful assortment of vegetables that may vary according to what is available or what the cook selects. I always expect eggplant, tomatoes, zucchini, onions, and garlic to be included, so I find the best time to make it is when summer's vegetables are at their prime and can be picked up fresh at farmer's markets.

1 Tbsp	olive oil	15 mL
2	onions, coarsely chopped	2
2	cloves garlic, minced	2
2	zucchini, cut in ¼-inch (5-mm) slices	2
1	medium eggplant, cubed	1
1	green sweet pepper, seeded and diced	1
¼ lb	mushrooms, quartered (about 12)	125 g
1	bay leaf	1
1 Tbsp	chopped fresh basil or	15 mL
	1 tsp (5 mL) dried	
1 tsp	granulated sugar	5 mL
½ tsp	crumbled dried thyme	2 mL
3	tomatoes, peeled and quartered	3
	or 1 can (19 oz/540 mL) tomatoes	
2 Tbsp	capers	25 mL
	Salt and freshly ground black pepper	
2 Tbsp	freshly grated Parmesan cheese	25 mL
	Chopped fresh parsley	

- In large nonstick skillet, heat oil over medium heat. Cook onions and garlic for 4 minutes or until just tender.

- Add zucchini, eggplant, green pepper, mushrooms, bay leaf, basil, sugar, and thyme. Cook over medium heat, stirring occasionally, for 10 minutes or until some moisture evaporates.

- Stir in tomatoes. Simmer, stirring occasionally, for about 30 minutes or until eggplant is tender and mixture is thickened. Stir in capers, if desired. Season to taste with salt and freshly ground black pepper. Discard bay leaf.

- Sprinkle with Parmesan cheese and parsley.

Makes 8 servings.

Imam Bayeldi (Middle Eastern)

Swooning Priest

Apparently, this dish owes its name to a Muslim priest, a great gourmet, who was so overcome by its delicious smell that he fainted. But, some think it was the power of the garlic that affected him. It's been toned down for this version.

2	eggplants (1 lb/500 g each)	2
2 tsp	olive oil	10 mL
2	onions, chopped	2
2 to 3	cloves garlic	2 to 3
1	can (19 oz/540 mL) tomatoes, drained	1
½ cup	chopped fresh parsley	125 mL
½ tsp	paprika	2 mL
¼ tsp	ground cinnamon	1 mL
2 tsp	lemon juice	10 mL
	Salt and freshly ground black pepper	
1 Tbsp	raisins	15 mL
½ cup	hot water	125 mL
1 Tbsp	finely chopped hazelnuts or almonds	15 mL

▪ Cut each eggplant into quarters lengthwise. On the cut side of each quarter, make 2 long slashes. Sprinkle with salt. Let stand for 20 minutes.

▪ Meanwhile, in nonstick skillet, heat oil over medium heat. Cook onions and garlic for 5 minutes or until tender. Stir in tomatoes, breaking into pieces with fork, ¼ cup (50 mL) parsley, paprika, and cinnamon. Cook for 2 minutes. Stir in lemon juice. Season to taste with salt and pepper.

▪ Rinse eggplant; drain and dry well. Arrange skin side down, in baking pan. Fill slashes with half tomato mixture. Stir raisins and water into remaining tomato mixture. Spread over eggplants. Sprinkle with nuts. Cover.

▪ Bake in 350°F (180°C) oven for 30 minutes. Remove cover and bake for 15 minutes or until tender.

▪ Serve warm or cool sprinkled with remaining parsley.

Makes 4 servings.

EACH SERVING
¼ of recipe

1 Starch
2 Vegetable
½ Fat

147 calories
3 g total fat
0 g saturated fat
0 mg cholesterol
5 g protein
28 g carbohydrate
237 mg sodium
887 mg potassium

GOOD
Iron, Magnesium,
Vitamin C, Vitamin B$_6$

EXCELLENT
Folate

VERY HIGH
Fiber

Chinese Stir-Fried Vegetables

The Oriental technique of stir-frying quickly cooks vegetables, keeping them brightly colored, full of flavor, tender-crisp, and vitamin-rich.

SAUCE

2 Tbsp	cold water	25 mL
1 Tbsp	cooking sherry	15 mL
2 tsp	lite soy sauce	10 mL
1 tsp	cornstarch	5 mL

VEGETABLES

1 tsp	butter	5 mL
1 tsp	olive oil	5 mL
1	onion, coarsely chopped	1
2	stalks celery, diagonally sliced	2
1 cup	fresh cauliflower florets (½ lb/250 g)	250 mL
1 cup	fresh broccoli florets (⅓ lb/175 g)	250 mL
½ cup	chicken broth or water	125 mL
2 Tbsp	finely chopped red sweet pepper or fresh parsley	25 mL
	Salt and freshly ground black pepper	

▪ Sauce: In small dish or cup, combine water, sherry, soy sauce, and cornstarch; mix well.

▪ Vegetables: In large nonstick skillet or wok, heat butter and olive oil over medium-high heat. Stir-fry onion and celery for 4 minutes. Add cauliflower and broccoli; stir-fry for 4 minutes longer. Stir in broth, cover, and steam for 1 minute.

▪ Push vegetables to one side. Stir sauce mixture into pan juices. Cook, stirring, for 1 minute or until thickened. Fold into vegetables to lightly coat them. Stir in red pepper. Season to taste with salt and pepper.

▪ Serve immediately.

Makes 6 servings.

More Stir-fry Combinations

▪ Celery, onion, Bok choy or cabbage, red sweet pepper
▪ Celery, onion, zucchini, mushrooms, red sweet pepper

For taste variations, add one or more of the following:

▪ 1 clove garlic, minced
▪ 1 Tbsp (15 mL) grated fresh ginger root
▪ 1 Tbsp (15 mL) shredded lemon or orange rind
▪ a few grains cayenne or crushed red chili peppers

EACH SERVING
⅙ of recipe

1   Vegetable
½   Fat

42 calories
2 g total fat
0 g saturated fat
1 mg cholesterol
2 g protein
5 g carbohydrate
146 mg sodium
269 mg potassium

GOOD
Folate

EXCELLENT
Vitamin C

Sesame Snow Peas & Bean Sprouts (Japanese)

Sesame Snow Peas & Bean Sprouts

Since stir-frying is quick cooking, it is prudent to prepare everything ahead—trim and cut the vegetables and premeasure the other ingredients.

½ lb	snow peas	250 g
½ lb	bean sprouts	250 g
2	green onions	2
1 tsp	canola oil	5 mL
1 tsp	sesame oil	5 mL
2 tsp	grated fresh ginger root	10 mL
1 tsp	sesame seeds	5 mL

▪ Cut snow peas into julienne strips. Trim bean sprouts. Cut green onions into 2-inch (5-cm) lengths, then into julienne strips.

▪ In nonstick skillet, heat oils and ginger root over medium-high heat. Stir-fry snow peas, bean sprouts, and green onions for 2 minutes. Add sesame seeds. Stir-fry for 1 to 2 minutes or until tender-crisp.

Makes 6 servings.

Grilled Vegetables (Italian/Canadian)

Grilled Vegetables

Mix and match vegetables for grilling. The only caution is to make sure the vegetables and/or pieces are big enough that they will not fall through the grill.

The following vegetables are high in fiber, vitamins, and minerals but low in calories, which makes them ideal for grilling: Asparagus, broccoli, celery, cauliflower, cucumber, green onions, red, green, and yellow sweet peppers, mushrooms, snow peas, and zucchini.

Moderate amounts fit easily into the meal plans of individuals with diabetes.

To ensure vegetables stay moist, blanch asparagus, broccoli, and green onions before grilling; leave skin on zucchini, cucumbers, and mushrooms; start with crisp celery, fennel, green, red, and yellow peppers, and snow peas.

▪ To grill: Arrange vegetables on lightly greased grill or shallow foil baking dish. Cook over medium-hot coals or medium setting, turning once or twice and brushing with a mixture of water and lemon juice, for 10 to 15 minutes (depending on vegetable) or until lightly browned and tender but still firm.

EACH SERVING
⅛ of recipe

1   Vegetable

    37 calories
    0 g total fat
    0 g saturated fat
    0 mg cholesterol
    0 g protein
    7 g carbohydrate
   17 mg sodium
  152 mg potassium

EXCELLENT
Vitamin A

Tzimmes (Jewish)

Carrot, Beet, & Apple Medley

When we tested this combination, cooking carrots and beets together seemed unusual. But the flavorful and rather sweet-tasting result won my praise. Now tzimmes joins the others in my file of favorite veggie dishes.

1 tsp	olive oil	5 mL
2	onions, thickly sliced	2
3	carrots, sliced	3
3	beets, cooked and sliced	3
1	apple, shredded	1
1 cup	water	250 mL

▪ In nonstick skillet, heat oil. Cook onion for 5 minutes or until translucent. Add carrots, and cook for 5 minutes.

▪ Add beets, apple, and water. Bring to boil. Reduce heat, cover and simmer for 30 minutes or until tender.

Makes 8 servings.

EACH SERVING
¼ of recipe

1   Starch

    86 calories
    2 g total fat
    0 g saturated fat
    0 mg cholesterol
    1 g protein
   15 g carbohydrate
  198 mg sodium
  415 mg potassium

Oven-Crisp Chips (American/Canadian)

Oven-Crisp Chips

This recipe proves that very little fat is required to give potatoes a crisp finish. These potatoes sometimes puff, making them similar to French souffled potatoes. For garlic-scented ones, cut a garlic clove in half and rub it in the pan before adding the oil.

3	potatoes (1 lb/500 g)	3
2 tsp	canola oil	10 mL
	Salt	
	Paprika	

▪ Peel potatoes; cut into ½-inch (1-cm) slices, or lengthwise into ½-inch (1-cm) thick sticks.

▪ Soak in ice water for 10 minutes. Drain and thoroughly pat dry. Place in dry bowl. Drizzle oil over top, and, with hands, rub oil all over potato pieces.

▪ Arrange in single layer on nonstick jelly roll pan or baking sheet.

▪ Bake, turning occasionally, in 425°F (210°C) oven for 30 to 35 minutes or until golden brown. Sprinkle to taste with salt and paprika.

Makes 4 servings.

Gratin Dauphinois (French)
Potatoes with Goat Cheese

For French cooks, this qualifies as a gratin, because the sprinkling of Parmesan cheese forms a golden crust on top of the potatoes.

5	potatoes, scrubbed	5
1	clove garlic, halved	1
1	onion, thinly sliced	1
2 tsp	butter, melted	10 mL
	Salt and freshly ground black pepper	
¼ cup	crumbled goat cheese	50 mL
½ cup	skim milk	125 mL
2 Tbsp	shredded Parmesan cheese	25 mL

▪ Microwave potatoes on high for 10 minutes. Cool under cold running water. Peel and slice.

▪ Rub 8-inch (20-cm) square or round baking dish or casserole with cut sides of garlic; discard garlic.

▪ Arrange half potato and onion slices in dish. Drizzle with half the butter. Sprinkle with salt and pepper. Top with half goat cheese. Repeat layers.

▪ Bring milk to a boil. Pour over potato mixture. Sprinkle with Parmesan cheese.

▪ Bake, uncovered, in 400°F (200°C) oven for 20 minutes or until top is crusty and golden brown.

Makes 6 servings.

VARIATION
Jansson's Temptation (Scandinavian)
Potatoes with Anchovies

This classic potato casserole is usually one of the hot dishes served at an authentic Swedish smorgasbord.

▪ Substitute 2 anchovy fillets for goat and Parmesan cheeses. Rub 1 tsp (5 mL) butter into 2 Tbsp (25 mL) dry bread-crumbs and sprinkle over potatoes.

Makes 6 servings.

EACH SERVING
⅙ of recipe

½ Starch
½ Fat

66 calories
3 g total fat
2 g saturated fat
11 mg cholesterol
3 g protein
6 g carbohydrate
134 mg sodium
169 mg potassium

EACH SERVING
⅙ of recipe

½ Starch

42 calories
1 g total fat
0 g saturated fat
4 mg cholesterol
1 g protein
6 g carbohydrate
30 mg sodium
141 mg potassium

Raita (East Indian)

Cucumber Yogurt Sauce

Serve this refreshing East Indian relish or salad with lively curry dishes. It cools the palate and complements the spicy fare.

1	English cucumber, unpeeled	1
1	onion, finely chopped	1
1½ cups	low-fat yogurt	375 mL
½ tsp	salt	2 mL
½ tsp	ground cumin	2 mL
Pinch	each cayenne and white pepper	Pinch

▪ Cut cucumbers in half lengthwise. Discard seedy center. Finely chop or coarsely grate cucumbers into bowl. Stir in onion, yogurt, salt, cumin, cayenne, and white pepper until well mixed.

▪ Cover and chill for at least 2 hours before serving.

Makes 3 cups (750 mL), 6 servings.

Salsa Picante (Mexican)

Salsa Picante

For the Mexican cook, sauces came from the Spanish cuisine and were also part of the Indian kitchen. Today, there are many brands of commercial salsa, but still, Mexican cooks have their la salsa de la casa—their own homemade tomato sauce. The sauce adds additional flavor and often the fire to Mexican foods.

2	tomatoes, peeled, chopped, and drained	2
1	small onion, finely chopped	1
1	jalapeno pepper, seeded and chopped or 1 Tbsp (15 mL) chopped pickled jalapeno	1
1	clove garlic, minced	1
½	green sweet pepper, seeded and chopped	½
2 tsp	lime juice	10 mL
¼ cup	chopped fresh cilantro or 1 Tbsp (15 mL) dried Salt	50 mL

▪ In bowl, combine tomatoes, onion, jalapeno pepper, garlic, green pepper, lime juice, and cilantro; mix well. Season to taste with salt.

▪ Let stand for 2 hours to blend flavors.

▪ Serve at room temperature.

Makes 2 cups (500 mL), 10 servings.

Breads, Cookies, & Cakes

Bannock - *Canadian Aboriginal*

Sour Cream Pastry - *Middle European*

Irish Soda Bread - *British*

Cream Tea Scones - *British*

Oatcakes - *British*

Oatcake Cookies - *British*

Drop Biscuits - *Canadian/American*

Broa - *Portuguese*

Pizza - *Italian*

Focaccia - *Italian*

Pumpernickel - *German*

Naan - *East Indian*

Biscotti - *Italian*

Biscotti All'Anise - *Italian*

Amaretti - *Italian*

Xing Ren Bing - *Chinese*

Bolo de Leite & Cupcakes - *Portuguese*

Lemon Chiffon Cake - *American/Canadian*

Chocolate Chiffon Cake - *American/Canadian*

Lemon Butter/Lemon Cream - *British*

Bûche de Noël - *French Canadian*

Chocolate Angel Food Cake - *American/Canadian*

Schwarzwalder Kirschtorte - *German*

Swiss Roll - *British*

Raspberry Ribbon Cake - *British*

Bannock (Canadian Aboriginal)

Bannock

As soon as flour became available to Canada's natives, they started to make bannock, just as the first fur traders and buffalo hunters did. Now, we think of the quick bread as traditional Canadian aboriginal bread.

1¾ cups	all-purpose flour	425 mL
2 Tbsp	baking powder	25 mL
1 tsp	salt	5 mL
1 cup	water	250 mL
1 Tbsp	melted butter or canola oil	15 mL

▪ In bowl, combine flour, baking powder, and salt; mix until well blended.

▪ In measuring cup, whisk together water and melted butter. Stir into flour mixture until just mixed.

▪ Turn out onto lightly floured surface. Knead 12 to 15 times until dough feels fairly smooth.

▪ Pat out roll into ½-inch (1-cm) thick round shape; cut into 8 wedges. Place on lightly buttered nonstick baking sheet. Or, alternatively, pat into lightly buttered 9-inch (23-cm) square or round nonstick baking pan.

▪ Bake in 350°F (180°C) oven for 20 minutes or until golden.

Makes 8 servings.

EACH SERVING
1 biscuit

1½ Starch

117 calories
1 g total fat
0 g saturated fat
0 mg cholesterol
2 g protein
21 g carbohydrate
488 mg sodium ✴
32 mg potassium

Sour Cream Pastry (Middle European)

Light Sour Cream Pastry

Ukrainian and Russian cooks seem to have a magic touch with this type of pastry.

2 cups	all-purpose flour	500 mL
1 tsp	salt	5 mL
½ cup	vegetable shortening	125 mL
¾ cup	1% sour cream or yogurt	175 mL

▪ In food processor, combine flour and salt. Add shortening. With on/off pulses, cut in shortening until coarse crumbs form. Add sour cream, and process until ball of dough forms. Or, alternatively, in bowl, combine flour and salt. With pastry blender, cut in shortening, then stir in sour cream until well mixed.

▪ Shape dough into even cylinder. Cut evenly into thirds. Form into 3 flattened balls.

▪ Use 1 ball for single crust 9-inch (23-cm) pie shell. Use 2 balls for double crust 9-inch (23-cm) pie crust.

Makes 3 single 9-inch (23-cm) pie crusts, 8 servings each.

EACH SERVING
1/24 of recipe

½   Starch
1   Fat

80 calories
4 g total fat
1 g saturated fat
0 mg cholesterol
1 g protein
8 g carbohydrate
102 mg sodium
26 mg potassium

Irish Soda Bread (British)

Irish Soda Bread

Irish soda bread is a quick bread rather than a yeast bread, making it quick and easy to make. It is rugged and grainy, perfect as the bread to go with meal-size salads, soups, and stews.

1 cup	all-purpose flour	250 mL
1 cup	whole-wheat flour	250 mL
1 tsp	baking powder	5 mL
1 tsp	baking soda	5 mL
2 tsp	granulated sugar	10 mL
½ tsp	salt	2 mL
2 Tbsp	butter	25 mL
1 cup	sour milk* or buttermilk	250 mL

▪ In mixing bowl, combine flours, baking powder, baking soda, sugar, and salt.

▪ With pastry blender or 2 knives, cut in butter until mixture resembles fine crumbs.

▪ Stir in sour milk, all at once, to make a soft dough (a little sticky).

▪ Turn out onto lightly floured surface. Knead about 10 times. Form into ball. Place on nonstick baking sheet. Flatten into 3-inch (7.5-cm) thick round. With sharp knife, cut large "X" about ¼ inch (5 mm) deep in top of dough.

▪ Bake in 375°F (190°C) oven for about 40 minutes or until golden brown.

Makes 1 large loaf, 12 pieces.

EACH SERVING
¹⁄₁₂ of recipe

1   Starch
½   Fat

    96 calories
     2 g total fat
     1 g saturated fat
     4 mg cholesterol
     3 g protein
    16 g carbohydrate
   215 mg sodium
    75 mg potassium

*TIMELY TIP
To make sour milk: Measure 1 Tbsp (15 mL) vinegar into a 1-cup (250-mL) measure then add milk to make 1 cup (250 mL).

Cream Tea Scones (British)
Cream Tea Scones

Scottish cooks take pride in their scones. Their ancestors, from before the days of the kitchen stove (with its oven), cooked them on a griddle pan over the hot embers of a fire.

2 cups	all-purpose flour	500 mL
1 tsp	granulated sugar	5 mL
1 Tbsp	baking powder	15 mL
½ tsp	baking soda	2 mL
½ tsp	salt	2 mL
¼ cup	cold butter	50 mL
½ cup	currants or dried cranberries	125 mL
1	egg	1
⅔ cup	low-fat sour cream	150 mL
GLAZE		
1 Tbsp	low-fat sour cream	15 mL
1 Tbsp	orange juice	15 mL

- In mixing bowl, combine flour, sugar, baking powder, baking soda, and salt.
- With pastry blender or 2 knives, cut in butter until mixture is crumbly. Stir in currants.
- In another bowl, beat egg lightly with sour cream; pour over crumbly mixture. With fork, quickly stir to make a soft dough. Form into a ball.
- Turn out onto floured surface. Dust lightly with flour. Knead 10 to 12 times. With floured rolling pin, roll out to ¾-inch (1-cm) thickness. With floured 2- to 2½-inch (5- to 6-cm) round cookie cutter, cut out 12 biscuits. Place on nonstick baking sheet.
- Glaze: Whisk together sour cream and orange juice. Brush onto tops of biscuits.
- Bake in 425°F (210°C) oven for about 15 minutes or until lightly browned.

Makes 12 biscuits.

EACH SERVING
1 scone

1½ Starch
½ Fat

150 calories
5 g total fat
2 g saturated fat
32 mg cholesterol
3 g protein
22 g carbohydrate
202 mg sodium
88 mg potassium

Oatcakes (British)

Scottish Oatcakes

*Traditional Scottish oatcakes were made from oatmeal only,
since oats grew better than wheat in Scotland. Originally,
they were also "baked" on a griddle pan. This variation,
made with half oatmeal and half wheat flour, can be rolled
thin to make crisp cakes that are more like crunchy crackers
than cookies.*

1 cup	quick-cooking oats	250 mL
1 cup	all-purpose flour	250 mL
½ tsp	baking soda	2 mL
¼ tsp	salt	1 mL
¼ cup	butter	50 mL
¼ cup	cold water	50 mL

▪ In mixing bowl, combine oats, flour, baking soda,
and salt. With pastry blender, cut in butter until mixture
resembles fine crumbs.

▪ Stir in water until ingredients hold together and mixture
forms stiff dough.

▪ Shape into 2 balls. (Dough can be prepared ahead,
wrapped in plastic wrap, and refrigerated for up to 48
hours. Bring to room temperature to roll.)

▪ On lightly floured surface, roll out ⅛ inch (3 mm) thick.
Cut into 2-inch (5-cm) squares or rounds (using cookie
cutter). Place on nonstick baking sheets.

▪ Bake in 350°F (180°C) oven for about 12 minutes or
until golden brown. Cool on wire rack.

Makes 24 oatcakes.

Oatcake Cookies (British)

Oatmeal Cookies

*Adding just a small amount of brown sugar to the oatcake
mixture turns the baked biscuit into a sweet cookie.*

▪ Add ¼ cup (50 mL) packed brown sugar to the oats and
flour mixture.

Makes 24 cookies.

EACH SERVING
1/24 of recipe

½ Starch

48 calories
2 g total fat
1 g saturated fat
5 mg cholesterol
1 g protein
6 g carbohydrate
47 mg sodium
16 mg potassium

EACH SERVING
1/24 of recipe

½ Starch
½ Fat

57 calories
2 g total fat
1 g saturated fat
5 mg cholesterol
1 g protein
8 g carbohydrate
47 mg sodium
23 mg potassium

Drop Biscuits (Canadian/American)
Shortcake Biscuits

Real tea biscuits or baking powder biscuits are a little firmer than these, and the dough is kneaded to develop the characteristic flaky texture. These are simply the stir and bake kind.

1 cup	all-purpose flour	250 mL
½ cup	whole-wheat flour	125 mL
1 Tbsp	baking powder	15 mL
1 tsp	granulated sugar	5 mL
½ tsp	ground cinnamon	2 mL
½ tsp	salt	2 mL
⅔ cup	1% milk	150 mL
1	egg	1
1 Tbsp	butter, melted	15 mL
1 Tbsp	finely chopped pecans or walnuts	15 mL

▪ In mixing bowl, combine flours, baking powder, sugar, cinnamon, and salt.

▪ Whisk together milk, egg, and butter.

▪ Make a well in flour mixture; pour in milk mixture. Stir quickly, just until dry ingredients are moistened. Do not overmix or beat. (Batter should be rough and lumpy.)

▪ Drop 2-Tbsp (25-mL) portions, about 2 inches (5 cm) apart, onto nonstick baking sheets. With back of spoon, flatten slightly into flatter cake. Sprinkle lightly with pecans.

▪ Bake in 400°F (200°C) oven for 20 minutes or until golden brown.

Makes 12 biscuits.

Broa (Portuguese)
Cornbread

Portuguese cornbread calls for corn flour rather than cornmeal. The corn flour blends with the wheat flour and bakes into a pale yellow, evenly grained, crusty loaf that is a little sweeter than regular wheat-flour bread. It is good with fish soups or Caldo Verde (recipe p. 28).

1	pkg quick-rise yeast (1 Tbsp/15 mL)	1
2 cups	all-purpose flour	500 mL
¾ cup	corn flour (not cornmeal)	175 mL
1 tsp	granulated sugar	5 mL
1 tsp	salt	5 mL
1 cup	warm water (120°F/50°C)	250 mL
1 Tbsp	olive oil or canola oil	15 mL
	Cornmeal	

- In large bowl, combine flours, yeast, sugar, and salt until well blended.
- In measuring cup, combine water and oil. Stir into flour mixture until well mixed.
- Turn out onto lightly floured surface. Knead for about 5 minutes or until smooth and elastic. (If dough sticks, sprinkle on a little additional all-purpose flour.) Form into ball; place in bowl. Cover and let stand for 15 minutes.
- Form into round loaf. Place on nonstick baking pan sprinkled lightly with cornmeal. Cut three shallow slashes into top of loaf.
- Cover lightly with waxed paper and light cloth. Place in warm place to rise for about 45 minutes or until doubled in bulk.
- Bake in 350°F (180°C) oven for 40 minutes or until golden brown.
- Transfer to wire rack to cool.

Makes 1 loaf, 12 pieces.

EACH SERVING
¹/12 of recipe

1½ Starch

115 calories
1 g total fat
0 g saturated fat
0 mg cholesterol
2 g protein
22 g carbohydrate
195 mg sodium
57 mg potassium

GOOD
Folate

Pizza (Italian)

Pizza Crust

Pizza dough is as versatile as any bread dough. Use it for pizzas or make crusty Italian rolls or loaves with it.

1 tsp	granulated sugar	5 mL
1	envelope active dry yeast or 1 Tbsp (15 mL)	1
1½ cups	warm water	375 mL
1 tsp	salt	5 mL
3½ cups	all-purpose flour	875 mL
	Cornmeal	

▪ In mixing bowl, combine sugar, yeast, and ½ cup (125 mL) warm water; let stand for 10 minutes until foamy.

▪ Stir in remaining warm water and salt. Beat in half the flour until smooth. Gradually stir in remaining flour until dough comes away from sides of bowl.

▪ Turn out onto lightly floured surface; let stand for 8 minutes. With floured hands, knead dough for 5 minutes or until smooth and elastic. Cut in half. Form each half into ball. Cover and rest for 10 minutes.

▪ For each pizza crust, sprinkle 12-inch (30-cm) pizza pan or 11 x 15 inch (28 x 38 cm) jelly roll pan sparingly with cornmeal.

▪ Roll out and stretch one ball of dough to fit pan. Let rise for 15 minutes. Bake ahead, or top with toppings of your choice.

▪ Bake in 400°F (200°C) oven for 20 minutes or until golden brown.

Makes two 12-inch (30-cm) pizza crusts, 16 servings.

VARIATION

Focaccia (Italian)

Italian Flat Bread

To change the flavor of this Italian flat bread, replace the rosemary with other herbs.

▪ Prepare Pizza Crust as directed. Do not divide. Knead 1 Tbsp (15 mL) chopped fresh rosemary, or 1 tsp (5 mL) dried, into dough.

▪ Sprinkle nonstick jelly roll pan with cornmeal. Pat dough into rectangle. Place on top of cornmeal. Poke all over with finger tips to dimple surface. Brush lightly with 2 tsp (10 mL) olive oil and sprinkle lightly with small amount of chopped fresh or dried rosemary.

▪ Bake and cut into 16 squares to serve.

Makes 16 servings.

Pumpernickel (German)

Grainy Pumpernickel

This recipe is based on one given to me by my friend Ruth Anderson, who lives near us in Campbellville. She serves it with fruit and cheese for an appetizer or a small meal. At first, it may look like an unlikely combination, but once the batter has a chance to sit, the texture changes and it bakes into a dark, dense, chewy loaf.

2½ cups	Ralston cereal (450 g)	625 mL
½ cup	whole-wheat flour	125 mL
½ cup	rye flour	125 mL
1 Tbsp	caraway seeds, crushed	15 mL
1 tsp	baking soda	5 mL
1 tsp	baking powder	5 mL
½ tsp	salt	2 mL
⅓ cup	dark molasses	75 mL
3 cups	boiling water	750 mL

- In bowl, combine cereal, flours, caraway seeds, baking soda, baking powder, and salt; mix well.

- Stir boiling water into molasses until mixed. Pour all at once into dry ingredients. Stir well. Cover and let stand, at room temperature, for 8 hours or overnight.

- Lightly grease 8 x 4 inch (20 x 10 cm) loaf pan, and line bottom with waxed paper cut to fit.

- Spoon cereal mixture into pan, and smooth top. Cover pan with foil.

- Bake, covered with foil, in 275°F (140°C) oven for 3 hours or until tester inserted in middle comes out clean. Cool on rack.

- Remove from pan, discard waxed paper, wrap in plastic wrap, and allow to mellow for 1 day before cutting.

Makes 1 loaf, 24 thin slices.

EACH SERVING
¹⁄₂₄ of recipe

1   Starch

85 calories
0 g total fat
0 g saturated fat
0 mg cholesterol
2 g protein
17 g carbohydrate
94 mg sodium
54 mg potassium

Naan (East Indian)

Indian Flat Bread

In India, this flat bread is baked in the barrel-shaped tandoori oven. Flattened ovals of the dough are popped onto the very hot sides of the tandoori from a small pillow, which saves fingertips from scorching. The bread stretches into an elongated shape as it hangs there, puffs slightly as it bakes quickly, and takes on a slight smoky flavor. This modification replaces some of the white flour with whole-wheat flour and uses yogurt for the sour tang found in the naan made in India.

1 cup	all-purpose flour	250 mL
1 cup	whole-wheat flour	250 mL
1 Tbsp	baking powder	15 mL
½ tsp	granulated sugar	2 mL
½ tsp	salt	2 mL
½ cup	low-fat yogurt	125 mL
½ cup	1% milk	125 mL
1	egg white	1

TOPPING

2 tsp	butter, softened	10 mL
2 tsp	poppy seeds	10 mL

▪ In mixing bowl, combine flours, baking powder, sugar, and salt.

▪ Whisk together yogurt, milk, and egg white. Add to flour mixture, stirring to make fairly light dough.

▪ Turn out onto lightly floured surface. Knead well. Let stand, covered with a damp cloth, for 30 minutes.

▪ Divide dough evenly into 8 pieces. Roll into balls, then pat out into elongated leaf shapes, round at one end, flat at the other. Place on nonstick baking sheets. With dull side of knife, press 3 to 4 creases along length of each leaf.

▪ Topping: Brush with butter and sprinkle with poppy seeds.

▪ Bake in 425°F (210°C) oven for 12 minutes or until golden brown.

Makes 8 flat breads.

Biscotti (Italian)

Italian Biscotti

My Italian friends tell me it is perfectly correct to dunk these crunchy biscuits (I call them cookies) into coffee or dessert wine. The crispness develops in the second baking. Happily, they keep for months in airtight containers.

½ cup	granulated sugar	125 mL
2 Tbsp	soft butter	25 mL
1	egg	1
2	egg whites	2
1 tsp	vanilla	5 mL
¼ tsp	almond extract	1 mL
1½ cups	all-purpose flour	375 mL
1½ tsp	baking powder	7 mL
Pinch	salt	Pinch
½ cup	chopped toasted slivered almonds	125 mL

▪ In mixing bowl, cream sugar and butter. Beat in egg and egg whites. Continue beating until mixture is almost white. Stir in vanilla and almond extract.

▪ Combine flour, baking powder, and salt. In batches, sift and fold into egg mixture until blended.

▪ Turn out onto floured surface. Sprinkle with almonds. Knead until nuts are evenly distributed in dough.

▪ Divide dough into 2 pieces. Form each one into roll about 6 inches (15 cm) long. Place on nonstick baking sheet. Press the top of each roll to flatten slightly. Let stand for 5 minutes.

▪ Bake in 375°F (190°C) oven for 20 minutes or until golden brown.

▪ Remove from oven. Cut into ¾-inch (1-cm) slices.

▪ Return slices to baking sheet. Bake for 5 minutes on each side or until slices are dry and golden.

▪ Store in airtight container for up to 6 weeks.

Makes 36 biscuits.

VARIATION

Biscotti All'Anise (Italian)

Anise Biscotti

Nuts are wonderful in biscotti. However, the biscotti I prefer over all others are the ones flavored with the essence of anise, the traditional flavoring for these biscuits.

▪ Add 2 tsp (10 mL) anise seed, crushed, with the almonds.

EACH SERVING
⅟₃₆ of recipe

½ Starch
½ Fat

56 calories
2 g total fat
0 g saturated fat
7 mg cholesterol
1 g protein
7 g carbohydrate
28 mg sodium
31 mg potassium

Calculations same as above.

Amaretti (Italian)

Almond Macaroons

My mom taught me how to make macaroons, one of our favorite company cookies. They are like amaretti, but ours were always made with coconut rather than almonds.

2	egg whites	2
Pinch	salt	Pinch
⅓ cup	granulated sugar	75 mL
1 tsp	vanilla	5 mL
⅔ cup	chopped toasted sliced almonds	150 mL

- In bowl, beat egg whites with salt until soft peaks form.
- Gradually add sugar and vanilla, beating constantly, until stiff peaks form. Fold in almonds.
- Drop by spoonfuls, about 2 inches (5 cm) apart, onto nonstick or brown paper-lined baking sheet, to make 24 equal mounds.
- Bake in 325°F (160°C) oven for 20 minutes or until lightly browned and firm. For chewy cookies, remove immediately; for crisp macaroons, turn off oven and let cookies dry as oven cools.
- Remove from pan or paper when cool. Store in airtight container.

Makes 24 small macaroons.

Xing Ren Bing (Chinese)

Almond Cookies

These almond cookies are usually eaten as a between-meal snack by the Chinese. They make a wonderful accompaniment to one of my favorite canned fruit combinations, chilled lychees and mandarin oranges.

⅓ cup	butter	75 mL
2 Tbsp	granulated sugar	25 mL
2 Tbsp	brown sugar	25 mL
Pinch	salt	Pinch
1 tsp	almond extract	5 mL
1	egg white, beaten	1
1 cup	all-purpose flour	250 mL
1 tsp	baking powder	5 mL
Pinch	salt	Pinch
¼ cup	ground almonds	50 mL
18	blanched whole almonds	18

▪ In bowl, cream together butter and sugars until light and fluffy. Beat in salt and almond extract.

▪ In bowl, whisk egg white until frothy. Divide, and add half to the creamed mixture. Reserve remaining egg white for later use.

▪ Combine flour, baking powder, and salt; stir into creamed mixture. Stir in ground almonds. Form into 36 small balls. Place 2 inches (5 cm) apart on nonstick baking sheet. With fingertips, slightly flatten each ball.

▪ Split almonds in half lengthwise. Press half almond into each cookie.

▪ Stir 2 tsp (10 mL) water into remaining egg white. Lightly brush onto tops of cookies.

▪ Bake in 350°F (180°C) oven for 15 minutes or until golden.

Makes 36 cookies, 18 servings.

EACH SERVING
1/18 of recipe

½ Carbohydrate
1 Fat

86 calories
4 g total fat
2 g saturated fat
8 mg cholesterol
2 g protein
8 g carbohydrate
52 mg sodium
62 mg potassium

Bolo de Leite (Portuguese)

Milk Cake

In my baking experience, this is like a two-egg butter cake. However, this variation uses very little butter. Because of that, it is best eaten when it is fresh, even warm. To keep any that is left over, wrap it well and freeze it to maintain as much moisture as possible, then serve as soon as it is defrosted. This cake is a great base for that comfy, colonial family dessert, cottage pudding. To make it, top a piece of cake with light and fruity Berry Sauce (recipe p. 197).

EACH SERVING
¹⁄₁₂ **of recipe**

2   Carbohydrate

     167 calories
       2 g total fat
       1 g saturated fat
      40 mg cholesterol
       3 g protein
      32 g carbohydrate
     167 mg sodium
      57 mg potassium

1 cup	1% milk	250 mL
2	eggs	2
2 Tbsp	melted butter	25 mL
1 tsp	grated lemon rind	5 mL
1 tsp	vanilla	5 mL
2 cups	cake and pastry flour	500 mL
1 cup	granulated sugar	250 mL
1 Tbsp	baking powder	15 mL
½ tsp	salt	2 mL

- Line bottom of 8-inch (20-cm) round or square cake pan with waxed paper cut to fit.
- In mixing bowl, beat together milk, eggs, butter, lemon rind, and vanilla until well blended.
- Combine flour, sugar, baking powder, and salt. Beat into milk mixture until smooth.
- Pour into prepared cake pan.
- Bake in 350°F (180°C) oven for 35 minutes or until top springs back when touched and cake tester comes out clean.
- Cool cake for 30 minutes. Loosen edges. Invert onto cake plate; remove waxed paper.

Makes 1 cake, 12 servings.

VARIATION

Cupcakes (Portuguese)

Portuguese Cupcakes

- Line muffin cups with paper liners. Fill ¾ full with batter.
- Bake in 350°F (180°C) oven for 18 minutes or until tops spring back when touched.

Calculations same as above.

Lemon Chiffon Cake

This versatile, low-fat cake may be dressed up for celebrations and parties or served on its own as the finale for a family meal.

1 cup	sifted cake and pastry flour	250 mL
⅔ cup	granulated sugar	150 mL
2 tsp	baking powder	10 mL
½ tsp	salt	2 mL
¼ cup	canola oil	50 mL
2 Tbsp	lemon juice	25 mL
2 Tbsp	water	25 mL
2 tsp	grated lemon rind	10 mL
2	egg yolks	2
4	egg whites	4
¼ tsp	cream of tartar	1 mL

- Line bottom only of 8-inch (20-cm) cake pan with waxed paper cut to fit. Or, alternatively, have 10-inch (25-cm) tube pan ready.

- In medium bowl, combine flour, ⅓ cup (75 mL) sugar, baking powder, and salt; mix well. Pour in oil, lemon juice, water, lemon rind, and egg yolks. Beat for 1 minute or until very smooth. Wash beaters.

- In large bowl, and with clean beaters, beat egg whites and cream of tartar until soft peaks form. Add remaining sugar and beat until stiff peaks form.

- Pour egg yolk mixture evenly over stiffly beaten egg whites. Fold in until blended and evenly colored.

- Pour into prepared pan. With knife, cut through batter to remove air bubbles. Smooth top.

- Bake in 350°F (180°C) oven for 40 minutes or until tester inserted in center comes out clean.

- Cool on wire rack. (Or, if tube pan is used, invert pan and allow to hang upside down on its own rack or funnel.) Loosen around edge of cake; invert onto cake plate. Remove waxed paper.

Makes 16 pieces, 16 servings.

VARIATION

Chocolate Chiffon Cake (American/Canadian)

Chocolate Chiffon Cake

Unsweetened cocoa powder supplies a rich, chocolaty taste without adding extra calories.

- Substitute ¼ cup (50 mL) unsweetened cocoa powder for ¼ cup (50 mL) cake flour; use water instead of lemon juice; delete lemon rind and add 1 tsp (5 mL) vanilla to egg yolk mixture.

EACH SERVING
1/16 of recipe

1   Carbohydrate
½   Fat

103 calories
4 g total fat
0 g saturated fat
26 mg cholesterol
1 g protein
15 g carbohydrate
100 mg sodium
23 mg potassium

EACH SERVING
1/16 of recipe

1   Carbohydrate
½   Fat

96 calories
4 g total fat
0 g saturated fat
26 mg cholesterol
1 g protein
13 g carbohydrate
109 mg sodium
28 mg potassium

Lemon Butter (British)

Lemon Butter

In English cookbooks, lemon butter is also referred to as lemon curd and lemon cheese. It is handy to keep on hand, refrigerated, for filling jelly rolls and small pastries and for spreading on bread or crackers.

2	eggs	2
⅓ cup	lemon juice	75 mL
2	egg whites	2
	Sugar substitute equivalent to ⅓ cup (75 mL) sugar	

▪ In heavy saucepan or top of double boiler, whisk eggs, egg whites, and lemon juice until smooth. Cook over medium-low heat or boiling water, stirring, for 4 to 5 minutes or until mixture thickly coats metal spoon. Remove from heat.

▪ Beat egg white until stiff but soft peaks form. Fold into hot mixture. Cool for 10 minutes. Stir in sugar substitute.

▪ Spoon into covered container. Refrigerate for up to 4 weeks.

Makes 1 cup (250 mL), 12 servings.

Lemon Cream (British)

Lemon Cream

Turn the Lemon Chiffon Cake (p. 175) into a special treat by splitting it, spreading this filling between the layers, and dusting the top layer with icing sugar. Or fill Phyllo Shells (recipe p. 17) with it to make Lemon Cream Phyllo Tarts.

| 2 cups | low-calorie dessert topping | 500 mL |
| ⅓ cup | Lemon Butter (recipe above) | 75 mL |

▪ In bowl, fold together dessert topping and Lemon Butter until smooth.

Makes 2⅓ cups (575 mL), 12 servings.

Bûche de Noël (French Canadian)

Chocolate Log

For this classic, bake the chocolate chiffon cake batter as a jelly roll, fill it with light dessert topping, then spread chocolate frosting on it, creating a surface that looks like the bark of a tree. In French Canadian homes, it is traditionally served as a Christmas dessert.

1	Chocolate Chiffon Cake (recipe p. 175)	1
2 cups	low-calorie dessert topping	500 mL

FROSTING

⅔ cup	semisweet chocolate chips	150 mL
½ cup	low-fat cream cheese	125 mL
2 Tbsp	corn syrup	25 mL

■ Line bottom only of 12 x 15 inch (28 x 38 cm) jelly roll pan with waxed paper, cut to fit.

■ Prepare Chocolate Chiffon Cake batter. Pour into waxed paper-lined pan; smooth top.

■ Bake in 350°F (180°C) oven for 15 minutes or until tester inserted in center comes out clean.

■ Loosen edges of cake and invert onto clean tea towel; peel off paper. Immediately cut ¼-inch (5-mm) strip off all four sides (the crusty edges). Starting at wide side, roll up cake and towel. Let cool on rack. (Do not refrigerate.)

■ When cake is cool, unroll and remove cloth. Spread cake evenly with dessert topping. Reroll and (at this point roll can be wrapped and frozen for up to 4 weeks) place seam side down on serving plate.

■ Frosting: In small microwaveable bowl, microwave chocolate chips at medium-high (70%) for about 1½ minutes or until melted. Or, melt chocolate in top of double boiler over boiling water. Cool for 5 minutes. Beat in cream cheese and corn syrup until smooth and creamy.

■ Spread thin layer of frosting over chocolate roll. With knife or fork, mark with lines to make the roll look like the bark on a tree.

■ Cut into slices to serve.

Makes 16 servings.

EACH SERVING
1/16 of recipe

1½ Carbohydrate
1 Fat

167 calories
8 g total fat
3 g saturated fat
32 mg cholesterol
3 g protein
19 g carbohydrate
169 mg sodium
73 mg potassium

Chocolate Angel Food Cake

This lofty number has the rich taste of milk chocolate, but the texture is as light as a cloud and the calorie count low.

1½ cups	egg whites (approximately 12), at room temperature	375 mL
¼ cup	water	50 mL
1 tsp	cream of tartar	5 mL
½ tsp	salt	2 mL
1 cup	granulated sugar	250 mL
¾ cup	sifted cake and pastry flour	175 mL
¼ cup	unsweetened cocoa powder	50 mL
1 tsp	vanilla	5 mL

▪ In mixer bowl, beat egg whites, water, cream of tartar, and salt until frothy. Gradually add ¾ cup (175 mL) sugar and continue beating just until stiff, shiny peaks form and sugar is dissolved. (A bit of the mixture feels smooth when squashed between finger and thumb.)

▪ In another bowl, lightly combine flour, cocoa, and remaining sugar. Sift over egg white mixture in 3 batches, and after each addition, with wire whisk, fold in until there are no little lumps of flour.

▪ Spoon into ungreased 10-inch (25-cm) tube pan. With knife, cut through batter to remove bubbles. Smooth top.

▪ Bake in 350°F (180°C) oven for 50 minutes or until a cake tester comes out clean and top springs back when lightly touched.

▪ Invert pan, allowing cake to hang upside down on its own stand or funnel for at least 1 hour to cool. With sharp knife, loosen around edge; transfer to cake plate.

Makes 1 angel food cake, 16 servings.

EACH SERVING
¹⁄₁₆ of recipe

1   Carbohydrate

83 calories
0 g total fat
0 g saturated fat
0 mg cholesterol
3 g protein
17 g carbohydrate
111 mg sodium
50 mg potassium

Schwarzwalder Kirschtorte (German)

Black Forest Cake

This German specialty has gained popularity in American and Canadian restaurants, especially among diners who love chocolate cake. This variation, pared of calories and added fat, is easy to make at home and is bound to bring forth compliments for the dessert maker.

1	Chocolate Chiffon Cake (recipe p. 175), baked and cooled	1
2 Tbsp	cherry, raspberry, or orange juice	25 mL
1 cup	pitted fresh Bing cherries or unsweetened frozen cherries	250 mL
¼ cup	water	50 mL
2 Tbsp	all-purpose flour	25 mL
½ tsp	cinnamon	2 mL
	Sugar substitute	
2 cups	low-calorie dessert topping	500 mL
½ tsp	almond extract	2 mL
¼ cup	grated semisweet chocolate (1 square)	50 mL

▪ Split cake into two even layers. Sprinkle cut sides with juice.

▪ Place bottom half, cut side up, on cake plate.

▪ In saucepan, heat cherries to boiling. Combine water, flour, and cinnamon; stir until smooth. Add to cherries, stirring, for 2 minutes or until thickened. Sweeten to taste with sugar substitute.

▪ Spread over bottom layer. Place remaining cake layer, top side up, on top. Gently press in place. Set aside for 10 minutes to cool.

▪ Beat almond flavoring into dessert topping. Spread evenly over top and sides of cake. Sprinkle with grated chocolate. Refrigerate until serving time.

▪ Cut into wedges to serve.

Makes 16 servings.

EACH SERVING
¹⁄₁₆ of recipe

1 Carbohydrate
1 Fat

136 calories
6 g total fat
2 g saturated fat
27 mg cholesterol
2 g protein
18 g carbohydrate
116 mg sodium
74 mg potassium

Swiss Roll (British)

Lemon Jelly Roll

This jelly roll freezes well. Once frozen, single servings can be cut from the roll, and the remainder may be refrozen for another time. As such, it is a perfect dessert to have handy, to be removed from the freezer whenever the desire for such a dessert arises.

1	Lemon Chiffon Cake (recipe p. 175)	1
1 cup	Lemon Butter (recipe p. 176)	250 mL
	Ground cinnamon	

▪ Line bottom only of 12 x 15 inch (28 x 38 cm) jelly roll pan with waxed paper cut to fit.

▪ Prepare chiffon cake batter. Pour into prepared jelly roll pan; smooth top.

▪ Bake in 350°F (180°C) oven for 15 minutes or until tester inserted in center comes out clean.

▪ Loosen edges of cake and invert onto clean tea towel; peel off paper. Immediately cut ¼-inch (5-mm) strip off all four sides (the crusty edges). Starting at wide side, roll up cake and towel. Let cool on rack. (Do not refrigerate.)

▪ When cake is cool, unroll and remove cloth. Spread Lemon Butter evenly on cake; roll up. Place seam side down on serving plate. Dust lightly with cinnamon.

▪ Cut in slices to serve.

Makes 16 servings.

VARIATION

Raspberry Ribbon Cake (British)

Raspberry Ribbon Cake

When layers of thin cake are sandwiched together with fruit-flavored spreads, it is possible to cut them into little ribbon cakes that make a pretty, dainty treat for teatime.

▪ Prepare Lemon Chiffon Cake, as directed above. Once baked, trim, and cut in half crosswise. Do not roll. Spread one half, top side up, with 1 cup (250 mL) raspberry dietetic spread. Top with remaining half, placed top side down.

▪ Wrap with plastic wrap, and allow to mellow for 6 hours or overnight.

▪ To serve, cut into rectangular pieces. Place cut side down on cake plate to show raspberry ribbon in center.

English Tea Cream Tea Scones, Oatmeal Cookies, Amaretti, Xing Ren Bing (Almond Cookies), Lemon Cream Phyllo Tarts, Raspberry Ribbon Cake

Desserts

Wild Berry Dumplings - *Canadian Aboriginal*

Ris à L'Amande - *Scandinavian*

Ba Bao Fan - *Chinese*

Kheer - *East Indian*

Pouding au Pain à la L'Erable - *French Canadian*

Gajar Halva - *East Indian*

Gingered Orange Slices - *Chinese*

Macedonia - *Greek*

Khoshaf - *Middle Eastern*

Rabarbragrot - *Scandinavian*

Berry Fool/Kiwi Fool/Peach Fool - *British*

Pudim de Morangos - *South American*

Kissel - *Russian*

Rodgrod - *Scandinavian*

Hsing-jen-tou-fu - *Chinese*

Biscuit Tortoni - *Italian*

Almond Cream Filling - *Canadian*

Profiteroles - *French*

Crostata di Ricotta - *Italian*

Berry Sauce - *Canadian*

Meringue Torte - *French*

Meringues Schalen - *Swiss*

Oeufs à la Neige - *French Canadian*

Strawberry Shortcake - *Canadian/American*

Peach Shortcake/Orange Shortcake - *Canadian/American*

Akwadu - *African/Caribbean*

Caffe Latte Granita - *Italian*

Frozen Berry Yogurt - *American*

Sharbatee Gulab - *Middle Eastern*

Wild Berry Dumplings

Wild Berry Dumplings

Freshly picked wild blueberries are wonderful for this easy-to-make dessert. The batter for the dumplings is a variation of basic bannock with an egg added. The dessert is best served hot; they are not as good rewarmed.

2 cups	wild blueberries, raspberries, or elderberries	500 mL
1½ cups	water	375 mL
⅓ cup	granulated sugar	75 mL
DUMPLINGS		
1 cup	all-purpose flour	250 mL
1 Tbsp	granulated sugar	15 mL
1 Tbsp	baking powder	15 mL
1 tsp	salt	5 mL
⅔ cup	water	150 mL
1	egg	1

- In deep skillet (10- to 12-inch/25- to 30-cm) with lid, combine blueberries, water, and sugar. Bring to boil. Reduce heat and simmer for 5 minutes or until berries are tender.

- In bowl, combine flour, sugar, baking powder, and salt.

- Whisk together water and egg until well blended.

- Stir into flour mixture until well mixed.

- Drop by dessertspoonful onto hot berry mixture. Cover and cook at simmer for 15 minutes (without peeking) until dumplings puff and are coated with sauce. If they require more cooking, cover and simmer for 5 minutes longer.

- Serve immediately. Dumplings are best before they have cooled; they do not reheat well.

Makes 6 servings.

EACH SERVING
⅙ of recipe

2½ Carbohydrate

167 calories
1 g total fat
0 g saturated fat
35 mg cholesterol
3 g protein
36 g carbohydrate
533 mg sodium ✪
72 mg potassium

Ris à L'Amande (Scandinavian)

Danish Rice Pudding

*Rice pudding is a popular comfort dessert for many
nationalities. When raisins, cinnamon, mace, and pistachios are added, it becomes keskul for Turkish families.
Caribbean cooks make it with evaporated milk and
pineapple. The Portuguese add a bit of lemon rind and
cinnamon and call it arroz doce. According to tradition in
Danish families, the person who finds the almond in his or
her serving of this version will have a period of good luck.*

2 cups	cooked long- or short-grain rice	500 mL
2 cups	1% milk	500 mL
1 tsp	almond extract	5 mL
	Sugar substitute equivalent to ¼ cup (50 mL) sugar	
2 cups	low-calorie dessert topping	500 mL
1	whole almond	1
	Raspberries or blueberries	
	Mint leaves	

▪ In saucepan, heat rice and milk over medium heat,
stirring occasionally, for about 15 minutes or until
mixture is thick and creamy. Do not boil.

▪ Remove from heat. Stir in almond flavoring. Set aside
to cool.

▪ Sweeten to taste with sugar substitute. Fold dessert
topping into cooled rice mixture. Stir in almond.

▪ Spoon into pudding bowl. Garnish with raspberries and
mint leaves.

Makes 8 servings.

EACH SERVING
⅛ of recipe

1½ Carbohydrate
½   Fat

135 calories
3 g total fat
2 g saturated fat
4 mg cholesterol
4 g protein
22 g carbohydrate
43 mg sodium
126 mg potassium

Ba Bao Fan (Chinese)

Eight Treasures Pudding

Traditionally, this pudding is made for Chinese festive occasions, such as banquets, weddings, or Chinese New Year. The mosaic made by the eight different fruits placed around the bowl makes it both attractive and delicious.

1 cup	Chinese glutinous rice (opaque short-grain rice)	250 mL
	Sugar substitute equivalent to ⅓ cup (75 mL) sugar	
1 tsp	butter	5 mL
3	candied red cherries, sliced	3
3	pitted dates, quartered lengthwise	3
2 Tbsp	golden raisins	25 mL
2 Tbsp	dark raisins	25 mL
1 Tbsp	diced candied citron	15 mL
1 Tbsp	diced candied orange peel	15 mL
1 Tbsp	diced preserved ginger	15 mL
6	blanched almonds, cut in half lengthwise	6

- Rinse rice under cold running water; drain.
- In saucepan, combine rice and 2 cups (500 mL) lightly salted water; bring to boil. Reduce heat, cover, and simmer for about 15 minutes or until tender. Cool for 5 minutes. Stir in sugar substitute.
- Lightly brush small round bowl with butter.
- Arrange cherries in center and other fruits and nuts in circles around them, on the bottom and up the sides of bowl, in the order given.
- Spoon in rice, taking care not to disturb fruit.
- Cover bowl with foil. Steam in steamer or covered Dutch oven in 2 inches (5 cm) of simmering water for 30 minutes. Cool for 10 to 15 minutes.
- Unmold onto serving plate and serve warm.

Makes 8 servings.

EACH SERVING
⅛ of recipe

2   Carbohydrate

134 calories
1 g total fat
0 g saturated fat
1 mg cholesterol
2 g protein
28 g carbohydrate
12 mg sodium
108 mg potassium

Kheer (East Indian)

Noodle Pudding

For East Indian cooks, this is an aromatic milk dessert. For Jewish cooks, it is not unlike their famous kugel. Their recipes call for cottage cheese to replace the cream cheese and some of the milk, currants in place of raisins, and cinnamon as the spice of choice. With few changes, this low-calorie version of kheer could also become light kugel.

1½ cups	fine egg noodles or vermicelli	375 mL
3 cups	milk	750 mL
½ cup	raisins	125 mL
¼ cup	chopped slivered almonds	50 mL
2 Tbsp	low-fat cream cheese	25 mL
Pinch	each ground cardamom, cinnamon, and nutmeg	Pinch
2	egg whites	2
2 Tbsp	granulated sugar	25 mL
	Sugar substitute	

▪ In large heavy saucepan, combine noodles, milk, raisins, and almonds over medium heat. Bring to boil, stirring occasionally. Cook, stirring constantly, for 5 to 7 minutes or until noodles are tender. Stir in cream cheese, cardamom, cinnamon, and nutmeg until well blended.

▪ In bowl, beat egg whites until foamy. Add sugar and beat until stiff peaks form. Fold into hot noodle mixture until well blended. Remove from heat. Cool to warm. For added sweetness, sweeten to taste with sugar substitute.

▪ Pour into serving dish. Serve warm or cold.

Makes 8 servings.

EACH SERVING
⅛ of recipe

1½ Carbohydrate
½ Fat

151 calories
4 g total fat
2 g saturated fat
16 mg cholesterol
6 g protein
21 g carbohydrate
71 mg sodium
249 mg potassium

GOOD
Vitamin D, Riboflavin, Vitamin B₁₂

Pouding au Pain à la L'Erable (French Canadian)

Maple, Bread, & Apple Pudding

The small amount of maple syrup used in this version of "pouding" is there just to tease. Traditional recipes use three or four times the amount for a syrupy sweetness.

1 cup	fresh whole-wheat breadcrumbs	250 mL
3 cups	chopped peeled apples	750 mL
Pinch	salt	Pinch
1 cup	water	250 mL
⅓ cup	maple syrup	75 mL
2 Tbsp	finely chopped nuts	25 mL

- In bowl, combine breadcrumbs, apples, and salt. Spoon into lightly buttered 8-inch (20-cm) square baking dish.

- In saucepan, combine water and syrup. Bring to a boil. Pour over apple mixture. Sprinkle with nuts.

- Bake in 350°F (180°C) oven for 20 minutes or until apples are tender.

Makes 8 servings.

Gajar Halva (East Indian)

Carrot Pudding

This pudding, with its natural sweetness from the raisins and carrots, is great for soothing the palate following richly spiced East Indian curries and vindaloos. Greek cooks make their halwa using semolina rather than vegetables. Some East Indian cooks use squash in place of the carrots.

4	carrots, grated	4
1 cup	1% milk	250 mL
2 Tbsp	raisins	25 mL
½ tsp	ground cardamom	2 mL
	Sugar substitute	
¼ cup	chopped pistachios or almonds	50 mL

▪ In saucepan, combine carrots and milk over medium heat. Bring to boil. Reduce heat, cover and simmer, stirring frequently, for about 40 minutes or until milk is absorbed.

▪ Stir in raisins and cardamom. Cook over low heat for 15 minutes, adding a bit of milk if mixture seems dry. Cool for 5 minutes. Sweeten to taste with sugar substitute.

▪ Spoon into one large or 6 small pudding dishes. Garnish with pistachios.

▪ Serve warm, at room temperature, or chilled.

Makes 6 servings.

EACH SERVING
⅙ of recipe

½ Carbohydrate
½ Fat

79 calories
3 g total fat
0 g saturated fat
1 mg cholesterol
3 g protein
11 g carbohydrate
39 mg sodium
286 mg potassium

EXCELLENT
Vitamin A

Gingered Orange Slices (Chinese)

Gingered Orange Slices

Variations of this pleasant refreshing dessert are also found in Greek and Middle Eastern cuisines, in which the spice is likely to be cardamom or ginger. In Chinese culture, the orange symbolizes happiness and prosperity.

3	oranges	3
2 Tbsp	finely chopped candied ginger	25 mL
½ tsp	ground cinnamon	2 mL
	Sugar substitute equivalent to 2 tsp (10 mL) sugar	

▪ Peel oranges, removing the outside white membrane. Cut into ½-inch (1-cm) slices over dish to collect juice. Reserve juice; arrange slices on serving plate or platter.

▪ Combine candied ginger, cinnamon, and reserved juice. Sweeten with sugar substitute. Sprinkle over orange slices. Cover lightly with plastic wrap or waxed paper. Allow to marinate at room temperature for at least 30 minutes or up to 1 hour before serving.

Makes 6 servings.

EACH SERVING
⅙ of recipe

1 Fruit

45 calories
0 g total fat
0 g saturated fat
0 mg cholesterol
0 g protein
11 g carbohydrate
2 mg sodium
229 mg potassium

EXCELLENT
Vitamin C

Macedonia (Greek)

Fresh Fruit Cup

Greek markets always have an abundance of fresh fruit for making succulent fruit cups—the easiest and most refreshing desserts to make. Combining three or four fruits at a time, no more, in a glass bowl, ensures a pretty and delicious concoction every time.

1 cup	diced peaches or pineapple or orange sections	250 mL
1 cup	diced honeydew melon or cantaloupe	250 mL
½ cup	seedless red or green grapes, halved	125 mL
2 tsp	lemon or lime juice	10 mL
	Sugar substitute	

▪ In glass bowl, combine peaches, honeydew melon, and grapes. Sprinkle with juice; toss lightly. Sweeten to taste with sugar substitute.

▪ Serve at room temperature or chilled.

Makes 6 servings.

EACH SERVING
⅙ of recipe

1 Fruit

45 calories
0 g total fat
0 g saturated fat
0 mg cholesterol
1 g protein
12 g carbohydrate
4 mg sodium
251 mg potassium

GOOD
Vitamin A, Vitamin C

Khoshaf (Middle Eastern)

Turkish Fruit Compote

Since top-quality dried fruits come to us from the Middle East, it seems fitting to include this easy-to-make compote. It is the answer for dessert when the assortment of fresh fruit is somewhat limited. And the apricots and figs certainly add fiber to the diet. Since the fruit-filled concoction keeps well in the refrigerator for at least a week, it is worth making even if you are cooking for two or just for you.

12	dried apricots	12
6	dried figs	6
¼ cup	raisins	50 mL
¼ cup	chopped slivered almonds	50 mL
2	whole cloves	2
2	whole cardamom pods	2
1	small stick cinnamon	1
1 cup	water	250 mL
½ cup	orange juice	125 mL
	Sugar substitute	

- In bowl, pour boiling water over dried apricots, figs, and raisins. Set aside for 15 minutes to soften. Drain and discard water.

- In saucepan, combine fruit, almonds, cloves, cardamom, and cinnamon stick. Cover with water and orange juice. Bring to boil.

- Reduce heat, simmer, stirring occasionally, for 20 minutes.

- Remove and discard cloves, cardamom, and cinnamon stick.

- With slotted spoon, transfer fruit to serving dish.

- In saucepan, bring juice to boil. Reduce liquid by half. Cool for 5 minutes. For added sweetness, sweeten to taste with sugar substitute. Pour over fruit.

- Serve warm, at room temperature, or chilled.

Makes 6 servings.

EACH SERVING
⅙ of recipe

1½ Fruit
½ Fat

125 calories
2 g total fat
0 g saturated fat
0 mg cholesterol
2 g protein
26 g carbohydrate
4 mg sodium
376 mg potassium

Rabarbragrot (Scandinavian)
Rhubarb & Strawberry Mold with Yogurt Sauce

Here is a fragrant, red fruit presentation similar to ones that are served frequently in Scandinavian homes. In this recipe, strawberries and rhubarb, always pleasing partners, provide the rosy color and fruity tartness.

2	envelopes unflavored gelatin (2 Tbsp /25 mL)	2
½ cup	orange juice	125 mL
3 cups	chopped rhubarb	750 mL
1½ cups	sliced strawberries	375 mL
	Sugar substitute	

YOGURT SAUCE

2 cups	low-fat yogurt	500 mL
1 tsp	cinnamon	5 mL
	Sugar substitute	

- Sprinkle gelatin over orange juice. Let stand for 5 minutes to soften.

- Meanwhile, in heavy nonreactive saucepan over medium heat, cook rhubarb, stirring occasionally, for 5 minutes or until tender. Stir in strawberries; bring to boil. Stir in gelatin. Remove from heat, and cool for 5 minutes. Sweeten to taste with sugar substitute.

- Pour into 6-cup (1.5-L) stainless steel, glass, or plastic mold. Or pour evenly into 8 individual molds or fruit dishes or sherbet glasses. Cover and refrigerate mold for at least 4 hours or up to 2 days. Dip bottom of bowl in hot water for a few seconds to loosen mold. Invert onto serving plate.

- Yogurt Sauce: In bowl, combine yogurt and cinnamon; mix well. Sweeten to taste with sugar substitute. Drizzle over mold or pass separately.

Makes 8 servings.

EACH SERVING
⅛ of recipe

½ Fruit
½ Milk, skim

64 calories
0 g total fat
0 g saturated fat
1 mg cholesterol
5 g protein
11 g carbohydrate
47 mg sodium
302 mg potassium

GOOD
Vitamin B$_{12}$

Berry Fool

The first "fools" were made with gooseberries and thick cream. Fortunately, there are some food products that work in making a low-calorie copy of the old-fashioned specialty, as this recipe proves. For me, the kiwi version seems to exude the same taste sensation as the rich gooseberry classic.

1½ cups	raspberries, blueberries, or blackberries	375 mL
1 tsp	finely grated orange or lemon rind	5 mL
	Sugar substitute	
2 cups	low-calorie dessert topping	500 mL
6	sprigs fresh mint	6
	Whole raspberries, blueberries, or blackberries	
	Mint sprigs	

▪ In coarse sieve, food mill, or food processor, puree berries. Sieve to remove seeds, if you wish. Add orange rind. Sweeten to taste with sugar substitute. Cover and chill for at least 2 hours.

▪ Prepare dessert topping. Gently fold raspberry puree into dessert topping. Spoon into serving bowl or 6 individual dessert dishes.

▪ Garnish with raspberries and mint springs.

Makes 6 servings.

VARIATIONS

Kiwi Fool (British)
Kiwi Fool

▪ Substitute 1½ cups (375 mL) diced kiwifruit for the raspberries.

Peach Fool (British)
Peach Fool

▪ Substitute 1½ cups (375 mL) diced raw or canned peaches (no sugar added) for the raspberries.

EACH SERVING
⅙ of recipe

½ Fruit
1 Fat

71 calories
3 g total fat
2 g saturated fat
2 mg cholesterol
1 g protein
9 g carbohydrate
17 mg sodium
61 mg potassium

Calculations approximately the same as above.

Pudim de Morangos (South American)

Strawberry Cream Mold

Light is the operative word for this dessert, which is similar to a Spanish or Bavarian cream. The scent from the added strawberries makes it luscious as well as creamy.

½ cup	water	125 mL
1	package low-calorie strawberry gelatin	1
½ cup	ice cold water	125 mL
2 cups	low-calorie dessert topping	500 mL
2	egg whites, beaten	2
1 cup	sliced fresh or frozen strawberries	250 mL

▪ Boil water; stir in strawberry gelatin until dissolved. Stir in cold water. Refrigerate for about 15 minutes or until partially set. Prepare dessert topping. Fold into gelatin until smooth. Chill for 15 minutes.

▪ Beat egg whites until stiff peaks form. Fold into strawberry gelatin mixture. Set aside 12 strawberry slices for garnish. Fold remaining strawberries into gelatin mixture. Pour into ring mold.

▪ Cover and chill in refrigerator for 4 hours or until firm.

▪ Unmold onto serving plate. Garnish with reserved strawberry slices.

Makes 6 servings.

EACH SERVING
⅙ of recipe

½   Carbohydrate
½   Fat

     70 calories
      3 g total fat
      3 g saturated fat
   3 mg cholesterol
      3 g protein
      7 g carbohydrate
  36 mg sodium
  93 mg potassium

Kissel (Russian)

Apricot Pudding

European and Scandinavian cookbooks usually have an assortment of kissels or fruit soups made with different fresh or dried fruits, using cornstarch or arrowroot as the thickener. It is a dessert that knows no season and pleases all ages from youngsters to seniors.

2 cups	water	500 mL
16	dried apricot halves	16
¼ cup	cornstarch	50 mL
	Sugar substitute	

- In saucepan, combine water and apricots and bring to boil. Reduce heat, cover, and simmer for 15 minutes or until tender.
- Transfer apricots and cooking liquid to food processor. Puree until smooth. Press through sieve back into saucepan.
- Mix cornstarch with ¼ cup (50 mL) cold water until well blended. Stir into pureed apricot mixture. Bring to boil, stirring constantly for 1 minute or until thickened. Press through sieve into bowl. Cool for 5 minutes.
- Sweeten to taste with sugar substitute.
- Pour into dessert dishes. Serve warm or chilled.

Makes 4 servings.

VARIATION

Rodgrod (Scandinavian)
Berry Pudding

- Substitute 2 cups (500 mL) fresh or unsweetened frozen sliced strawberries and 1 cup (250 mL) fresh or unsweetened frozen raspberries for the water and apricots.

EACH SERVING
¼ of recipe

2 Carbohydrate

130 calories
0 g total fat
0 g saturated fat
0 mg cholesterol
2 g protein
33 g carbohydrate
4 mg sodium
495 mg potassium

EXCELLENT
Vitamin A

HIGH
Fiber

EACH SERVING
¼ of recipe

1 Carbohydrate

76 calories
0 g total fat
0 g saturated fat
0 mg cholesterol
1 g protein
19 g carbohydrate
2 mg sodium
141 mg potassium

GOOD
Vitamin C

MODERATE
Fiber

Hsing-jen-tou-fu (Chinese)

Almond Custard with Lychees & Oranges

Most Chinese cooks think of this combination of fruit and squares of almond jelly as a fruit salad. In Chinese homes, it is more readily served as a refreshing snack rather than a dessert at the end of a meal.

½ cup	ground blanched almonds	125 mL
1 cup	boiling water	250 mL
1	envelope gelatin	1
¼ cup	cold water	50 mL
⅔ cup	evaporated milk	150 mL
	Sugar substitute equivalent to 2 Tbsp (25 mL) sugar	
3	drops almond extract	3
1 cup	fresh or canned lychees	250 mL
1 cup	fresh or canned mandarin orange sections	250 mL

- In bowl, pour boiling water over ground almonds. Cover and let stand for 30 minutes. Strain through cheesecloth-lined sieve into saucepan, squeezing to extract all liquid. Discard residue.

- Sprinkle gelatin over cold water; let stand for 5 minutes to soften.

- Stir evaporated milk and sugar substitute into almond liquid. Heat gently until sugar dissolves. Stir in gelatin until it melts. Let cool.

- Stir in almond extract. Pour into 8-inch (20-cm) square cake pan. Chill for at least 4 hours or until firmly set.

- Cut into ¾-inch (2-cm) squares. Pile in serving bowl.

- Arrange lychees and orange sections around almond squares.

Makes 6 servings.

Biscuit Tortoni (Italian)

Frozen Almond Cream

Italian cooks usually serve this frozen fantasy in pretty paper cups. Cooking lore tells us that it was created about 200 years ago for a chic Paris restaurant, the Cafe Tortoni, by its operator, a Neapolitan ice cream maker.

12	Amaretti (recipe p. 172), crumbled	12
2 cups	low-calorie dessert topping	500 mL
1 tsp	vanilla	5 mL
4	candied red cherries, finely chopped	4
2 Tbsp	chopped toasted almond slivers	25 mL

▪ Place large paper baking cups into muffin pan.

▪ In bowl, combine Amaretti crumbs, dessert topping, and vanilla until blended.

▪ Spoon into paper baking cups, filling ¾ full. Sprinkle evenly with cherry bits and almonds.

▪ Cover and freeze overnight or for up to 3 weeks. (Mixture will become firm but not solid.)

▪ Serve in paper cups or transfer to dessert dishes.

Makes 8 servings.

EACH SERVING
⅛ of recipe

½ Carbohydrate
1½ Fat

125 calories
8 g total fat
2 g saturated fat
1 mg cholesterol
3 g protein
10 g carbohydrate
45 mg sodium
114 mg potassium

Almond Cream Filling (Canadian)

Almond Cream Filling

Use as filling for profiteroles, meringues, or as an accompaniment for fresh fruit.

2 cups	low-calorie dessert topping	500 mL
½ tsp	almond extract	2 mL
2 tsp	finely chopped toasted almonds	10 mL

▪ Prepare dessert topping following package directions. Beat in almond extract. Fold in almonds.

Makes 2 cups, 12 servings.

EACH SERVING
1/12 of recipe

½ Fat

28 calories
2 g total fat
1 g saturated fat
1 mg cholesterol
1 g protein
2 g carbohydrate
8 mg sodium
23 mg potassium

Profiteroles (French)

Cream Puffs & Berry Sauce

Miniature cream puffs are the base for this easy-to-make glamorous dessert that is often a menu item in French restaurants. The little puffs can be made ahead then finished with flavored fillings or plain whipped dessert topping. Making them look like they are floating on fruit sauce on the dessert plate gives them a royal treatment that is both pretty and tasty.

1 cup	water	250 mL
¼ cup	butter	50 mL
Pinch	salt	Pinch
1 cup	all-purpose flour	250 mL
1	egg	1
3	egg whites	3
	Almond Cream Filling (recipe p. 195)	
	Berry Sauce (recipe p. 197)	
	Icing sugar	

▪ In saucepan, combine water, butter, and salt. Bring to rapid boil. As soon as butter melts, add flour all at once. With wooden spoon, stir quickly until mixture forms a cooked ball of dough and leaves the side of the pan. Immediately remove from heat. Cool for 5 minutes. Transfer to electric mixer bowl or food processor.

▪ Add egg and egg whites, one at a time; beat or process until mixture is smooth after each addition. Or beat by hand.

▪ Spoon into 24 small mounds onto nonstick baking sheets, leaving about 2 inches (5 cm) between to allow for expansion.

▪ Bake in 400°F (200°C) oven for 15 minutes. Reduce heat to 350°F (180°C). Bake for 20 minutes longer or until golden brown and firm to touch.

▪ Remove from oven, but leave oven on. With spatula, loosen each puff from pan. Cut a slash or small hole in the side of each puff to release steam.

▪ Leave puffs on baking sheet; return to oven. Reduce heat to 200°F (100°C). Leave puffs in oven for 1 hour to dry and crisp. Cool.

▪ Spoon or pipe filling into puffs to fill each one. Divide Berry Sauce evenly among dessert plates. Place 2 filled puffs on top. Sprinkle very lightly with icing sugar.

Makes 24 small puffs, 12 servings.

Crostata di Ricotta (Italian)

Ricotta Cheesecake

Italian cooks will probably recognize this as a lighter version of budino di ricotta (ricotta pudding), which is traditionally full of candied fruits. This slimmer version has a hint of citrus from the orange rind and fruitiness from serving it with sliced fresh fruit or berries and the fruit sauce.

2 cups	low-fat ricotta	500 mL
1 cup	1% cottage cheese, drained	250 mL
2	eggs	2
4	egg whites	4
⅓ cup	granulated sugar	75 mL
¼ cup	all-purpose flour	50 mL
2 tsp	grated orange or lemon rind	10 mL
2 tsp	vanilla	10 mL
	Berry Sauce (recipe below)	
	Fruit slices or berries	
	Mint sprigs	

- Line bottom and sides of 8½-inch (22-cm) spring form pan with waxed paper.
- In food processor or blender, process ricotta, cottage cheese, eggs, egg whites, sugar, flour, orange rind, and vanilla until very smooth. Pour into prepared pan.
- Bake in 350°F (180°C) oven for 30 to 35 minutes or until center is no longer shiny and feels firm.
- Turn off oven; let cool in oven for at least 30 minutes.
- Cut into wedges to serve with Berry Sauce. Garnish with fruit slices and mint.

Makes 8 servings.

EACH SERVING
⅛ of recipe

1 Carbohydrate
2 Meat, very lean
1 Fat

182 calories
7 g total fat
4 g saturated fat
74 mg cholesterol
14 g protein
16 g carbohydrate
238 mg sodium
132 mg potassium

GOOD
Calcium, Phosphorus, Riboflavin, Vitamin B$_{12}$

Berry Sauce (Canadian)

Berry Sauce

When fresh berries are out of season, use thawed frozen ones. Drain off the liquid before pureeing them to prevent the sauce from being too liquidy.

2 cups	raspberries, blueberries, saskatoons, or blackberries	500 mL
1 tsp	lemon juice	5 mL
	Sugar substitute equivalent to ⅓ cup (75 mL) sugar	

- In food processor or blender, combine strawberries, lemon juice, and sugar substitute. Process until sauce-like.

Makes about 1¾ cups (425 mL), 12 servings.

EACH SERVING
1/12 of recipe

1 Free

12 calories
0 g total fat
0 g saturated fat
0 mg cholesterol
0 g protein
3 g carbohydrate
0 mg sodium
31 mg potassium

Meringue Torte (French)

Meringue Torte

When light, crispy, flat rounds of meringue are layered with a creamy filling, the result is a torte or cake of a fashion—a truly fancy dessert. For perfect meringue, make sure the sugar is completely dissolved in the stiffly beaten egg white before forming it into torte layers or meringue nests.

2	egg whites	2
Pinch	cream of tartar	Pinch
Pinch	salt	Pinch
¼ cup	granulated sugar (fine, if possible)	50 mL
½ tsp	vanilla	2 mL
	Almond Cream Filling (recipe p. 195)	
	Raspberries	

▪ Line baking sheet with brown paper, baking paper, or lightly buttered and floured foil. Draw outlines for 2 circles, 7 inches (17.5 cm) in diameter.

▪ In electric mixer bowl, beat egg whites, cream of tartar, and salt until foamy. Gradually beat in sugar until stiff peaks form. Beat in vanilla. With spoon, spread meringue evenly within circles to make 2 round meringue layers.

▪ Bake in 200°F (100°C) oven for 35 to 40 minutes or until delicately golden. Turn off oven and leave meringues inside for 4 hours or overnight to dry thoroughly.

▪ Spread half of Almond Cream Filling on one meringue, top side up. Cover with second meringue, top side up. Spread top only with remaining filling. Garnish with raspberries. Serve immediately.

Makes 6 servings.

Meringues Schalen (Swiss)

Swiss Meringues

Once meringues are crisp and dry they will keep for weeks (8 to 10) in an airtight container. It is smart to keep them on hand so that desserts, such as this one, can be put together in minutes.

▪ Prepare meringue; spoon it into decorating bag fitted with large star tip. Pipe meringue (or spoon it) evenly into 12 mounds or ovals. Bake as directed.

▪ Spoon ⅙ of Almond Cream Filling on bottom of one meringue, top with second meringue. Place on side on serving plate to look like a meringue sandwich. Repeat with remaining meringues and cream filling.

Oeufs à la Neige (French Canadian)

Meringues on Custard

In some British, Canadian, and American families, this is called floating island, another variation of the meringue theme. Puffs of poached meringue float on a delicate custard sauce. Sounds complicated, but the step-by-step preparation is easy even for novice cooks.

1½ cups	1% milk	375 mL
2	egg whites	2
Pinch	salt	Pinch
2 Tbsp	granulated sugar	25 mL
1	egg yolk	1
1 Tbsp	cornstarch	15 mL
1 tsp	vanilla	5 mL
	Sugar substitute equivalent to ¼ cup (50 mL) sugar	

- In large skillet, heat milk just to boiling. Immediately reduce heat to simmering.
- In bowl, beat egg whites and salt until foamy. Gradually beat in sugar until stiff peaks form. Drop by the tablespoon (15 mL), 12 Tbsp total, onto hot milk. Cook gently over simmering milk for about 4 minutes or until firm. (Do not allow milk to boil.) With slotted spoon, lift from milk to paper towels.
- Strain milk into top of double boiler.
- In small bowl, whisk together egg yolk and cornstarch until smooth. Add about ½ cup (125 mL) hot milk to egg mixture, whisk until smooth. Return to hot milk. Cook in double boiler, stirring and not allowing water in bottom of pan to heat over simmering, for about 4 minutes or until mixture thickens and coats a metal spoon.
- Immediately remove from heat; stir in vanilla. Cool for 5 minutes. Sweeten to taste with sugar substitute.
- Pour egg custard into serving bowl. Carefully top with meringues. Chill well.

Makes 6 servings.

EACH SERVING
⅙ of recipe

½ Carbohydrate
½ Fat

64 calories
1 g total fat
0 g saturated fat
37 mg cholesterol
3 g protein
8 g carbohydrate
114 mg sodium
102 mg potassium

GOOD
Vitamin D, Vitamin B$_{12}$

Strawberry Shortcake

For generations, summertime family reunions, graduation parties, showers, and weddings have featured this old-fashioned combination. The light drop biscuits, especially when they are still warm, make ideal little cakes for the shortcake part of the dessert. Freshly picked juicy strawberries are rated as the best filling, but when they are not available, either of the variations is a delicious alternative.

6	Drop Biscuits (recipe p. 166)	6
2 cups	sliced strawberries	500 mL
	Sugar substitute	
2 cups	low-calorie dessert topping	500 mL
6	whole strawberries	6

▪ Bake biscuits.

▪ Sweeten strawberries with sugar substitute.

▪ To assemble shortcake, split biscuits in half. Place bottom halves on dessert plates. Spoon sliced strawberries, evenly divided, over top. Cover with biscuit tops. Top each with dollop of dessert topping. Garnish with strawberry.

Makes 6 servings.

VARIATIONS

Peach Shortcake (Canadian/American)
Peach Shortcake

▪ Substitute 1 cup (250 mL) sliced canned or fresh peaches for strawberries.

Orange Shortcake (Canadian/American)
Orange Shortcake

▪ Substitute 2 small oranges, sectioned or sliced, or 1 cup (250 mL) canned mandarin orange sections (with no sugar added).

EACH SERVING
⅙ of recipe

1   Starch
½   Fruit
1   Fat

148 calories
5 g total fat
4 g saturated fat
5 mg cholesterol
4 g protein
23 g carbohydrate
169 mg sodium
199 mg potassium

EXCELLENT
Vitamin C

MODERATE
Fiber

Calculations approximately the same as above.

Akwadu (African/Caribbean)

Baked Bananas

Few fruits are as mellow and satisfying as the banana. Still, Middle Eastern, African, Caribbean, and Mexican cooks turn it into something more than a quick snack in its own wrapper. Mexicans and Jamaicans season bananas with cinnamon plus a dash of rum; Africans sprinkle on coconut. Individuals from the Middle East add chopped dried fruits.

4	small bananas	4
¼ cup	orange juice	50 mL
2 Tbsp	rum, optional	25 mL
½ tsp	ground cinnamon	2 mL
2 Tbsp	desiccated coconut	25 mL

▪ Cut bananas in half lengthwise.

▪ Combine orange juice and rum. Pour half of mixture in 8-inch (20-cm) baking dish. Arrange banana halves in single layer on top. Cover with remaining orange juice mixture, and sprinkle with cinnamon and coconut.

▪ Bake in 375°F (190°C) oven for 10 minutes or until coconut is golden.

▪ Transfer to dessert plates. Spoon sauce from baking dish over top bananas.

Makes 4 servings.

EACH SERVING
¼ of recipe

2 Fruit

137 calories
1 g total fat
1 g saturated fat
0 mg cholesterol
1 g protein
30 g carbohydrate
7 mg sodium
442 mg potassium

EXCELLENT
Vitamin B_6

MODERATE
Fiber

Caffe Latte Granita (Italian)

Caffe Latte Ice

Caffe Latte, one of the favorites in coffee houses, turns into a refreshing ice made in the classic way of the Italian granita. The ice crystals are smaller and more even when a modern ice-cream machine is used.

2 cups	freshly brewed coffee or expresso	500 mL
1 cup	1% milk	250 mL
1 cup	evaporated skim milk	250 mL
	Sugar substitute equivalent to ¼ cup (50 mL) sugar	

▪ Combine all ingredients; stir well.

▪ Pour into ice-cream maker. Freeze following manufacturer's instructions. Or, alternatively, freeze for 30 minutes, stir well. Repeat 3 times, stirring or beating well to finely distribute ice crystals.

▪ Serve immediately, or freeze in covered freezer container for up to 4 weeks.

Makes 6 servings.

EACH SERVING
⅙ of recipe

½ Milk, skim

63 calories
0 g total fat
0 g saturated fat
2 mg cholesterol
5 g protein
10 g carbohydrate
22 mg sodium
106 mg potassium

EXCELLENT
Vitamin D

EACH SERVING
1/6 of recipe

1/2 Carbohydrate

43	calories
0 g	total fat
0 g	saturated fat
0 mg	cholesterol
3 g	protein
8 g	carbohydrate
28 mg	sodium
159 mg	potassium

MODERATE
Fiber

VARIATIONS

Frozen Berry Yogurt (American)

Frozen Berry Yogurt

Once yogurt with fruit earned its place as a popular snack and dessert in the Western world, in no time, it was put to the test to see how it would rate as a frozen treat. It won lots of approval. Now, we find it is easy to make in wonderful low-fat variations at home.

2 cups	fresh or frozen whole raspberries or blueberries	500 mL
1 cup	low-fat yogurt	250 mL
1/4 cup	water	50 mL
	Sugar substitute equivalent to 1/4 cup (50 mL) sugar	

- Follow instructions for making Caffe Latte Ice on p. 201.

Makes 6 servings.

EACH SERVING
1/6 of recipe

1 Carbohydrate

75	calories
0 g	total fat
0 g	saturated fat
0 mg	cholesterol
3 g	protein
16 g	carbohydrate
1 mg	sodium
85 mg	potassium

Sharbatee Gulab (Middle Eastern)

Pineapple Sherbet

Sherbet probably originated in the Middle East, where it was served as a cool refreshment in the harems. Rose petals were part of the potion. In this one, rose water adds its wispy, mystical scent.

1	can (14 oz/398 mL) crushed pineapple, in its own juice	1
3/4 cup	evaporated skim milk	175 mL
1/4 cup	water	50 mL
	Sugar substitute equivalent to 1/4 cup (50 mL) sugar	
1/2 tsp	rose water or vanilla	2 mL

- Follow instructions for making Caffe Latte Ice on p. 201.

Makes 6 servings.

MENU SUGGESTIONS

Chinese Banquet

Cha Yun T'uns – 20
Wontons

Jia Chang Pai Gu – 18
Shanghai Ribs

Hsia Ch'iu – 19
Cantonese Shrimp Balls

Hsing Jen Chi Ting – 105
Cantonese Chicken with Almonds

Hu Nan Yu – 140
Hoisin Salmon with Green Onion & Peas

Hsing-jen-tou-fu – 194
Almond Custard with Lychees & Oranges

Italian Pasta Party

Antipasto di Funghi Crudi – 6
Marinated Mushrooms

Giardinera – 47
Marinated Garden Vegetables

Pasta al Pomodoro e Basilico – 83
Pasta with Tomato & Basil Sauce

Fettucine alla Vongole Bianco – 85
Fettucine with White Clam Sauce

Insalata Mista – 39
Greens with Black Olives

Crostata di Ricotta – 197
Ricotta Cheesecake

Scandinavian Smorgasbord

Seinisalaatti – 39
Mushroom Salad

Kal-och Appelsalad – 41
Apple & Grape Coleslaw

Inkokta Rodbetor – 47
Pickled Beets

Frikadeller – 124
Danish Meatballs

Jansson's Temptation – 159
Potatoes with Anchovies

Rabarbragrot – 190
Rhubarb & Strawberry Mold with Yogurt Sauce

Spanish Tapas

Empanaditas – 10
Little Meat Pies

Salsa Picante – 160
Salsa Picante

Patéis de Bacalhoa – 142
Codfish Cakes

Antipasto di Funghi Crudi – 6
Marinated Mushrooms

Tortilla de Patatas – 64
Potato Omelette

Olives and Toasted Almonds*

Greek Yiasus "To your good health"

Dolmates – 14
Stuffed Grape Leaves

Souvlaki – 128
Skewered Meat

Horta – 152
Spinach with Lemon

Orzo Riganati – 86
Herb-Scented Orzo & Beans

Horiatiki Salata – 52
Hellenic Country Salad

Macedonia – 188
Fresh Fruit Cup

Middle Eastern Meze

Hummus – 2
Light Hummus

Baba Ghannooj – 3
Eggplant Dip

Falafel – 57
Falafel

Seekh Kabob – 123
Shish Kebob

Tabbouleh – 50
Bulgur Parsley Salad

Tzimmes – 158
Carrot, Beet, & Apple Medley

*Recipe not in book.

Portuguese Esfolhada

Caldo Verde – 28
Potato Soup with Greens

Arroz de Tomate cam Amêijoas – 74
Tomato Rice with Clams

Broa – 167
Cornbread

Salada Verde com Coentro – 38
Mixed Greens with Cilantro

Melon Wedges*

East Indian Meal

Korma – 101
Curried Chicken

Pilau – 80
Mushroom Cashew Pilaf

Dal – 72
Lentil Puree

Raita – 160
Cucumber Yogurt Sauce

Kheer – 185
Noodle Pudding

Mexican Comida

Guacamole – 4
Low-Fat Guacamole

Sopa Azteca – 22
Chicken Tortilla Soup

Mole Poblano – 103
Mexican Chicken Stew

Salsa Picante – 160
Salsa Picante

Cubed Mango or Mango Ice*

Canadian Aboriginal Dinner

Three Sisters Soup – 26
Squash, Bean, & Corn Soup

Bannock – 162

Grilled Rabbit – 114

Creamed Greens – 152

Wild Berry Dumplings – 182

German Octoberfest

Rouladen – 119
Braised Stuffed Beef Rolls

Kartoffelsalat – 44
Hot Bavarian Potato Salad

Rotkohlsalat – 41
Red Cabbage Salad

Schwarzwalder Kirschtorte – 179
Black Forest Cake

Japanese Supper

Sushi – 9

Matsukaze-yaki – 107
Flat Chicken Loaf

Åomame-gohan*
Steamed Rice with Peas

Yasai no Sokuseki-suke – 48
Japanese Pickled Vegetables

Sumashi-Jiru*
Sliced Mushrooms in Clear Broth

Mandarin Oranges and Persimmons*

African Feast

Couscous – 132

Salade Verte – 38
Lettuce with Vinaigrette

Steamed Yams*
Steamed Sweet Potatoes

Raita – 160
Cucumber Yogurt Sauce

Akwadu – 201
Baked Bananas

Caribbean Island Feast

Jerk Chicken – 93
Jamaican Jerk Chicken

Moros Y Cristianos – 71
Cuban Black Beans & Rice

Creamed Greens – 152

Sharbatee Gulab – 202
Pineapple Sherbet

*Recipe not in book.

TYPICAL FOODS & FLAVORS

Caribbean

Seafood, tropical fruits, and vegetables—taro, papaya, pumpkin, hot chilies, tomatoes, onion, avocado, bananas, sweet potatoes; food influenced by settlers from Africa, Britain, France, Spain, Portugal, India, and Holland.

Chinese

Fungi, sprouts, roots, stalks, seeds, buds, flowers, fruits; small amounts of pork, poultry, and fish; noodles, buns, and pancakes from wheat and other grains from the North; rice from the South, home of lightly seasoned Cantonese food; fiery Szechwan and Hunan dishes from inland; sweet and sour; soy sauce, onion, scallion, ginger, garlic, soybean and curd, ginger root, rice vinegar, bean pastes, sesame seeds, star anise, pepper, five spice powder (fennel, cloves, star anise, and Schezwan pepper); salty dried foods, such as shrimp paste, oyster sauce, and hoisin sauce; tea.

Eastern European

Many variations of borscht; basic grains, such as wheat, rye, corn, and barley used for dumplings, envelopes of dough, and yeast breads; cabbage, sauerkraut, potatoes, turnips, onions, beets, mushrooms, and cucumbers for salads and pickles; beef, veal, pork, mutton, chicken and goose, and fresh and salted fish; generous amounts of cream, sour cream, and butter; dill, mushrooms, garlic; indigenous fruits and berries (cranberries, lignonberries); pumpkin, squash, and sunflower seeds; ice cream.

German & Austrian

Filling, hearty food; delicate seasonings; pork and all the wursts (sausages), chicken and geese, beef; breads, especially dark ones made with rye flour; red and green cabbage, sauerkraut, turnips, boiled potatoes, and dumplings; sweet and sour; dill, caraway, lovage, mustard, juniper, horseradish, poppy seed, and sesame seed; apples, cherries, pears for fruit soups, pies, butters, cakes; raisins, currants, cinnamon, ginger, and nutmeg; beer and kaffe.

Greek

Food has Mediterranean flair; lots of vegetables—artichokes, okra, broad beans, lima beans, cauliflower, peas, tomatoes, cucumbers, onions, garlic, carrots, potatoes, legumes, and mustard, dandelion, and spinach greens (horta); bread; small quantities rice and pasta; goat, lamb, pork, chicken, fish, and seafood; no milk, but yogurt and cheese (feta); olive oil for cooking and salads; butter for pastries (phyllo); dill, mint, rosemary, oregano, cilantro, and spices—peppercorns, cinnamon, cloves, ginger; assorted olives, lemons, oranges, melons, figs, plums, peaches, and nuts—almonds, pine nuts, walnuts, pistachios, chestnuts; water and ouzo.

Portuguese

Simple and regional; fish, seafoods, dried salt cod and pork (often in the same dish); breads, especially cornbread (broa) at every meal; olive oil, potatoes, tomatoes, garlic, onion, pimientos; legumes, garbanzos; turnip greens, kale, tomatoes, pimientos, onions, scallions, and leeks; sea salt, lemons, garlic, mint, cilantro, parsley, vinegar, and the hot sauce (piri piri); cumin, saffron, nutmeg, and cinnamon; oranges, lemons, peaches, apricots, figs, dates, raisins, berries, grapes, melons, and candied fruits; rice desserts; eggs, butter, vanilla, lemon and orange rinds, almonds, chestnuts, and walnuts; wine and coffee.

East Indian

Combinations of freshly ground herbs and spices (marsala) that create the curry taste; cardamom, cinnamon, ginger, coriander, cumin, mustard, nutmeg, saffron, turmeric, garlic, mint, chilies, tamarind, and coconut milk; long-grain rice (basmati), wheat and other grains, flat breads, vegetables, and, especially, pulses; meat and fish are expensive and many religious taboos affect their use, so economical vegetarianism is popular; goat, lamb, and chicken, barbecued or finely chopped and ground; fish; yogurt; vegetable oils for regular cooking, ghee (clarified butter) used by upper class; potatoes, onions, tomatoes, cucumbers, cauliflower; mustard, fenugreek, spinach, radish greens, and pulses are sprouted for their greens; apples, pears, cherries, melons, mangoes, dates, lemons, persimmons; tea.

Italian

Olive oil and garlic add sustenance to pastas, risottos, cornmeal-based polentas, and even breads; from the North, rice, milk, butter, and polenta are common; from the South, olive oil and pasta (chewy not mushy); scampi, eels, mussels, mullet, and sole; pork, cured proscuitto, Parma hams, and ground pork in tomato-based pasta sauces (ragu); root vegetables, legumes, tomatoes, onion, cheese, and herbs; fruits indigenous to the Mediterranean; biscuit tortoni and granite; caffe latte, wine.

Japanese

Simple and artistic; dashi; shoyu (soy sauce); small bits of fish, seafood, and meat; large bowls of rice and lots of noodles from buckwheat (soba), wheat, and rice; tofu, nori (toasted seaweed), miso (bean paste), black and white sesame seeds, peanuts, walnuts, wasabi (horseradish), rice vinegar; fish with sake and mirin (rice wine); sushi and sashimi (raw fish); vinegared salads and pickles, ginger, carrot, daikon, cabbage; oranges and seasonal fruit; tea and sake.

Mexican

Corn in tortillas used for tacos, burritos, etc.; beans (frijoles); chicken, turkey, fish and seafood, chorizo, chilies, red and green tomatoes, sweet peppers, avocados, onions, limes; cilantro, mint; cinnamon, cloves, vanilla, nuts, lime, chocolate; fresh fruits, seeds, nuts; hot chocolate, beer, coffee.

Middle Eastern

Sun-ripened vegetables, eggplants, peppers, tomatoes, oregano, mint, basil, cilantro, garlic, onions; grains and breads (couscous, bulgar, pita); olive oil, tahini; salt, pepper, cinnamon, cayenne, cumin, saffron, ginger, cinnamon, sesame and anise seeds; seasonal fruits, dates, almonds; tea.

Scandinavian

Homey foods; pork, potatoes, breads, and grains; smoked meats and fish; pickles; legumes; dill, onion, juniper berries, pine needles, mustard, horseradish; cream and milk; assorted spices but with a light touch; pureed berries and cream; aquavit, beer, coffee.

REFERENCES

American Heritage. 1968, 1971. *The Horizon Cookbook*. Toronto: McGraw-Hill.

Barer-Stein, Thelma. 1979. *You Eat What You Are*. Toronto: McClelland and Stewart.

Bon Appetit. *Country Cooking*. 1978. New York: Viking Press.

Borghese, Anita. 1977. *Foods from Harvest Festivals and Folk Fairs*. Toronto: Fitzhenry & Whiteside.

Born, Wina. 1973. *Famous Dishes of the World*. New York: Macmillan.

Canadian Home Economics Association. 1979. *A Collage of Canadian Cooking*. Toronto: Webcom.

Chantiles, V.I. 1989. *Diabetic Cooking from Around the World*. New York: Harper & Row.

Child, Julia, and Simone Beck. 1973. *Mastering the Art of French Cooking*, Volume Two. New York: Alfred A. Knopf.

Child, Julia, Louisette Bertholle, and Simone Beck. 1961. *Mastering the Art of French Cooking*. New York: Alfred A. Knopf.

China and Its Cuisine. Hong Kong: Mallard Press.

Ferguson, Carol, and Margaret Fraser. 1992. *A Century of Canadian Home Cooking*. Toronto: Prentice-Hall.

General Mills. 1980 *Betty Crocker's International Cookbook*. Toronto: Random House.

General Mills. 1989, 1994. *Betty Crocker's New International Cookbook*. Toronto: Prentice Hall.

Gibbons, Barbara. 1978. *The International Slim Gourmet Cookbook*. New York: Fitzhenry & Whiteside.

Hansen, Barbara. 1980. *Mexican Cookery*. New York: Dell Publishing.

Hazelton, Nika. 1978. *The Regional Italian Kitchen*. New York: M. Evans.

Herbst, Sharon Tyler. 1990. *Food Lover's Companion*. New York: Barron's.

Jenkins, Nancy Harmon. 1994. *The Mediterranean Diet Cookbook*. New York: Bantam Books.

Kakonen, Ulla. 1974. *Natural Cooking the Finnish Way*. Toronto: Fitzhenry & Whiteside.

Kolpas, Norman. 1982. *The Gourmet's Lexicon*. Toronto: Prentice-Hall.

Konishi Kiyoko. 1983. *Japanese Cooking for Health and Fitness*. Tokyo: Gakken.

Larousse Treasury of Country Cooking. 1975. New York: Vineyard Books.

Lovesick Lake Native Women's Association. 1985. *The Gathering*. Burleigh Falls: Ontario Lovesick Lake Native Women's Association.

Mitchell, John. 1988. *The Best of Thai Cooking*. Bangkok: Asia Books.

Romagnoli, Margaret, and D. Franco. 1975. *The Romagnoli's Table*. Canada: Little, Brown & Company.

Salloum, Mary. 1986. *A Taste of Lebanon*. Regina, Canada: Centax.

Schlabach, Joetta Handrich. 1991. *Extending the Table*. Scottsdale: Herald Press.

Sevilla, Maria Jose. 1992. *Spain on a Plate*. London: BBC Books.

Simonds, Nina. 1994. *Classic Chinese Cuisine*. Vermont: Chapters Publishing.

Sirkis, Ruth. 1989. *A Taste of Tradition— The How and Why of Jewish Cooking*. Tel Aviv: R. Sirkis Publishers.

Times Inc. 1968. *Foods of the World Series: The Cooking of China; Italy; Latin America; Scandinavia*. New York: Time-Life Books.

Times Inc. 1969. *Foods of the World Series: The Cooking of Germany; Portugal and Spain*. New York: Time-Life Books.

Waldo, Myra. 1971. *Seven Wonders of the Cooking World*. New York. Dodd, Mead & Company.

Weight Watchers. 1977. *Weight Watchers International Cookbook*. New York: The New American Library.

Women's Day. 1966. *Encyclopedia of Cookery*. New York: Fawcett Publications.

World Cookery, the complete book of. 1972. London: Octopus Books.

INDEX

NEW BOOKS
from the American Diabetes Association

American Diabetes Association Complete Guide to Diabetes
The ultimate home diabetes reference. Complete, thorough chapters cover all areas of self-care: nutrition, blood glucose, exercise, complications, etc. Discover how to: handle emergencies, cope with depression, choose a health-care team, maximize your insurance coverage, and much more. #CSMCGD

Nonmember: $29.95; ADA Member: $23.95

How to Get Great Diabetes Care
This book explains the American Diabetes Association's Standards of Care and informs you—step-by-step—of the importance of seeking medical attention that meets these standards. You'll learn about special concerns and treatment options for diabetes-related diseases and conditions. #CSMHGGDC

Nonmember: $11.95; ADA Member: $9.55

101 Tips for Staying Healthy with Diabetes
Get the inside track on the latest tips, techniques, and strategies for preventing and treating diabetes complications. Learn how to treat and prevent skin infections, reduce the pain of frequent finger sticks, eat the foods you like while lowering your calorie intake, and more. #CSMFSH

Nonmember: $12.50; ADA Member: $9.95

101 Tips for Improving Your Blood Sugar
101 Tips offers a practical, easy-to-follow road map to tight blood sugar control. One question appears on each page, with the answers or "tips" below each question. Tips on diet, exercise, travel, weight loss, insulin injection, illness, sex, and much more. #CSMTBBGC

Nonmember: $12.50; ADA Member: $9.95

Reflections on Diabetes
A collection of stories written by people who have learned from the experience of living with diabetes. Selected from the *Reflections* column of *Diabetes Forecast* magazine, these stories of success, struggle, and pain will inspire you. #CSMROD

Nonmember: $9.95; ADA Member: $7.95

Diabetes Meal Planning Made Easy
Learn about the new diabetes nutrition recommendations and master the new Diabetes Food Pyramid. From starches, at the pyramid's base, to fats, sweets, and alcohol at the pyramid's tip, you'll learn how much of what foods to eat to fit your personal nutrition needs. #CCBMP

Nonmember: $14.95; ADA Member: $11.95

Sweet Kids: How to Balance Diabetes Control & Good Nutrition with Family Peace

Addresses the behavioral and developmental issues surrounding nutrition management in the families of children with diabetes. Based on a survey of 50 pediatric diabetes clinicians and parents of children with diabetes, *Sweet Kids* offers practical, reassuring advice for parents and caregivers of children with diabetes. #CSMSK

Nonmember: $14.95; ADA Member: $11.95

How to Cook for People with Diabetes

Finally, here's a collection of reader favorites from the delicious, nutritious recipes featured every month in *Diabetes Forecast*. You get not only ideas for pizza, chicken, unique holiday foods, vegetarian recipes and more, but also nutrient analysis and diabetic exchanges for each recipe. #CCBCFPD

Nonmember: $11.95; ADA Member: $9.55 *Available November 1996*

Diabetic Meals in 30 Minutes—Or Less

Put an end to bland, time-consuming meals with more than 140 fast, flavorful recipes. Complete nutrition information accompanies every recipe, and a number of "quick tips" will have you out of the kitchen and into the dining room even faster! #CCBDM

Nonmember: $11.95; ADA Member: $9.55

Flavorful Seasons

More than 400 unforgettable recipes that combine great taste with all the good-for-you benefits of a well-balanced meal, all-year round. Enjoy Black Bean, Corn, and Rice Chili, Tropical Mango Mousse, or Orange Sea Bass. Plus complete nutrition information—calories, protein, fat, carbohydrate counts, and diabetic exchanges —accompanies each recipe. #CCBFS

Nonmember: $16.95; ADA Member: $13.50

Southern-Style Diabetic Cooking

This cookbook takes traditional Southern dishes and turns them into great-tasting but good-for-you recipes you'll come back to again and again. Features more than 100 recipes including appetizers, main dishes, and desserts; complete nutrient analysis with each recipe and suggestions for modifying recipes to meet individual nutritional needs. #CCBSSDC

Nonmember: $11.95; ADA Member: $9.55 *Available November 1996*

Magic Menus for People with Diabetes

Like magic, this book figures fats, calories, and exchanges for you automatically! No matter how you combine the more than 50 breakfasts, 50 lunches, 75 dinners, and 30 snack recipes, the day's total calories will equal 1,500 and nutrients and exchanges will always be correct. Choices include: Blueberry Muffins, Pasta Salad, and Hawaiian Kabobs. #CCBMM

Nonmember: $14.95; ADA Member: $11.95

BESTSELLERS
from the American Diabetes Association

Diabetes A to Z
In clear, simple terms, you'll learn all about blood glucose, complications, diet, exercise, heart disease, insulin, kidney disease, meal planning, pregnancy, sex, weight loss, and much more. Alphabetized for quick reference. #CGFDAZ

Nonmember: $9.95; ADA Member: $7.95

Managing Diabetes on a Budget
For less than $10 you can begin saving hundreds and hundreds on your diabetes self-care. An inexpensive, sure-fire collection of "do-it-this-way" tips and hints to save you money on everything from medications and diet to exercise and health care. #CSMMDOAB

Nonmember: $7.95; ADA Member: $6.25

The Fitness Book: For People with Diabetes
You'll learn how to exercise to lose weight, exercise safely, increase your competitive edge, get your mind and body ready to exercise, and much more. #CSMFB

Nonmember: $18.95; ADA Member: $14.95

Raising a Child with Diabetes
Learn how to help your child adjust insulin to allow for foods kids like to eat, have a busy schedule and still feel healthy and strong, negotiate the twists and turns of being "different," accept the physical and emotional challenges life has to offer, and much more. #CSMRACWD

Nonmember: $14.95; ADA Member: $11.95

The Dinosaur Tamer
Enjoy 25 fictional stories that will entertain, enlighten, and ease your child's frustrations about having diabetes. Each tale warmly evaporates the fear of insulin shots, blood tests, going to diabetes camp, and more. Ages 8-12. #CSMDTAOS

Nonmember: $9.95; ADA Member: $7.95

The Healthy HomeStyle Cookbook
Choose from more than 150 good-for-you recipes you'd love to see on the dinner table. Each recipe is low in fat, cholesterol, sugar, and calories, and each includes American Diabetes Association-approved exchanges. Also includes energy- and time-saving tips, how-to's for microwaving and freezing, and good ideas for cutting fat and calories in your meals. Some homestyle favorites: Meatless Lasagna, Rhubarb-Banana Bake, and "Guiltless" Cheesecake. #CCBHHS

Nonmember: $12.50; ADA Member: $9.95

Month of Meals
When celebrations begin, go ahead—dig in! The original "automatic menu planner" includes a Special Occasion section that offers tips for brunches, holidays, parties, and restaurants to give you delicious dining options anytime, anywhere. Menu choices include Chicken Cacciatore, Oven-Fried Fish, Sloppy Joes, Crab Cakes, and many others. #CMPMOM

Nonmember: $12.50; ADA Member: $9.95

Month of Meals 2
Automatic menu planning goes ethnic! A healthy diet doesn't have to keep you from your favorite restaurants. Tips and meal suggestions for Mexican, Italian, and Chinese restaurants are featured. Quick-to-fix and ethnic recipes are also included. Menu choices include Beef Burritos, Chop Suey, Veal Piccata, Stuffed Peppers, and many others. #CMPMOM2

Nonmember: $12.50; ADA Member: $9.95

Month of Meals 3
Enjoy fast food without guilt! Make sensible but delicious choices at McDonald's, Wendy's, Taco Bell, Kentucky Fried Chicken, and other fast-food restaurants. Special sections offer valuable tips such as reading ingredient labels, preparing meals for picnics, and meal planning when you're ill. Menu choices include Fajita in a Pita, Seafood Stir-Fry, Stouffer's Macaroni and Cheese, and many others. #CMPMOM3

Nonmember: $12.50; ADA Member: $9.95

Month of Meals 4
Meat and potatoes menu planning! Beef up your meal planning with old-time family favorites like Meatloaf and Pot Roast, Crispy Fried Chicken, Beef Stroganoff, Kielbasa and Sauerkraut, Sausage and Cornbread Pie, and many others. Hints for turning family-size meals into delicious leftovers will keep generous portions from going to waste. Meal plans for one or two people are also featured. Spiral-bound. #CMPMOM4

Nonmember: $12.50; ADA Member: $9.95

Month of Meals 5
Meatless meals picked fresh from the garden. Choose from a garden of fresh vegetarian selections like Eggplant Italian, Stuffed Zucchini, Cucumbers with Dill Dressing, Vegetable Lasagna, and many others. Plus, you'll reap all the health benefits of a vegetarian diet, including less obesity, less coronary artery disease, less colon and lung cancer, less osteoporosis, and more. #CMPMOM5

Nonmember: $12.50; ADA Member: $9.95

Great Starts & Fine Finishes
Try Crab-Filled Mushrooms, Broiled Shrimp, or Baked Scallops for an appetizer. Dig into Cherry Cobbler or Chocolate Chip Cookies for dessert. #CCBGSFF

Nonmember: $8.95; ADA Member: $7.15

Easy & Elegant Entrees

Enjoy Fettucini with Peppers and Broccoli, Steak and Brandied Onions, Shrimp Creole, many more. You'll also enjoy peace of mind knowing your meals are low in fat and calories. #CCBEEE

Nonmember: $8.95; ADA Member: $7.15

Savory Soups & Salads

Pasta-Stuffed Tomato Salad, Mediterranean Chicken Salad, Seafood Salad, many others. Hungry for soup? Try a bowl of Clam Chowder, Gazpacho, Mushroom and Barley, many others. #CCBSSS

Nonmember: $8.95; ADA Member: $7.15

Quick & Hearty Main Dishes

Try Spicy Chicken Drumsticks, Apple Cinnamon Pork Chops, Chicken and Turkey Burgers, Macaroni and Cheese, Beef Stroganoff, and dozens more. #CCBQHMD

Nonmember: $8.95; ADA Member: $7.15

Simple & Tasty Side Dishes

Add just the right touch to any meal with Sautéed Sweet Peppers, Onion-Seasoned Rice, Parsley-Stuffed Potatoes, Brown Rice with Mushrooms, Broccoli with Lemon Butter Sauce, and a pantry of others. #CCBSTSD

Nonmember: $8.95; ADA Member: $7.15

HOW TO ORDER

To order by phone: just call us at **1-800-ADA-ORDER** (232-6733) and have your credit card ready. VISA, MasterCard, and American Express are accepted. Please mention code CKA96WC when ordering.

To order by mail: on a separate sheet of paper, write down the books you're ordering and calculate the total using the shipping & handling chart below. (NOTE: Virginia residents add 4.5% sales tax; Georgia residents add 6.0% sales tax.) Then include your check, written to the American Diabetes Association, with your order and mail to:

American Diabetes Association
Order Fulfillment Department
P.O. Box 930850
Atlanta, GA 31193-0850

Shipping & Handling Chart

up to $30.00	$30.01–$50.00	over $50.00
add $3.00	add $4.00	add 8%

Allow 2–3 weeks for shipment.
Add $3.00 to shipping & handling for each extra shipping address.
Add $15 for each overseas shipment.

PRICES SUBJECT TO CHANGE WITHOUT NOTICE.